*Research Guide to
Corporate Acquisitions,
Mergers, and Other
Restructuring*

RESEARCH GUIDE TO CORPORATE ACQUISITIONS, MERGERS, AND OTHER RESTRUCTURING

Michael Halperin

AND

Steven J. Bell

GREENWOOD PRESS

NEW YORK • WESTPORT, CONNECTICUT • LONDON

016.6581
H 195

Library of Congress Cataloging-in-Publication Data

Halperin, Michael.
  Research guide to corporate acquisitions, mergers, and other
restructuring / Michael Halperin and Steven J. Bell.
     p.   cm.
  Includes bibliographical references and index.
  ISBN 0-313-27220-4 (alk. paper)
  1. Consolidation and merger of corporations—Information services.
I. Bell, Steven. II. Title.
HD2746.5.H357   1992
016.6581'6—dc20   91-24199

British Library Cataloguing in Publication Data is available.

Library of Congress Catalog Card Number: 91-24199
ISBN: 0-313-27220-4

First published in 1992

Greenwood Press, 88 Post Road West, Westport, CT 06881
An imprint of Greenwood Publishing Group, Inc.

Printed in the United States of America

The paper used in this book complies with the
Permanent Paper Standard issued by the National
Information Standards Organization (Z39.48-1984).

10 9 8 7 6 5 4 3 2 1

To Mina and Laura
for their support and encouragement

Contents

Tables and Figures   xi

Preface   xiii

1. Coping with Corporate Change   1

2. Monitoring Corporate Change with Print Resources   17

3. Monitoring Corporate Change with Electronic Resources   27

4. Williams Act Filings: Public Disclosure of M&A   53

5. M&A Transaction Databases   79

6. Finding Acquisition Candidates   97

7. The Muddled Corporate Identity   123

8. International M&A: A Cross-Border Perspective   143

9. Information Checklist   177

Appendix 1:
Online Database Chart   189

Appendix 2:
Directory of Time-Sharing Database Systems   195

Glossary   197

Select Bibliography   201

Index   205

Tables and Figures

TABLES

1.1	M&A Activity, 1979-1990	7
1.2	Bibliographic Measures of M&A Activity, 1979-1990	8
1.3	Transactions in Related M&A Areas, 1979-1990	9
2.1	Printed Resources for Monitoring Corporate Change	18
2.2	Time Lag of Selected Corporate News Releases	20
3.1	Newswire Retrieval and Frequencies	40
4.1	Total M&A Filings since 1985	55
6.1	Standard Business Directories in Print, Online, and in CD-ROM	99
6.2	Industrial Valve Manufacturers in D&B—DUNS MARKET IDENTIFIERS	102
6.3	Industrial Valve Manufacturers in TRINET U.S. BUSINESSES	104
6.4	Employee Size Classes in DUN'S ELECTRONIC BUSINESS DIRECTORY	106
6.5	Industrial Valve Manufacturers in DUN'S ELECTRONIC BUSINESS DIRECTORY	106
6.6	Philadelphia Area Facility Rental and Party-Planning Companies from DUN'S ELECTRONIC BUSINESS DIRECTORY	108
6.7	Screening Report from DISCLOSURE	109

6.8   COMPUSTAT Report on U.S. Companies with High EPS
      Growth Rates   111

6.9   TRINET Share of Market Report   113

6.10 TRINET Line of Business Report   114

7.1   TRINET Report Format   135

7.2   Public Companies That Went Private, 1985-1987   137

FIGURES

1.1   Business Information Availability Grid   13

8.1   Sample Page from *Merger & Acquisition Sourcebook*   148

8.2   Sample Page from *International Merger Yearbook*   150

8.3   Sample Page from *Mergerstat Review*   152

8.4   Sample Page from *Mergers & Acquisitions*   154

Preface

The volume of information on corporations is staggering. Each year in the United States there are typically 600,000 incorporations, 60,000 business failures, and 2,000 merger/acquisition announcements. Almost all of these events require official records. Many generate published stories in newspapers, journals, and books. The 12,000 U.S. public companies alone submit 3 million pages of documents annually to the Securities and Exchange Commission. The rest of the industrialized world is producing business information at a comparable rate.

Sifting through this mass of material for information concerning mergers and acquisitions (M&A) presents several problems for the researcher. These include:

- Specialized Vocabulary. Some understanding of financial terms associated with M&A (for example, "LBO" and "junk bond financing") is vital for effective research. In addition, the phrases used to describe M&A activities, while often colorful ("white knight defense" and "greenmail" are examples) can be confusing to the uninitiated.

- Unique Document Types. The U.S. federal government often requires that companies involved in acquisitions file reports. The researcher must be aware of these documents, their contents, and how they can be searched.

- Variety of Formats and Search Systems. The material for research is available in a bewildering variety of formats: print, microform, online, CD-ROM (Compact Disc-Read Only Memory) text, and CD-ROM image. Nearly identical computer databases are often available on several online or ondisc systems, each with its own searching procedure. The choice of format and system can determine speed of retrieval, update frequency, searching power, and cost.

- M&A Databases. There are several specialized machine-readable databases of M&A transactions and filings that are central to serious M&A research.

We have designed the *Research Guide to Corporate Acquisitions, Mergers, and Other Restructuring* to help the researcher cope with the special characteristics of M&A research. Throughout the *Guide* we stress the importance of computer-readable databases—in particular, commercial online (time-sharing) systems. Begun in the early 1970s as a limited and expensive adjunct to printed libraries, commercial time-sharing systems have replaced print sources as the preferred mode of business research. Searched through modems attached to personal computers, time-sharing systems such as DIALOG, DOW JONES, and NEXIS are supermarkets of business information. The DIALOG system alone has some fifty business-related databases.

To illustrate the use of online systems in M&A research, we give examples of dozens of online searches. With few exceptions, our sample searches are done using a system's "command" language rather than "menu" choices. For example, although DIALOG offers menu-driven access to many of its business databases our illustrations use the command versions of the databases. Command languages are usually superior to menus in their flexibility and in the speed with which searches can be entered. If you are unfamiliar with any of the time-sharing systems we discuss, consult Appendix 2 for a directory of time-sharing services. More information on subscription costs and training is available directly from these companies.

When an online database was available on two or more systems, we usually used DIALOG's version of the file. This use reflects the fact that DIALOG is a popular system that supports many of the databases we described. To have repeated our examples on the many other excellent online systems would have been unwieldy and confusing. Appendix 1 lists the databases we have discussed.

Discussing the current state of business databases has been compared to trying to change the tire on a moving car. Corporate change also affects the electronic and print publishing industries. While writing this book, there were scores of changes occurring in the industry. These changes included the addition and deletion of electronic databases, the modification of searching systems, the proliferation of business databases on CD-ROM, and the publication and suspension of printed sources. A major change occurred in early 1991, when Disclosure Inc. acquired Bechtel Information Services. Bechtel had been the contract provider of corporate filings with the U.S. Securities and Exchange Commission.

This *Guide* is designed to be a practical manual for M&A research. It is not intended as an exhaustive list of merger sources. Although we discuss some sources for law, our expected reader is a business (not legal) researcher.

We want to thank the many people who encouraged the writing of this book. We are particularly grateful for the careful reading of the manuscript by Martin Sikora, editor of *Mergers and Acquisitions.* His encouragement, editorial skill, and encyclopedic knowledge of M&A helped us greatly. Of course, the final result is ours as is the responsibility for any errors.

*Research Guide to
Corporate Acquisitions,
Mergers, and Other
Restructuring*

1

Coping with Corporate Change

In 1988, a cartoon in the *New Yorker* showed Girl Scouts plotting to take over Mrs. Fields Cookie Company with the caption "Acquisition Fever Hits the Girl Scouts."[1] In the more sober 1990s, acquisition fever has cooled, at least in the United States. In 1990, the dollar value of announced U.S. merger and acquisitions dropped about 16 percent compared to the previous year. Merger activity may simply be shifting to Europe. European merger announcement increased almost 50 percent in 1990 compared to 1989.[2]

Although the 1980s are being characterized as a "decade of excess," the symbols of this excess, junk bonds and leveraged buyouts, will continue to be important instruments of corporate change. Despite occasional periods of slowdown, corporate change continues. Even when the headlines are devoid of megamerger news, many transactions take place. From divestitures and spinoffs, to buyouts and bankruptcies, these changes are a constant force in the restructuring of the corporate world.

Consider some statistics from the high point of M&A activity in 1988:

- at least $226.3 billion changed hands in mergers, acquisitions, and divestitures, setting a yearly record for dollar value of activity
- a record was set for megadeals, with 41 transactions priced at $1 billion or more
- a new record was set for the dollar value of U.S. foreign acquisitions, with $60.8 billion in transactions
- a new record was set for the dollar value of leveraged buyouts, with $42.6 billion in transactions (this figure does not even include the biggest deal of all time, the $24.7-billion leveraged buyout of RJR Nabisco by Kohlberg Kravis Roberts[3])

• Not only mammoth public companies fueled the boom in acquisitions and mergers. Since 1981, 56 percent of reported private deals were valued at less than $10 million.

Corporate change includes several kinds of restructuring activities. Their common thread is that they lead to the creation of different corporate entities (and, in some cases, may lead to the end of them). These changes confuse existing corporate identities. This, in turn, creates problems for the business researcher. In this chapter we will identify and define specific types of change and provide definitions and examples. We will also present several measures for gauging levels of corporate change.

DEFINING CORPORATE CHANGE

What is corporate change? While no business dictionary defines it, we know that it involves activities that alter the structure of corporations. This change can be as broad as a total corporate restructuring or as specific as a change in an executive position. We define corporate change as events that significantly alter a corporation's identity.[4]

Terms that describe corporate change are sometimes used interchangeably in the business literature. In fact, these terms can involve subtle distinctions. We often see the words "acquisition," "merger," or "consolidation" used to describe any activity where companies join. "Reorganization" and "restructuring" are often used interchangeably to refer to acquisition activity. Restructuring is sometimes used as a "catch-all" term for any type of corporate change.

Our terms are used for corporate change activities in which (in our experience) business researchers show the most interest. Most of the terms are adapted from definitions in either the *Dictionary of Banking and Finance*[5] or the *Business and Investment Almanac*.[6] Coming from dictionaries, these definitions are provided in their classic form, which we recognize may be slightly different from the definitions an M&A practitioner might provide. We also present examples of company change to illustrate or elaborate on the definitions.

Acquisition is the acquiring of control of one corporation by another. An acquisition may be friendly or hostile. Companies may be acquired for cash or stock. Depending on the nature of the acquisition, the acquirer may need to pay a price higher than the current market value of the stock. The added cost is called a "premium." Premiums may be used to induce stockholders to give up their claims to future dividends, or to outbid competitors vying for the same target. A merger is similar because the result is the same—one company takes control of another. The term "acquisition" is often used to describe a friendly deal, while a hostile acquisition is usually referred to as a "takeover."

EXAMPLE: After winning one of the longest and most fiercely contested takeovers in any industry, Bank of New York acquired Irving Bank
Corporation. The acquisition took place during a fourteen-month
struggle that saw Irving Bank take various defenses. These included
lobbying legislators, weakening the balance sheet, and seeking an al-
ternate, more friendly acquirer. Irving Bank resisted the acquisition
because its management believed that the two companies did not fit
together.[7]

Bankruptcy occurs when the conditions under which the financial
position of an individual corporation, or other legal entity are such as to
cause actual or legal insolvency. Involuntary bankruptcy occurs when
one or more creditors of an insolvent debtor file a petition having the
debtor declared bankrupt. Voluntary bankruptcy occurs when a debtor
files a petition claiming inability to meet debts and willingness to be declared bankrupt. When a bankruptcy is declared three basic resolutions
are possible: liquidation, acquisition, or reorganization. In a Chapter 11
filing the roles of all interested parties—creditors, stockholders, and
management— are specifically defined. Chapter 11 refers to the section
of the Bankruptcy Reform Act of 1978 that permits corporate restructuring. Since stockholders cannot receive any funds until the claims of
creditors are satisfied, they usually prefer reorganization to liquidation.
Management preference is for reorganization rather than liquidation.[8]

EXAMPLE: In 1982, Johns-Manville Company escaped into the safety of Chapter 11 in the face of $2 billion in asbestos health lawsuits. After six
years in bankruptcy, a reorganization plan has created a healthy
Manville Corporation. Manville will pay the claims of asbestos
victims and the cost of future cleanups out of corporate profits, but
has had to cut payroll by one-third and move to cheaper offices as
part of the reorganization plan.[9]

Consolidation is a combination of two or more organizations into one, to
form a new entity. Consolidation, in that it creates a new corporate
entity, is similar to both an acquisition and a merger. Consolidation is
considered a more friendly, cooperative deal than either a merger or acquisition. It gives equal footing in the new firm to each corporation.
Again, this is a classic definition. In reality a consolidation may be no
more friendly than any deal type, nor is there a guarantee that the two
firms will have equality in the new entity.

EXAMPLES: A strategic gain hoped for in consolidations is greater competitive
strength in an industry. Two of the "Big Eight" accounting firms,
Arthur Young and Ernst & Whinney, consolidated in 1989 to form
Ernst & Young. They created the larger accounting firm to combine

their strengths in claiming a greater share of the decreasing pool of corporate clients.[10] Baker International Corporation and Hughes Tool Company also consolidated to gain competitive advantage in the oil drill bit market. Both firms were performing poorly prior to the consolidation, and hoped the resulting organization, Baker-Hughes, would become a dominant firm in the oil exploration and production equipment industry.[11] Because of the imprecise use of corporate change terminology in the business literature both of these deals were frequently referred to as "mergers."

Divestiture is the process of disposing of all or part of a business. There are variations on a divestiture. A "selloff" involves the sale of a business for cash. A divestiture can be accomplished by a "spinoff" to shareholders in the formation of a new firm. A business unit can be divested to create a joint venture with another company.

EXAMPLE: One of the most well-known divestitures in business history was conducted by AT&T in 1984. AT&T was required to divest itself of its seven regional operating companies. Each of the divested subsidiaries became an independent, publicly held telecommunications company. Many more divestitures occur as the result of mergers and leveraged buyouts. This strategy reduces large debt incurred in the transaction. Campeau Corporation of Canada acquired both the Allied and Federated Department Stores. Campeau, in one of its restructuring moves, sold off seventy-six stores of the Gold Circle chain to Kimco Development Corporation.[12]

Initial public offering (IPO) is the sale of new issues of stock to the public to raise capital for corporate development. An IPO leads to the creation of a new publicly held corporation.

EXAMPLE: IPOs are primarily of interest to investors looking for bargain-priced companies. For example, a $10,000 investment in King World Productions in 1984 was worth $115,000 in 1988. These gems are difficult to find. Of all IPOs issued between 1982 and 1988, only 41 percent now sell for more than their original issue price.[13] Since the 1987 stock market crash, fewer IPOs come to market. There were 280 IPOs in 1988 compared with 541 in 1987.[14]

Leveraged buyout (LBO) is the acquisition of a business primarily with borrowed funds that are repaid from the target company's earnings and/or sale of excess assets. An LBO differs from a typical acquisition in that, along with transfer of ownership, there is also a complete restructuring of the target company's balance sheet. An LBO often transforms a target company's balance sheet from a largely debt-free condition to a highly leveraged state.[15]

EXAMPLE: To foil a takeover attempt, the Southland Corporation, owner of the 7-Eleven convenience store chain, went through a leveraged buyout in 1987. Southland repurchased all of its stock, going from public to private status. The LBO left Southland $4 billion in debt.[16]

In an LBO, a public company often goes private. Going private gives a company some advantages. It eliminates the burdens of public disclosure and the necessity to produce short-term results to please shareholders. An LBO may be used as a takeover defense. A related type of deal is the management buyout (MBO), in which a team of internal managers take a company division and operate it as a separate, privately run company.

Liquidation is the winding up of the affairs of a business by converting all assets into cash, paying off all outside creditors in the order of their preference, and distributing the remainder, if any, to the owners in proportion and in the order of preference.

EXAMPLE: Most liquidations are among private companies, or the subsidiaries of larger companies. In fact, since 1983 only three fortune 500 companies have liquidated: Uniroyal, Household Manufacturing, and American Bakeries.[17]

Merger is the combining of two or more entities through the direct acquisition by one of the net assets of the other. In a deal in which the companies are of equal size, one will still act as the acquirer. Also, an important distinction that characterizes a merger is that the deal usually involves an exchange of stock. Regardless of the format of the deal, a merger is the final legal requirement for the completion of the deal.

EXAMPLE: The merger of Smithkline Beckman and Beecham Group, two pharmaceutical firms, created the world's second largest prescription drug firm. Smithkline stockholders received shares in the new Smithkline Beecham PLC, plus a one-time special dividend of $5.50. Although Beecham was acquiring Smithkline, the deal gave Smithkline stockholders equality with owners of Beecham stock.[18]

Recapitalization involves altering the capital structure of a firm by increasing or decreasing its capital stock. In doing so, a firm also may increase its debt or leverage. In a leveraged recapitalization, stock is exchanged for debt securities and leverage becomes a greater percentage of the total capitalization. Methods of decreasing stock to defend against takeovers or to increase stock value are referred to as stock buybacks or stock repurchases. The stocks are bought back from existing shareholders, which shrinks outstanding shares.

EXAMPLE: To defend against a takeover threat in 1988 from United Kingdom raider James Goldsmith, Goodyear Tire & Rubber Company went through a $2.6-billion recapitalization. Goodyear emerged as a smaller and more efficient operation.[19]

Reorganization is the altering of a firm's capital structure, often resulting from a merger, that affects the rights and responsibilities of the owners. In a Chapter 11 bankruptcy, the objectives of a reorganization are to eliminate the cause of failure, settle with creditors, and allow the firm to remain in business. Alternatively, a company may undergo a nonlegal reorganization that may result only in changes to the organizational chart through a shuffling of subsidiaries and divisions.

EXAMPLE: As a result of a staggering $3-billion penalty Texaco was forced to pay to Pennzoil, it went into Chapter 11 bankruptcy. Texaco reorganized by selling some $6 billion worth of assets. In addition, many layers of management were shed.[20] Although this reorganization was related to emergence from Chapter 11, the term is often used in the literature to refer to corporate strategies for overhauling or turning around troubled companies. For example, Sears Roebuck focused its reorganization on a plan to offer "everyday low prices" and national brands as a discount retailer. Sears also had a 10 percent stock buyback and sold off assets such as the Sears Tower.[21] Even IBM, as a result of slumping sales, reorganized its operations into five independent organizations designed to be more responsive to customer needs.[22]

Restructuring is a collection of activities designed to increase shareholder wealth by maximizing the value of corporate assets. These activities may include divestiture of underperforming businesses, spinoffs to shareholders, stock repurchases, recapitalization, or acquisitions.

EXAMPLE: Kaufman & Broad, a large homebuilding company, underwent a corporate restructuring into two separate companies—Kaufman & Broad Home Corporation and Broad Incorporated.[23] The strategy behind the restructuring focused on the separation of the company's housing and financial services businesses to enhance stockholder value. Broad Inc. is more aggressive in the insurance and financial services businesses. The company will add to its financial services through strategic acquisitions. One of the positive effects of the restructuring was an unprecedented six-level increase in Broad Inc.'s Standard & Poor investment rating, from BB– to A–.[24]

A *Spinoff* is the separation of a subsidiary or division of a corporation from its parent by issuing shares in a new corporate entity. Shareowners in the parent receive shares in the new company in proportion to their original holding and the total value of the shares remains about the same.

EXAMPLE: Honeywell spun off its defense business into a new company called Alliant Techsystems, which immediately began trading on the New York Stock Exchange; Cooper Development spun off both Cooper LaserSonics and CooperVision, two divisions originally belonging to Cooper Laboratories, a health and personal care business; and May Department Stores spun off its discount chain, Venture Stores, to concentrate on May's main business, department stores.

LEVELS OF CORPORATE CHANGE ACTIVITY

There were thousands of M&A transactions in the decade of the 1980s. The record for total number of transactions was set in 1986, when hundreds of deals were rushed to completion before tax advantages expired at the end of the year. M&A activity continued at high levels—well over 3,000 deals a year—through 1988. The total dollar value of the deals showed strong growth until the end of the 1980s (see Table 1.1 for measures of U.S. M&A activity for the period 1979-1990).

Note the discrepancies between some of the numbers reported in Table 1.1 and the figures provided at the beginning of this chapter. For example, two different dollar amounts are given for the total dollar value of deals in 1988. Table 1.1 shows the value is $246.9 billion, but a figure of $226.3 billion was cited in the text. We point this out to illustrate the fact that the statistical data provided on M&A activity will often be reported differently in different sources.

The figures in Table 1.1 come from the *Mergerstat Review* while the figures at the beginning of the chapter come from MLR Publishing Com-

Table 1.1
M&A Activity, 1979-1990

	Deal Announcements	Total Value (in billions of dollars)	Deals Valued over $100 Million
1979	2128	43.5	83
1980	1889	44.3	94
1981	2395	82.6	113
1982	2346	53.8	116
1983	2533	73.1	138
1984	2543	122.2	200
1985	3001	179.8	270
1986	3336	173.1	346
1987	2302	163.7	301
1988	2258	246.9	369
1989	2366	221.1	328
1990	2074	108.2	181

Source: Mergerstat Review (1990).

pany, the firm that publishes *Mergers & Acquisitions*. It is important to determine the criteria publishers use when they collect M&A data. For example, do they include only deals over a certain dollar amount in value? Do they include all announced deals or only those that were actually completed? Do they include U.S. deals or worldwide deals? Understanding the data collection methods of the statistical source helps to ensure accuracy.

Accompanying the growing number of M&A deals is an increasing body of literature about this business phenomenon. News items about the transactions appear in scores of newspapers and magazines. Scholarly literature and practitioner-oriented articles are published frequently. Table 1.2 shows the growing interest in M&A as reflected in the literature produced on the subject.

Column 1 shows the number of completed deals in each year from 1979 to 1990 as recorded by the M & A DATABASE, an electronic database for acquisitions and merger research. This is not a bibliographic database; we provide it in the table as a comparative measure of actual transactions. Column 2 shows the number of bibliographic records retrieved from the database ABI/INFORM when searching the index term "acquisitions & mergers." ABI/INFORM indexes and abstracts articles from over 700 business journals. Column 3 shows the number of bibliographic records retrieved from the database NATIONAL NEWSPAPER INDEX (NNI) when searching the index term "consolidation and merger of corporations." NNI indexes articles published in the *New York Times, Wall Street Journal, Washington Post, Los Angeles Times*, and *Christian Science Monitor*. Column 4 shows the number of bibliographic records retrieved from the Predicasts' F & S INDEX when searching the event

Table 1.2
Bibliographic Measures of M&A Activity, 1979-1990

	M&A	ABI/INFORM	NNI	F&S	LC-MARC
1979	1547	220	208	N/A	28
1980	1545	255	115	11,675	29
1981	2336	449	320	13,907	29
1982	2289	473	315	11,415	37
1983	2392	611	276	12,476	55
1984	3178	768	562	18,823	33
1985	3441	901	741	19,793	61
1986	4403	1098	757	28,746	53
1987	3948	1062	833	32,352	57
1988	3678	1362	1301	32,434	63
1989	3719	1405	1966	31,364	68
1990	3216	1224	789	23,441	34

code for M&A activity. The F & S INDEX covers 2,500 business publications, including journals, trade magazines, newspapers, newsletters, and press releases. Column 5 shows the number of bibliographic records retrieved from the LC MARC-BOOKS database on DIALOG. It contains bibliographic records for monographs catalogued by the Library of Congress. This should provide a measure of the number of books published on M&A.

We find it interesting that the literature published on M&A topics reflects the actual number of transactions. Periods of increased transactions are mirrored by increased numbers of books and articles in the literature. With decreases in transactions in 1990, citations in significant databases have dropped. Even with the decrease in the M&A literature, researchers working in this area must still contend with a large pool of literature and transaction data.

Most of the data presented in this section have focused on M&A. Corporate change, as we have defined it, includes more specialized aspects of M&A. Table 1.3 shows some statistics for transactions in related areas. There is also strong growth of transactions in these areas. In particular, the growth in private acquisitions indicates there has been a change in the financing of deals. More transactions are financed through private sources than through the previously popular use of debt instruments, such as junk bonds.

Corporate name changing is also on the upswing. Consider the following statistics:

Table 1.3
Transactions in Related M&A Areas, 1979-1990

	Divestitures	LBOs (going private)	Private Acquisitions	Public Acquisitions
1979	752	16	1,049	248
1980	666	13	988	173
1981	830	17	1,330	168
1982	875	31	1,222	168
1983	932	36	1,316	180
1984	906	57	1,351	190
1985	1,218	76	1,358	211
1986	1,259	76	1,598	336
1987	807	47	855	286
1988	894	125	836	464
1989	1,055	80	867	328
1990	940	20	821	185

Source: Mergerstat Review (1990).

- According to *Graphic Design: USA*, 931 American companies changed names in the first six months of 1988.
- Predicasts' *Index of Corporate Change* lists about 650 occurrences of name change in the 1988 cumulative index.
- A report in the June 27, 1988 issue of *U.S. News & World Report* showed that 1,753 companies took new names in 1987—up 27 percent from 1986.

The result of much of this activity is often general confusion about who is in what business and who owns whom. An example of the turmoil caused by corporate change was Time's planned merger with Warner Communications in mid-1989. The peaceful deal was suddenly shattered when a hostile bid for Time was made by Paramount Communications. The confusion was such that Time reporters leaving for lunch would tell their secretaries, "If my boss calls, find out his name."[25] The deal also caused confusion for business researchers. Initially, we could find no listing of Paramount Communications in several sources. Only after more detailed accounts of the takeover became available was it revealed that Paramount Communications was the new corporate name for Gulf & Western. Gulf & Western had changed its name one week before announcing its plan to acquire Time.

The volatile impact of corporate change was profiled in an article about the displacement of major companies from the Fortune Industrial 500. Between 1983 and 1988, 143 or nearly 30 percent of the 500 corporations were eliminated from the Fortune 500 as a result of some type of corporate change activity. By comparison, during the 500's first 25 years (1955-1980), only 238 companies were eliminated. Some of the companies still exist, but have altered their businesses significantly enough to lose eligibility for the Industrial 500; some are now on the Service 500. Others no longer do enough business to qualify as Fortune 500 level firms. It is clear that the volume of corporate deal making is the reason that many companies left the Industrial 500. More than 100 of 1983's Fortune Industrial 500 have been acquired, merged, or taken private. Most of these, 67 in all, are now subsidiaries of other companies on the 500.[26]

BUSINESS INFORMATION ACCESS

At one extreme, business information is ordinarily not available to the public. Examples of highly restricted information include trade secrets such as Coca Cola's formula for its soft drink and the income tax statements of private corporations. Information such as this can be obtained only by industrial espionage or court-ordered disclosure. "Insider information" (information known only by directors and officers of corporations) is another example of knowledge available to only a few. Insiders face stiff jail sentences if they attempt to profit from their privileged information by manipulating stocks. At the other end of the availability spectrum is information that is well known. Between the extremes of privileged information and common knowledge are a wide range of facts.

Access to information is often restricted by those who control it. We have already mentioned examples of trade secrets and insider information. Some government data can be described as "semisecret." U.S. government agencies often must disclose data through the Freedom of Information Act. Governments are not the only agencies to restrict information. Corporations typically will not reveal financial or marketing details unless required by law to do so. Associations frequently restrict commissioned marketing or financial studies to their membership. Another obvious restriction on information availability is its cost.

The availability of information frequently changes over time. If General Motors' management were making plans to acquire Ford, the information would initially be secret. If GM then made an offer to purchase stock from Ford stockholders, the information would become public. Time may affect the method by which information is disseminated. For example, the details of a General Motors patent filed within the last fifteen years is available through several online and CD-ROM databases. The availability of a GM patent filed in 1940, on the other hand, is limited to a few patent depositories.

BUSINESS INFORMATION COMPLEXITY

Business researchers supply information on topics ranging from single facts to complex theories.

Consider these three questions:

1. What were the annual sales of company X in 1990?
2. How many leveraged buyouts (LBOs) were there in the packaging industry in 1990?
3. Does a company's research and development (R&D) expenditure increase or decrease following its acquisition by another company?

Facts such as the sales figures in question 1 often serve as the building blocks of answers to more complex questions. Question 2 is more complex because it requires us to define both leveraged buyouts (it is not always clear that a transaction is an LBO) and packaging industry. To answer question 3 requires extensive empirical research and expert analysis. On this particular question, expert opinion is divided.[27] Usually, the more complex the question, the more difficult is the research required. Yet even uncomplicated questions are not necessarily easy questions. For example, the annual sales figures for many private companies are not publicly available.

We have illustrated the combination of business information availability and complexity in Figure 1.1. The horizontal axis represents the continuum from unavailable to widely known information. The vertical axis shows the increase in complexity from isolated facts to general theories. We have represented types of information as areas on the graph.

USERS OF CORPORATE CHANGE INFORMATION

Economists, accountants, lawyers, financial officers, and managers frequently have an interest in aspects of corporate change. Academics and business students are also active in collecting M&A data.

The information these different professions seek is varied. We find all of the following of concern to individuals tracking acquisitions and mergers:

Management
- motivation and strategy in mergers
- synergistic effects of mergers

Finance
- details of historical transactions
- news about ongoing activity involving specific deals or industries
- M&A techniques/methods
- names of acquisition, merger, and buyout specialists
- aggregate statistical data on M&A deals
- company information (profiles, financial data, news) for analyzing acquisition candidates
- financial statements for previously acquired companies
- comparable deal data

Law
- SEC regulations on M&A and tender offer activity
- legal and legislative news related to regulation of M&A
- state laws related to M&A activity

Economists
- antitrust implication of individual acquisition
- market share changes as result of M&A

Figure 1.1
Business Information Availability Grid

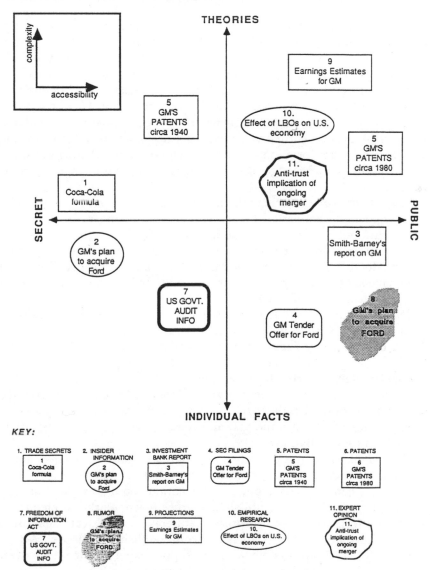

Accounting
- tax implications of mergers
- valuation of mergers

RESEARCHING CORPORATE CHANGE

Researching corporate change requires familiarity with a wide range of information sources in both print and electronic form. We have organized these sources into seven database categories. (Here, the term "database" includes both print and electronic sources.)

Filings databases contain the complete text or abstracts of documents filed by public companies with the U.S. Securities and Exchange Commission or other government agencies. They are primary source material for descriptions of a company's finances, lines of business, officers, and subsidiaries. They provide details of such corporate change events as tender offers, name change, security registration, and change of public status.

Transaction databases bring together the main facts concerning individual merger and acquisition deals. Transaction databases include both private and public companies and are international in scope.

Directory databases for companies include descriptions of companies, their products, and chief officers. Machine-readable company directories often have special features, such as the ability to link corporate families or to calculate share of market.

Monitoring databases follow day-to-day (or even minute-to-minute) corporate changes. Online newswire services are particularly useful in this regard because they focus on the events of interest as they become public.

Finance databases bring together company financial statements. They allow us to see corporation changes over time and to compare individual companies with their industry.

Legal databases contain the text and commentaries on administrative, judicial, and legislative law.

Bibliographic databases provide access to books, journal articles, newsletters, and report literature that discuss corporate change.

Databases can be used to obtain information about corporate change. Our emphasis will be on published sources, particularly on electronic access to information. We recognize that people sources can sometimes supply information that is missing from published sources. We do describe directories of people who can supply expert advice. However, we do not discuss techniques such as the use of the Freedom of Information Act to elicit information from U.S. federal agencies, nor do we discuss methods of soliciting information by telephone. For excellent advice on tapping people sources, we recommend the series produced by Washington Researchers Publishing.[28]

NOTES

1. *New Yorker* 64(9):31 (April 18, 1988).

2. "U.S. Merger and Acquisition Activity Drops 16 Percent; European M&A Is Up 50 Percent," *PR Newswire* (November 8, 1990).

3. Martin Sikora, "M&A Activity Hit a Record $226.3 Billion in 1988," *PR Newswire* (January 26, 1989).

4. Steven J. Bell, "Corporate Change: Impact on the Corporate Document Collection," *Special Libraries* 79(4):265-70 (1988).

5. Jerry M. Rosenberg, *Dictionary of Banking and Finance* (New York: Wiley, 1982).

6. Sumner N. Levine, *Business and Investment Almanac* (Homewood, Ill.: Dow Jones-Irwin, 1987).

7. Peter Finch, "Joe Rive's Fight to Fend Off the Bank of New York," *Business Week* 3044 (Industrial/Technology ed.):44 (1988).

8. George E. Nagler and Kenneth B. Schwartz, "Choosing the Best Alternative in a Chapter 11 Case," *Journal of Commercial Bank Lending* 70(2):48-53 (1987).

9. Mark Ivey, "Manville Starts to See a Glimmer of Daylight," *Business Week* 3074 (Industrial/Technology ed.):58, 60 (1988).

10. Jeffrey Laderman, "When One Plus One Equals No. 1," *Business Week* 3108:92, 94 (1989).

11. Baker-Hughes Tool Merger. Dow Jones News Retrieval; Wall Street Journal Full Text Database. Document Number 870406-0150. April 6, 1987.

12. "Target and Hills Get Gold Circle," *Discount Merchandiser* 28(10):14, 16 (1988).

13. Charles M. Bartlett, "When the Broker Calls with a Hot New Issue," *Forbes* 141(14):290-92 (1988).

14. "1988: The Market Struggles Through," *Going Public: The IPO Reporter* 13(1):1427-28 (1989).

15. J. T. Greve, *How to Do a Leveraged Buyout*, 3d ed. (San Diego, Calif.: Business Publications, 1987), pp. 3-4.

16. "Retailers of the Year: Post-LBO 7-Eleven Gets Tough," *Chain Store Age Executive* 64(2):367-42 (1988).

17. John Paul Newport, "A New Era of Rapid Rise and Ruin," *Fortune* 119(9):77-88 (1988).

18. SmithKline Beckman Corp. Merger Completed to Form Prescription Drug Company. Dow Jones News Retrieval. Wall Street Journal Full Text Database. Document Number 890727-0066. July 27, 1989.

19. Marcia Parker, "Goodyear Ready to Roll Again," *Pensions & Investment Age* 16(17):30-31 (1988).

20. "Texaco: Catch a Fallen Star," *Economist* 310(7585):66-67 (1989).

21. Michael O'Neal, "Sear Faces a Tall Task," *Business Week* 3079 (Industrial/Technology ed.):54-55 (1988).

22. Philip Dorn, "Change and Change Again at IBM," *Computerworld* 22(44):19 (1988).

23. Alfred C. Haggerty, "Broad Inc. to Quicken Financial Services Pace," *National Underwriter (Life/Health/Financial Services)* 93(2):19-20 (1989).

24. Jana W. Greer, "Broad Inc. Announces Move of Its $7 Billion Financial Services Operation to Los Angeles," *PR Newswire* (April 27, 1989).

25. Warren Bennis, "Leading Questions," *World*, 2 1990:46 (April 18, 1990).

26. Newport, "New Era."

27. H. Bronwyn Hall, et. al., "The Impact of Corporate Restructuring on Industrial Research and Development," *Brookings Papers on Economic Activity*, 85-135 (1990).

28. Washington Researcher Publishing, *How to Find Information about Divisions, Subsidiaries, and Products* (Washington, D.C.: Washington Researchers, Ltd., 1990).

2

Monitoring Corporate Change with Print Resources

Megamergers are always big news. When RJR Nabisco is involved in a $25-billion merger, it makes the front page of the popular press and is announced on the nightly news. If all M&A activity involved billions of dollars, monitoring corporate change would require little more than reading the headlines. In reality, for every billion-dollar transaction there are hundreds of smaller deals. Most deals attract little attention, even in business publications. Only diligent monitoring efforts will lead to the capture of information about smaller or industry-specific events.

Monitoring corporate change allows the business professional

- to gain general business awareness
- to observe active acquirers in a specific industry
- to know who in an industry is making acquisitions
- to know if business associates are being acquired or changing the nature of their company
- to know current prices being paid for specific types of companies
- to take advantage of opportunities to participate in or profit from deals through correctly timed stock purchases
- to undertake industry studies or market analysis

This chapter discusses strategies for monitoring corporate change with printed resources. These resources include corporate news releases, newspapers, business magazines, trade and industry literature, and newsletters.

Print resources differ from one another primarily in the speed, accuracy, and comprehensiveness that they bring to the delivery of M&A news. No printed resources can provide all three qualities. Resources often trade off accuracy and comprehensiveness for speed. Monitoring corporate change requires the development of a reading strategy or regimen covering a mixture of sources. This should ensure no important deal goes unnoticed. Table 2.1 summarizes the approximate time lag of several printed resources in reporting corporate change events.

NEWS RELEASES

Companies use news releases to publicize their activities. A news release is issued before or shortly after a corporate change occurs. It alerts the business community, shareholders, and media about events occurring within the company. News releases are a worthwhile medium for monitoring corporate change because virtually every development, from a change in executive personnel to an acquisition or divestiture, will be announced. Since the release is issued by the corporation, it can substantiate facts about a change.

Table 2.1
Printed Resources for Monitoring Corporate Change

Resource	1 - 5 days	1 - 3 weeks	1 month	Beyond 1 month
News Release	X	X		
Daily Newspaper	X			
Weekly News Magazine		X		
Trade/ Industry Magazines		X	X	
General News Magazines		X	X	
Monthly Business Magazines				X
M&A Journals				X
Business Newsletters		X		

New releases offer several advantages over other print resources. They are easy to obtain. A phone call or letter to the company will add your name to the corporate mailing list. A corporation's address or phone number may be obtained in a company directory such as Standard and Poor's *Register of Corporations* or Dun and Bradstreet's *Million Dollar Directory.* News releases are free; there is no direct cost for obtaining them beyond the initial letter or phone call. Finally, news releases are easy to use. Beyond opening the envelopes and scanning, little effort is required to monitor corporate change.

Although news releases are easy to use, they can quickly become a burden. It will take too much time to process the mail when many corporate releases are received. In addition, this approach to corporate monitoring allows for little selectivity. You are as likely to receive a release about a corporate fund-raising campaign as you are news about an important change. You will have no control over the type of corporate news release you receive. As a result, you will have to scan much irrelevant material to find the few nuggets of information about corporate change. Another problem with relying on printed news releases is that an increasing number of companies are issuing their releases only via electronic news services such as PR NEWSWIRE. This indicates that fewer companies continue to print and mail news releases.

It might seem that a key strength of the news release for monitoring corporate change is speed of information delivery. Depending on the company and the mail service, however, news releases may take several days to appear. To measure the speed of corporate news transmitted by news release, we sampled releases dealing with corporate change to estimate the time lag between date of release and receipt. The results are displayed in Table 2.2

The releases were received within three to ten days after issue. Since our mail is first received by a central mail processing unit before it is sent to us, a day or two may have been added to delivery time. The time lag for news releases is small compared to other print resources. Yet if corporate change information must be digested and analyzed as it occurs, news releases may prove to be too slow. They are still useful for their accuracy, detail, and low cost, but the several-day wait may not be acceptable.

NEWSPAPERS

For monitoring corporate change, newspapers offer greater speed than other print resources. Corporate change is often reported in the next printed edition released after the event. Newspapers are also sources of comprehensive information on larger transactions. While many deals are reported in newspapers, the majority of the reports are brief and provide

Table 2.2
Time Lag of Selected Corporate News Releases

Company	News Item	Release Date	Receipt Date
Cooper Industries	completes acquisition	July 24	July 27
Southmark Corporation	files for Chapter 11	July 14	July 20
Neoax	Sells a subsidiary	July 10	July 20
Johnson Controls	Purchase a new subsidiary	May 31	June 6
Republic New York	Proposes bank merger	June 22	June 28
National Medical Ent.	To spinoff Hillhaven Co.	May 24	May 31
Digilog	Merges with CXR Telecomm	June 28	July 6

few details other than the names of the companies and a summary of the terms of the deal. Comprehensive reporting is reserved for megadeals or those with significant impact on an industry.

Newspapers may be divided into three classes: metropolitan, national business, and local/regional business. Metropolitan papers, such as daily local papers, are weak in their coverage of corporate change. Extremely large or significant deals (e.g., RJR Nabisco, Time-Warner, General Electric-RCA) usually receive front-page reporting. There may be additional reporting in the business section of the local metropolitan daily. The vast majority of corporate change however, escapes coverage by these newspapers. The business section is likely to provide detailed reports on major deals involving local firms. For example, the *Philadelphia Inquirer* provided extensive coverage of the merger of the pharmaceutical companies SmithKline Beckman and Beecham. SmithKline has its headquarters in Philadelphia and employs thousands of people living in the area.

Metropolitan papers often provide only scant details of important deals that occur in other regions of the country or abroad. The business section of metropolitan papers may include a business news column giving brief reports of corporate change. These reports may be mixed with reports of an increase in the treasury bill rate or a new product announcement. Overall, metropolitan papers, despite their availability and low cost, are not sufficient for complete monitoring of corporate change.

The daily business section of the *New York Times* (NYT) is an exception. This source should be required reading for corporate change monitoring. The "Business Digest" column on the front page of the business section is the first place to look. It gives brief reports of corporate changes. If a supplemental story is available, it is noted. If you want to monitor the actions of specific companies, the "Company Index," usually found on the second page of the business section, will be helpful.

The *Wall Street Journal* (WSJ) is America's premier daily business newspaper. It too is required reading for monitoring corporate change, and for some individuals it may be the only business paper they need to read. The WSJ does not report every corporate change, but among newspaper sources it reports on more changes than its competitors. It also provides more comprehensive reports than other sources. Reports of mergers, divestitures, and other deals are scattered throughout the paper.

The "What's News" column on the front page of the WSJ highlights the most newsworthy business developments of the day. It is often the first place to look to find the latest news on corporate change. This column is limited to only a few corporate change events. Initial reports of rumored deals and initial deal offers are often reported here. Despite its prominence as a business newspaper, even the WSJ must limit its comprehensive reporting to the handful of major deals occurring at any one time.

Like the NYT business section, the WSJ provides a corporate name index. This index is usually found on the second page of the second section and lists all companies mentioned in that day's paper and the page(s) on which stories about them are found. If you choose to monitor only specific firms, the index is a helpful resource. About the only thing the WSJ does not have is a separate section or column devoted to the reporting of corporate change.

The *Investor's Daily* (ID) is America's second major paper devoted to business. While its coverage is similar to that of the WSJ, it may, depending on the nature of the deal, provide additional news not found in the WSJ. However, in most situations, the WSJ is going to provide news on more corporate change. The ID has a "Today's News Digest" section on the front page of the paper. Here, most of the corporate change events are summarized. Unlike the NYT and WSJ, the ID does not offer a company name index.

Of less value for corporate change monitoring is the *Journal of Commerce and Commercial* (JCC), a daily business paper that focuses on events of intrest to the trade and commodities communities. The second page of the JCC does feature a "News Summary" section that is similar in design and purpose to those found in the other business papers. If you have access to the JCC, then consider it a supplement to your monitoring of other business dailies. It would not be worth the subscription cost to use the JCC for the sole purpose of monitoring corporate change.

Another daily business newspaper that could be part of your monitoring regimen is the *Financial Times* (FT). Published in the United Kingdom, the FT is a good source for stories involving deals between U.S. and non-U.S. companies. For quick monitoring, view the "Business Summary" column on the front page. The FT will provide comprehensive reporting of larger deals, particularly those involving U.K. or European firms. The FT has no company name index. Again, unless you have a particular need to monitor global change and want supplemental information to that found in the WSJ, you could do without the FT if you wish to avoid an additional newspaper subscription.

How do the daily business papers compare in their coverage of corporate change? When Walt Disney attempted to acquire Henson Associates (creators of the Muppet characters), the WSJ, ID, and NYT business section all carried the story the day following the announcement. All three had a brief item in their respective business summary columns. All three carried more detailed reports on the deal, with comments from executives of the companies and analysis on the impact of the deal (including speculation on a possible relationship between Mickey and Miss Piggy). Although not among the largest deals, the companies involved are important players in the entertainment industry. Neither the JCC or the FT carried news of the transaction.

Some disparity in reporting among newspapers may be found with other deals. When Prime Computer first announced that it had agreed to be acquired by J. H. Whitney, only the WSJ carried the story in its "What's News" column. There was also an additional story in the WSJ. The NYT business section and the ID did not report the event at the time. Several weeks later, when the transaction was officially completed after shareholder approval, the NYT and ID carried the Prime story. The fact that Prime had been the target of a takeover deal by MAI Basic Four for nearly a year before the acquisition by Whitney may have had some impact on the reporting. It is difficult to determine which paper has the most efficient coverage of corporate change without comparing the reporting of hundreds of deals. The example of Prime Computer shows that some discrepancy in reporting may occur. Depending on any one business paper for all monitoring may prove unreliable.

The last type of newspaper is the local or regional business newspaper. Their value for corporate change monitoring cannot be underestimated. Weekly papers provide extensive coverage of business developments at the local level—in particular the hundreds of deals that are ignored by the national business newspapers. Often the transactions involve two smaller firms, and only a regional paper may find such a deal newsworthy. Moreover, a deal that may receive only a few lines of coverage in a major business daily, could receive far more extensive reporting in a local business paper. There are about 150 local business papers in the United States. Some examples are *Crain's Chicago Business*, *Philadelphia Business Journal*, and *Seattle Business*. Most metropolitan areas may have one or more business newspapers, but in some lesser populated areas there may only be a state business paper or magazine. *Vermont Business Magazine* is an example.

As an example of local newspaper coverage, consider the acquisition of Cricket Software by Computer Associates International. Cricket is a company located in a suburb of Philadelphia. It is the producer of the popular Cricket Graph software package for the Apple MacIntosh. When Cricket was acquired, the story was covered in the WSJ, but was less than one column in length. The *Philadelphia Business Journal* carried a lengthy story on the deal. It featured quotes from executives at the acquirer and target, information on the acquirer's strategy, background information on each company, and other details.

BUSINESS MAGAZINES

While newspapers offer the advantage of speed in reporting, their distinct disadvantage is the time consumed in reading them. It is possible there will not be an opportunity to read a newspaper each day. Business magazines, particularly weekly and biweekly publications, represent a means to supplement newspaper reading, and when time for reading is scarce, they serve as substitutes for newspaper monitoring. The disadvantage of business magazines is their limited coverage of corporate change and slowness in reporting compared to newspapers.

Business Week is to the business magazine what the *Wall Street Journal* is to the business newspaper. It is a source that must be read each week. *Business Week* will usually provide detailed reporting for major deals, or the largest of multiple deals occurring at any one time. Analysis of these deals is a strength of this publication. Stories are likely to feature interviews with major players in the deal, impact on the industry, background on the companies, and expected repercussions of the deal. Given the nature of this magazine, however, only a few deals will receive detailed coverage in an issue, and sometimes no deals will be covered at all.

Business Week does not have a column or section devoted to corporate change events. It does have the "In Business This Week" feature, which gives a paragraph or two on current, completed, or rumored deals. This is always a good place to look for news of M&A activity, but comprehensive coverage is lacking. Only a few deals can be covered in each issue, and some of these are either rumored deals or updates to current deals. As a source for monitoring corporate change, *Business Week* would be a better monitoring source if a corporate change listing were available in each issue.

There are a host of other general business magazines a reader may want to choose from to supplement a monitoring strategy. Examples include *Fortune, Forbes, Financial World,* and *Institutional Investor.* None of these appears as frequently as *Business Week,* and all usually cover large deals. There may be deals that some will cover that will get overlooked by others. Since none of these magazines is devoted to the coverage of corporate change, they only report selectively on these events. Most individuals will be reading a few of these publications for general business knowledge. In so doing, they can supplement their monitoring of corporate change.

There are two business journals devoted to the acquisition and merger area that are good sources for a monitoring strategy. Because they are published less frequently, these journals are not useful for keeping current on important change. With their lists of deals, however, they are ideal sources for monitoring the many changes never covered in newspapers or business magazines. Both *Mergers & Acquisitions* (semimonthly) and *Corporate Growth Report* (monthly) contain "transaction rosters" in each issue. These rosters list all completed deals that exceed $1 million in value, and often provide information on ongoing deals. Deals may be of any type, and involve many industries, public and private companies, and deals between companies in different countries. Despite the significant time lag in the reporting of deals, *Mergers & Acquisitions* and *Corporate Growth* are valuable sources for monitoring M&A activity. Little news of other types of corporate change is reported.

TRADE AND INDUSTRY JOURNALS

For monitoring change in a specific industry, a newspaper or journal specific to that industry is an important source. A publication that focuses on a specific industry is referred to as a "trade" or "industry" journal. There are many hundreds (possibly thousands) of these journals. These publications provide more indepth reporting for important industry-related deals than do newspaper or business magazines, and are much more likely to cover deals that are not mentioned in the other sources. An example is smaller deals that may be overlooked by the major business press, but may have a significant impact on the industry.

Most of the trade and industry journals are weekly or monthly, implying a long time lag in the reporting of corporate change. *Computerworld* is an example. Some industries do have daily publications reporting business activity. These would include such publications as *American Metal Market* and *American Banker.* Another strength of the trade and industry journals is that they are much more likely to report on a wide range of corporate change events. Takeovers, divestitures, subsidiary changes, executive changes, and rumors about expected change are all reported.

NEWSLETTERS

For the best balance of speed and coverage, business newsletters are an excellent source to consider for monitoring. Newsletters are usually published weekly to provide recent information quickly. Some newsletters are published monthly. Be certain to check on publication frequency before subscribing. The degree of comprehensiveness in reporting is questionable. By their nature, newsletters report developments in brief, easily digestible snippets. A report is rarely longer than one page. Newsletters are useful as a means for getting quick news on rumored, in process, and completed deals, with some minor analysis provided.

There are hundreds of business newsletters. Of those, a small number focus on M&A activity. Some examples are:

Acquisition/Divestiture Weekly Report
Quality Services Company
5290 Overpass Road, Santa Barbara, CA 93111
(805)964-7841 $595.00

Business & Acquisition Newsletter
Newsletters International Inc.
2600 S. Gessner Road, Houston, TX 77063
(713)783-0100 $300.00   Monthly

Corporate Restructuring
MLR Publishing
220 South 18th Street, Philadelphia, PA 19103
(215)790-7000 $595.00   Monthly

Mergers & Corporate Policy
Securities Data Co.
40 West 57th Street, New York, NY 10019
(212)765-5311 $489.00   Semiweekly

Industry-specific newsletters are another possibility for monitoring corporate change. For example, a newsletter covering events in the chemical industry would be likely to report important corporate change, as that would have an impact on the industry. These newsletters often report on any rumored or ongoing deal likely to have some impact on the industry. They are unlikely to report on any deals outside the industry. Therefore whether you use these newsletters for your monitoring strategy depends on what deals you need to follow.

The primary disadvantage of business newsletters is their cost. With an average cost of $200 for an annual subscription, newsletters are considerably more expensive than the other print resources we have discussed.

In an age of electronic information retrieval, some might question if any monitoring activity involving a printed resource will be timely enough. Although electronic retrieval systems are fast, they are costly and, for some types of monitoring, may offer no advantage over other printed resources. News releases, newspapers, and magazines are for many businesspeople a regular part of required professional readiing. It only takes a short time each day to complete a scheduled regimen of corporate change monitoring. Regular reading of the resources mentioned in this chapter will improve knowledge of ongoing and planned corporate changes.

3

Monitoring Corporate Change with Electronic Resources

The ability to retrieve news about corporate change as it happens, or with minimal delay, is essential to corporate monitoring. Electronic information sources, represented primarily by time-sharing databases, make instantaneous news retrieval possible. In addition, databases that cover the business literature may, in some cases, be manipulated to retrieve articles and news stories on a specific topic regularly and automatically. We will refer to this as "current awareness" searching. For these reasons, electronic sources are the first choice for monitoring corporate change.

In this chapter we will describe several electronic databanks and some specific databases particularly useful for monitoring corporate change. Databases often contain hundreds of thousands of documents. Therefore, some experience is needed to retrieve efficiently only those documents related to corporate change. We will present strategies for finding appropriate documents quickly. In addition, we will discuss database cost and comprehensiveness, the currency of information delivery, and the unique features of specific databases. Finally, we will identify those databases offering current awareness capability, and give examples of search sessions in electronic databases to illustrate the creation and use of current awareness profiles.

THE TIME-SHARING ENVIRONMENT

If you are new to the concept of time-sharing databanks, it is useful to understand how these databanks are created, structured, and made available to the information seeker. It is also important to gain familiarity with the names and background of the more widely available databanks.

Time sharing is the simultaneous sharing of access to a computer databank with other searchers. The databank interacts with you and, perhaps, thousands of others in sequence, acknowledging your request for information and responding to it at blazing speed. You do not monopolize the computer's time; you share it with many others. Hence the term "time sharing."

Time sharing is made possible by telecommunications networks. Most databanks are located far from the user. If each caller had to place a long-distance call to use the databank the whole process would be too costly. Instead, it is possible to call a national telecommunications network at a local telephone number, and then be connected to a remote databank. BT TYMNET and SPRINTNET are two well known telecommunications networks. The cost of engaging the network averages $12.00 an hour. The cost is automatically calculated by the databank and added to your monthly time-sharing bill.

The earliest databases available through time-sharing networks were those produced by the federal government. Some of today's most common databases—ERIC (Educational Resources Information Center), NTIS (National Technical Information Services), and MEDLINE (National Library of Medicine)—were started in the 1960s by government agencies. Now, most databases are produced by independent information organizations. These database producers collect data, such as journal articles, financial statements, or the text of newspapers, convert it to machine-readable format, and then make it publicly available through a databank.

Establishing and maintaining a databank is complex and costly. Therefore it is difficult for most database producers to offer their own databank. Also, existing databanks may have thousands of subscribers, giving the database producer a ready market. Databanks are like supermarkets. They purchase and offer to the public the products of many different producers. Searchers use the databank to select the database most appropriate to their information needs. For electronic monitoring of M&A activity, it is important to know which databanks offer the databases with appropriate information. Finally, it is also important to know that each databank has its own unique protocols for searching. The searcher needs to learn the "search language" of each databank for successful interaction.

WHY USE ELECTRONIC SOURCES

Electronic sources offer a number of advantages over printed resources: Timeliness may be the strongest argument in favor of using electronic sources for monitoring corporate change. Speed is a priority in determining what sources to use. For example, the DOW JONES NEWS database on DOW JONES NEWS/RETRIEVAL makes business news available as it comes over the newswire. Other databases may make daily newspapers available within twenty-four hours or less. Often, news magazines such as *Business Week* or *Fortune* are available in an abstracted format within twenty-four hours of the time of publication.

There is also speed of use. Printed resources may require significant time to read because the entire source must be scanned to locate articles of interest. With their keyword search capability, electronic sources make it possible to identify quickly only those documents of significance. For example, there are hundreds of news releases issued regularly on the PR NEWSWIRE database. To retrieve only those news releases related to M&A, you simply type a search statement such as "mergers or acquisitions." In most databases, this statement will retrieve any document mentioning either or both of these terms. Documents retrieved may then be printed or captured on a disk. A search that is restricted to a time period (for example, the most recent six months) may only take a few minutes to perform.

Electronic sources are flexible. Keyword searching is an obvious way to retrieve documents on a specific subject. Electronic sources offer other methods to retrieve documents, such as by words appearing in headlines; by specific date limitations; by unique code schemes such as keyword, product, or industry classifications; or by company ticker symbol.

There is no print counterpart. Some sources of M&A information exist only in electronic format. If you want to track the acquisition documents being submitted to the Securities and Exchange Commission, you have only two practical choices. Use an electronic database such as M&A FILINGS, or use a document delivery service to screen the material as it is submitted to the SEC. Other examples include highly industry-specific newsletters that are available only electronically, or the database ABI/INFORM, which indexes and abstracts articles from hundreds of business magazines.

Electronic sources are getting easier to use. Many early cryptic search languages have been replaced with menu-driven interfaces or simpler search procedures. Consider DOW JONES NEWS/RETRIEVAL, which offers users three ways to search the TEXT database. There is a command-driven interface, a menu-driven interface, or DOWQUEST. DOWQUEST is a revolutionary approach to online searching that allows users to enter their search queries as English language questions. For example, in DOWQUEST the searcher may enter the question "Tell me about acquisitions or mergers in the airline industry." Any microcomputer equipped with a modem can serve as a database search terminal. With toll-free or interactive assistance, user newsletters and magazines, and other incentives designed to make database searching appeal to the public, electronic sources are easier to use than ever.

Electronic searching has some disadvantages. Electronic sources cost more to use than print sources. In fact, the cost of a single issue of the *Wall Street Journal* will not buy one minute's worth of search time in the electronic version of the paper available in DOW JONES NEWS/ RETRIEVAL. The fees charged by electronic sources vary. Usually fees are based on per hour rates and possibly added costs for retrieving individual documents from the database. Typically, searches that monitor corporate change are brief and their cost reasonable. Because monitoring must be done regularly, perhaps daily or weekly, the cost of even short searches can add up quickly.

Not every database is available from every vendor of electronic databases. For example, only DOW JONES NEWS/RETRIEVAL has the electronic full-text versions of the *Wall Street Journal* and *Barron's*. Similarly, only Mead Data Central's NEXIS Service has the electronic, full-text version of the *New York Times.* In addition, each of the electronic sources may have its own search language and other important protocols. Gaining expertise in one electronic source may not prepare you to use another. There is an analogy here with using word processing software. If you know how to use WordPerfect you understand the features offered by word processing, but you will not be able to use Microsoft Word immediately because its interface and commands are completely different. The lack of standardization in search languages and features offered by electronic sources has hindered the widespread use of these systems.

Database searchers must also be aware that online time is money. For this reason, casual browsing through text on databases is expensive. To reduce total costs, you should formulate a search strategy before you do the search, and quickly perform the search once connected to the database. Print resources make casual browsing practical, since you alone determine the time constraints involved in using them.

Should you use electronic resources for monitoring corporate change? Print resources do offer low or no-cost means for monitoring, and they are readily available. However, if speed, direct access to source information, and the timeliness of that information is critical to your monitoring needs, electronic databases should be your choice.

PRIMARY TIME-SHARING DATABANKS

Databank popularity is often measured by the numbers of individual and corporate subscribers. By that measurement, the most well known databank is COMPUSERVE. A recent survey of database size showed that COMPUSERVE has about 500,000 active users. The next largest is

DOW JONES NEWS/RETRIEVAL (312,000 users), followed by DIALCOM (280,000 users), the LEXIS and NEXIS Services (216,000 users), and EASYLINK (210,000 users).[1]

DOW JONES NEWS/RETRIEVAL (DJNR) is a highly important source for retrieving financial and current events information. DJNR offers both menu- and command-driven searching. Some of the databases offered, such as the full text of the *Wall Street Journal*, are unique to DJNR. Others, such as the DISCLOSURE database, are available through multiple databanks. The majority of the databases in DJNR are searched by either a publicly held company's ticker symbol or by a DJNR industry/event code. These databases include DOW JONES NEWS, HISTORICAL QUOTES, and MEDIA GENERAL FINANCIAL SERVICES. For example, to find information on Exxon you would type XON, the ticker symbol. To find information on the latest M&A activity you would type, .I/TNM, the event code for tenders, mergers, and acquisitions.

For keyword searching of the complete text of hundreds of business newspapers and magazines, DJNR offers the TEXT database. These publications may be searched with conventional time-sharing search features, such as keyword searching, use of logical and proximity operators, and date or author searching. Source publications in TEXT include *Barron's*, *Fortune*, *Forbes*, *Business Week*, and regional business newspapers.

A wholly owned subsidiary of Knight-Ridder, DIALOG provides the world's largest and most comprehensive online databank. It offers nearly 300 databases covering many disciplines, and has 80,000 subscribers. DIALOG, along with DJNR, is a major provider of online information to the business community. In recent years, DIALOG has strongly emphasized the introduction of databases that make business news available with as little delay as possible. DIALOG is also a leader in designing products for end-users.

End-users are individuals who do their own database searching. DIALOG offers several versions of their databank that appeal to end-users. Both KNOWLEDGE INDEX and DIALOG MENUS are alternatives to DIALOG's regular command-driven databases. They use either simple commands or menus for easy online searching. The key tradeoffs for simplicity are limited database selection and some loss of search flexibility. DIALOG offers bibliographic databases, numeric databases, and full-text databases.

The LEXIS and NEXIS Services consist of two databanks. The LEXIS Service focuses on providing statutes and case law at the national and state levels. It also has a collection of databases containing Securities and Exchange Commission documents. The NEXIS Service focuses on news publications such as magazines and newspapers. Both databanks emphasize providing the complete text of documents. For M&A monitoring, NEXIS is more useful than LEXIS. Many of its hundreds of magazines and newspapers are business publications. The NEXIS Service is unique among databanks in having the full text of the *New York Times.* It also contains a good selection of wire services. Publications may be searched individually or in groups such as "finance," "business," or "government." For federal government documents, particularly Securities and Exchange Commission corporate documents, the LEXIS Service would be more appropriate.

Unlike some of its competitors, Mead Data Central (which produces the LEXIS and NEXIS Services) does not offer a separate end-user version, although their "NEXIS Plus" search software offers a more user-friendly interface. Historically, practicing attorneys were the target market for these databanks. The search language is considered simple enough for those without extensive database searching experience. It too offers conventional keyword search, logical operators or proximity operators, and many other searchable segments (date, author, words in a headline, etc.). Mead offers free training to all subscribers.

NEWSNET is an unusual databank. Its market niche is full-text business and industry newsletters. Many of the publications in NEWSNET are available only in electronic format, and those that are in print are usually available to NEWSNET subscribers before the print edition is mailed to subscribers. Because NEWSNET is designed primarily for end-users, using it is straightforward. You can scan newsletters by headlines or search them by keyword; search only the latest issue of a newsletter; or specify any period.

NEWSNET offers the complete text of over 300 newsletters. Most of the newsletters are industry-specific. Some examples are *Fiber Optic News, Health Care Competition Week,* and *Nuclear Waste News.* Unfortunately, NEWSNET does not contain any of the M&A newsletters mentioned in the chapter on print monitoring sources. However, because industry newsletters report on significant deals, a source such as *Telecommunications Week* would be useful for monitoring events related to the telecommunications industry. DISCLOSURE SEC FILINGS INDEX, because it lists documents submitted to the SEC that relate to takeover activity, is applicable to corporate change monitoring. Disclosure Index is not a full-text database. A more detailed discussion of its role in acquisitions and mergers is in the following chapter. NEWSNET also features several of the major newswire services, including BUSINESSWIRE, PR NEWS-WIRE, and UPI BUSINESS & FINANCIAL WIRE.

NEWSNET may have the largest database of electronic newsletters, but it does not have a monopoly on them. PREDICASTS offers its NEWS-LETTER DATABASE on DIALOG (file 636). There is one newsletter on NEWSLETTER DATABASE of particular interest to M&A researchers. *Buyouts,* published seventeen times a year by Venture Economics, Inc., covers the management buyout and leveraged acquisition industries. Use this newsletter to keep abreast of recent LBO deals, new equity partnerships being raised, and plans by LBO funds to sell investments.

To search this newsletter effectively, begin in File 636 and type the command S JN = BUYOUTS. This will retrieve all articles published in the newsletter. You may then use the DIALOG update command to limit the retrieval to the most recent update of the database. For example, UD = 9999 will retrieve only those articles from *Buyout* added in the last file update. To limit retrieval to articles on M&A in any of the newsletters, use the code "MA" with the industry prefix "IC." For example:

S IC = MA

The NEXIS Service also includes selected newsletters. For example, *Mergers & Acquisitions Reports* provides a weekly industry snapshot of U.S. and international M&A, restructurings, and buyouts.

DJNR provides access to many databases. DJNEWS is a continuously updated database of corporate news. The items in the database are taken from Dow Jones News Wire stories and *Wall Street Journal* articles. Any breaking news items related to acquisitions, takeovers, buyout offers, or other corporate changes will usually find their way onto DJNEWS. Articles are retained in DJNEWS for ninety days. This is useful if you need limited retrospective searching. As with most DJNR databases, DJNEWS may only be searched by using either a publicly held company's ticker symbol or a Dow Jones news code. This database cannot be searched by keyword. Therefore, tracking news of private companies or subsidiaries would not be an appropriate use of this database.

To illustrate how DJNEWS can be used in monitoring corporate change, we provide some examples of searches from the database. In Example 3.1, the use of the DJNR news code for acquisitions, mergers, or tender offers (.I/TNM) is demonstrated.

Use of the TNM code retrieves any story in DJNEWS related to M&A activity. The report on SKF's bid to purchase McGill Manufacturing is just one example. As the headline list shows, there are many reports, from just one day, about corporate change. The TNM code is useful if there is no particular company or industry being followed, and you just want to monitor current developments in many areas.

Example 3.2 shows how DJNEWS can be used to monitor corporate change affecting an individual company. UAL was attempting a leveraged buyout, but was having difficulty arranging financing for the deal. Anyone interested in following this deal, whether for general information or for potential stock transactions, would have found ample information on UAL's situation with DJNEWS. Since the airline industry is dominated by a few major players, it may also have been worthwhile to locate stories concerning other actions related to the UAL buyout. To

Example 3.1
Use of DJNR NewsCode

//DJNEWS [the DJNR code for accessing the DJNEWS database]

DOW JONES NEWS

ENTER A PERIOD (.) FOLLOWED BY A STOCK

SYMBOL OR NEWS/RETRIEVAL CATEGORY

CODE FOUND IN //SYMBOL.

    ENTER   .AAPL 01

    FOR   THE FIRST PAGE OF COMPANY

        HEADLINES ABOUT APPLE

ENTER REQUEST OR SEE //DJNEWS HELP.

  .I/TNM 01 [User enters code for acquisitions, mergers or tenders

        followed by "01" which retrieves a list of available

        stories]

   CATEGORY I/TNM   HEADLINE PAGE 01 OF 59

```
WK 10/24   Sheraton - Pan Am Moscow
   (DJ)       Hotel Venture
WJ 10/24   AXA-MIDI Pledges To Retain
   (DJ)       Farmers Group Management
WI 10/24.  Rally's Franchisee Sues
   (DJ)       Sugarman
WH 10/24   Raven Industries Director
   (DJ)       Resigns; To Sell 9.6 PC Stake
WG 10/24   Okabe - Elco Indus Stake
   (DJ)
WF 10/24   Group - Sealed Air Stake
   (DJ)
WE 10/24   Hart-Scott - Graphic Tech.
   (DJ)       Acquisition
WD 10/24   Okabe Lifted Stake In Elco
   (DJ)       Indus Last Month To 18.96%
WC 10/24   Delmed Exploring Possible
   (DJ)       Sale Of Ogden, Utah Plant
WB 10/24   Rally's Franchisee Sues To
   (DJ)       Bar Sugarman From Buying Shares
WA 10/24   SKF To Continue McGill Mfg
   (DJ)       Bid
```

WA [User selects story about SKF bid by entering two letter
      code "WA" which corresponds to that story]

```
CATEGORY I/TNM                                      STORY WA
/SKFRY MGLL            /TNM     /
10/24 (DJ) SKF To Continue McGill Mfg Bid
```

    KING OF PRUSSIA, Pa. -DJ- SKF U.S.A. Inc. said its SKF
Acquisition Corp. is continuing its $72-a-share cash offer for all
shares of McGill Manufacturing Co.
    SKF said that it was "disappointed" that McGill's board
rejected its offer. SKF said it believes the offer "is in the best
interests of McGill shareholders, employees and the communities in
which it operates."
    "McGill's board is offering no concrete alternative to our
offer, while its management has continued to refuse our repeated
requests to meet," SKF said.
    As reported, McGill's board today called the bid inadequate and
recommended that holders not tender their shares.
    SKF, a unit of AB SKF of Sweden, began its offer on Oct. 11; it
is scheduled to expire on Nov. 7, the company said.
    12:48 PM
                   -END-

Example 3.2
Monitoring Individual Companies with DJNEWS

```
ENTER ANOTHER REQUEST.

   .UAL 01 [User enters ticker symbol for UAL, the parent

           company of United Airlines, along with the "01"

           to retrieve a list of recent headlines]

     CATEGORY UAL       HEADLINE PAGE 01 OF 19

   HV 10/24 UAL Corp Has No Comment On
     (DJ)     Activity In Its Stock
   HU 10/24 UAL Opened On 400,000 Shrs At
     (DJ)     150 Dn 28 (NYSE)
     .
     .

   HA 10/18  Davis Withdraws Backup Bid
     (DW)     For UAL; May Make Other Offer
     HA
   CATEGORY UAL                                        STORY HA
   /UAL   BAB   LABOR      /TNM AIR/
   10/18 (DW) Davis Withdraws Backup Bid For UAL; May Make Other
   Offer
        LOS ANGELES -DJ- Marvin Davis said he has decided to
   withdraw his backup bid for UAL Corp.
        He added, however, that he will "continue working with our
   financing sources in order to determine at what price a bid can
   be financed."
        Davis said despite withdrawing his backup bid, "we remain
   very interested in acquiring UAL Corp."
        Davis said he has been informed by his agent bank that in
   light of Friday's announcement that Airline Acquisition Corp.
   failed to secure financing for the $6.9 billion buyout, the bank
   is "currently exploring the level of bank financing that will be
   available" for his proposed acquisition of UAL.
```

search by industry, find the appropriate code (e.g., .I/AIR for the airline industry), and search in the same way as by event code or ticker symbol.

These searches took about five minutes, including time for accessing the database, capturing the information, and logging off. There is little search flexibility, but the database requires no knowledge of a special command language. It is extremely easy to operate. Using DJNEWS, it takes only a few minutes a day to keep abreast of corporate change.

While DJNEWS may satisfy most monitoring needs, there are other useful sources on DJNR. In the last chapter, we discussed the merits of news releases. DJNR enhances this valuable information resource by making them available in full text, within hours of their release. Again, as with DJNEWS, this database, called RELEASE, is searchable only by ticker symbol or news code. The releases available in the database come from two important newswire services, PR NEWSWIRE and BUSINESS-WIRE. Both transmit news releases from many U.S. corporations. Example 3.3 illustrates the use of the DJNR code for acquisitions, mergers, and tenders to scan a day's press releases, indicating hour of release, on ongoing deals. Any of these stories may be displayed by typing in the corresponding three-letter code in the far left column.

Example 3.3
Monitoring News Releases

```
//RELEASE [the DJNR code for accessing the RELEASE database]

                    PRESS RELEASE WIRES

                    Copyright (C) 1989

                 PR Newswire, Business Wire

     .N/TNM [RELEASE news code for acquisitions, mergers, tenders]

N/TNM ACQUISITIONS & MERGERS RELEASES                HEADLINE PAGE

     1 OF 151

     DAH 18:39 Belvedere Corporation announcements
     DAG 18:29 Correcting Lawrence Insurance Group
     DAF 17:47 ASSOCIATION OF FLIGHT ATTENDANTS RESPONDS TO UAL BOARD
     DAE 17:36 INTEGRATED RESOURCES REPORTS
     AGREEMENT IN PRINCIPLE
     DAD 17:33 FISCHBACH CORP., APL CORP. AND FAC ACQUISITION TO END
     PLAN OF
     DAC 17:33 Lawrence Insurance Group acquires United Republic
     Reinsurance
     DAB 17:14 TELEPHONE AND DATA SYSTEMS ANNOUNCES PROPOSED PUBLIC
     OFFERING
     DAA 17:11 ENERGEN TO DISPOSE OF DRILLING OPERATIONS
     CZZ 17:09 GALAXY CABLEVISION ANNOUNCES AGREEMENT WITH CAPITAL
     CABLE
     CZY 16:50 ENRON FILES WITH FERC TO PURCHASE INCREMENTAL CANADIAN
     CZX 16:47 CONTINENTAL ILLINOIS HOLDING CORPORATION STOCKHOLDERS
     CZW 16:44 Transmed Express makes announcement
     CZV 16:38 Enron files with FERC to purchase incremental Canadian
     CZU 16:14 WESTINGHOUSE TO ACQUIRE THE SHAW-WALKER COMPANY
     CZT 15:26 KENNAMETAL INC. ISSUES ANNOUNCEMENT
     CZS 15:15 ASSOCIATED MARINER FINANCIAL GROUP BUYS INDEPENDENT
     CZR 15:13 Vacuum General to hold news conference
     CZQ 15:09 BARDEN COMMUNICATIONS ACQUIRES 181,900 SHARES OF FIRST
```

   DJNEWS or RELEASE cannot supply corporate change information on
a private company or a complete story as it appeared in the *Wall Street
Journal* because of the way the databases are constructed. However,
DJNR provides access to a library of business news databases jointly
referred to as TEXT. TEXT is a valuable resource because it allows
sophisticated keyword searching, including use of logical operators and
proximity operators.

   TEXT contains the complete text of the *Wall Street Journal, Washington
Post, Fortune, Forbes, Business Week,* several hundred trade and industry
journals, and other regional papers. One tradeoff for the search flexibility and diversity of sources is the database's lack of currency. With
the exception of the *Wall Street Journal,* which is updated daily, most of
the TEXT databases are updated only once a month. The material found
online may be two months behind its print counterpart. Despite this
limitation, searching the electronic versions means spending much less
time identifying corporate change news on specific industries or companies and eliminating the need to subscribe to different news magazines.

   Example 3.4 illustrates a search in the full text of the *Wall Street Journal:*

Example 3.4
A WSJ Search

```
THE WALL STREET JOURNAL
COPYRIGHT (C) 1989 DOW JONES & COMPANY, INC.

DJ/NRS   - SEARCH MODE - ENTER QUERY
    1_:        TNM.IN. AND UAL.CO. [search for articles from the
                                    acquisitions and mergers
                                    category that also discuss
                                    UAL Corporation]

RESULT         180 DOCUMENTS
    2_:        ..CP HL,DD,SO/DOC=1  [print the headlines, dates and
                                    source for the first two
                                    documents]

               DOCUMENT=       2
HL             UAL Directors
               Dash Prospects
               For a Buy-Out
               ---
               Wolf Pulls Out of Group;
               Management Faces Task
               Of Restoring Credibility
               ----
               By Judith Valente and Randall Smith
               Staff Reporters of The Wall Street Journal
DD             10/24/89
SO             WALL STREET JOURNAL (J)

               END OF DOCUMENT


      ..CP/DOC=2 [display document number 2 in full text]

               DOCUMENT=       2
AN             891024-0077.
HL             UAL Directors
               Dash Prospects
               For a Buy-Out
               ---
               Wolf Pulls Out of Group;
               Management Faces Task
               Of Restoring Credibility
               ----
               By Judith Valente and Randall Smith
               Staff Reporters of The Wall Street Journal
DD             10/24/89
SO             WALL STREET JOURNAL (J)
CO      *      UAL LABOR BAB
IN      *      TENDER OFFERS, MERGERS, ACQUISITIONS (TNM)
               AIRLINES (AIR)
TX   UAL Corp.'s board quashed any prospects for an immediate
revival of a labor-management buy-out, saying United Airlines'
parent should remain independent for now. As a result, UAL's
chairman, Stephen M. Wolf, pulled out of the buy-out effort to
focus on running the company. The two developments put the
acquisition attempt back to square one and leaves the airline
with an array of unresolved matters, including an unsettled labor
situation and a management scrambling to restore its damaged
credibility...
```

This article was retrieved because the UAL ticker symbol is included in the company name field, shown by the "CO" in the far left column, and the "TNM" code is included in the index term field, indicated by the "IN" in the far left column.

The TEXT search offers several advantages over other DJNR databases. It is a more direct way to locate relevant articles because it allows combinations of search terms. Unlike DJNEWS, you are not restricted to searching by one general code and then scanning a list of headlines to find the relevant articles. In addition, the full-text database provides articles with more detailed reporting. TEXT also allows the flexibility to research both private and public companies. Other DJNR databases are limited to research on public companies.

To simplify and speed access to corporate change news, use Dow's current awareness service called TRACK. TRACK allows you to create a custom portfolio of companies and news categories. After creating a "profile" (a list of the companies and codes being monitored), you will be able to view any new stories about the companies and events in the profile since your last log-on to DJNR. TRACK eliminates the need to access DJNEWS and search on individual codes.

For example, to follow M&A activity, create a profile called "MERGE." Enter the code .I/TNM into the profile. To view the full stories added to the database since your last profile review, enter the command string //TRACK MERGE NS NO (where MERGE is the name of the profile, NS is for full news story retrieval, and NO is for stories added since the last review of the profile). Profiles may include a mix of companies, industry codes, and news event codes. Just use TRACK to have the information delivered to you more efficiently. There is a nominal per-month charge to store any number of profiles on TRACK.

DIALOG is an essential resource for the business community. Among existing databanks, it offers the most databases for business research. Combine this fact with DIALOG's wide offering of databases that are updated either continuously, daily, or weekly, and you have an important tool for monitoring corporate change. Appropriate databases in DIALOG fall into one of the following categories: general newswire service, business newswire service, bibliographic database, industry-specific database, and merger and acquisition database. Among the many newswire service databases that DIALOG offers, we will describe four of particular importance.

NEWSWIRE ASAP provides the complete text and comprehensive indexing of news releases and wire stories from three news organizations: PR Newswire, Kyodo, and Reuters. The file offers both current and retrospective information on companies, industries, products, economics, and finance. News releases contain announcements of new products and services, quarterly earnings reports, S&P (Standard & Poor's) Credit Wire ratings, and other business news. Stories cover mergers, trade, commodities, stock markets, world news, and political events. NEWSWIRE ASAP is File 649 on DIALOG (all DIALOG databases are identified by their individual file number). It is updated daily.[2]

PR NEWSWIRE (File 613) contains the complete text of news releases prepared by companies, public relations agencies, trade associations, city, state, federal, and non-U.S. government agencies, and other sources covering the entire spectrum of the news. There are more than 12,000 participating client news sources adding hundreds of releases to the database each day. About 80 percent of the records in PR NEWSWIRE are related to business. The complete text of a news release typically contains details or background information that is not published in newspapers. Every release carries the name and telephone number of a spokesperson who can be contacted for additional information. PR NEWSWIRE is updated continuously throughout the day.[3]

AP NEWS (Files 258, 259) provides the full text of national, international, and business news from the AP DataStream service. AP NEWS is compiled by more than 1,000 journalists in 135 U.S. news bureaus and 83 overseas news bureaus. In addition, as a U.S. news cooperative, the AP has access to the news compiled by more than 1,300 newspaper members and 5,700 radio-television members in the United States. File 258 is the current file; it is updated daily and contains up to three months of news. A companion file (259) contains accumulated retrospective releases.[4] UPI NEWS (Files 260, 261) contains the full text of news stories carried on the United Press International wire, including domestic general news, columns, standing features, financial news, international news, commentaries, and Washington, D.C. news. This database is divided into two files. File 261 is the current file with daily updates; up to six months of information is available within 48 hours of the present date. File 260 contians the backfile. File 261 can be searched to obtain the latest in general and business news and current affairs.[5]

Although similar in design and content, the newswire databases differ in the amount of information they provide and in the number of available search methods. If you want to retrieve any document record that contains terms relating to a corporate change, then any of the newswire databases could be appropriate. For example, you may want to conduct a search to retrieve any document with any of the following words: acquisition, merger, or takeover. In DIALOG, you would use the search statement "acquisition or merger or takeover."

An initial search in the wire service databases will retrieve thousands of articles mentioning any of these terms. Because we want to review only those documents most recently added to the database, we can limit the search with a feature common to all four of the general newswire databases. It is called the "update" command. The command can be used to retrieve only the most recent documents added to the database. An alternative is to specify the number of updates to search. For monitoring, use of the update command will allow you to quickly home in on only the most current information in the database. How much is added to the database with each update will depend on whether the update frequency is daily or weekly.

Table 3.1 shows the results from the initial search, which retrieves any document in the database containing any of the specified terms. The column to the far right indicates how many documents remained after the initial search was modified with the update command.

NEWSWIRE ASAP and PR NEWSWIRE had a much higher initial retrieval because these databases cover a longer time period (several years versus several months) than do the AP and UPI wires used in this example.

Total retrieval is not necessarily the best way to judge any database. It is also important to consider how much flexibility and control the searcher has. The databases from AP and UPI are limited in how they may be searched. The searcher can enter keywords and combine them with logical or proximity operators, but beyond searching by publication date or section heading (e.g., business; international) there is little else to work with.

Search flexibility is important because it reduces the number of irrelevant documents retrieved. PR NEWSWIRE and NEWSWIRE ASAP, in contrast, allow the searcher to limit retrieval by company name, industry or product codes, state (PR), and ticker symbol. These search features allow for further narrowing of broad retrieval to yield more precise results. For example, in our search using the keywords "acquisition or merger or takeover," we could further refine retrieval by limiting to a specific industry, such as manufacturing pharmaceutical preparations (Standard Industrial Classification code 2834). Example 3.5 shows NEWSWIRE ASAP on DIALOG.

The complete text of both documents is available online. We know this because the last line of each record, the "availability" field, indicates that full text is available in the database. To retrieve the full text of the document we would request output in a different format (a short format is used in the example).

Another way to make general searches more precise is to use a more specialized database. For example, DIALOG offers two U.S.-based news-

Table 3.1
Newswire Retrieval and Frequencies

Newswire Retrieval and Frequencies			
Database	Update Frequency	Initial Search	After Use of Update
AP NEWSWIRE	DAILY	2,111	79
UPI NEWS	DAILY	339	14
PR NEWSWIRE	CONTINUOUS	9,551	85
NEWSWIRE ASAP	DAILY	96,034	701

Example 3.5
NEWSWIRE ASAP on DIALOG

```
File 649:NEWSWIRE ASAP - 01/12/90

   (COPR.1990 IAC)

   Set   Items  Description

   ---   -----  -----------

?SS MERGER? OR ACQUISITION? OR TAKEOVER? [input search terms with the
                                  "?" symbol for truncation]

   S1    74024  MERGER?
   S2    91356  ACQUISITION?
   S3     6982  TAKEOVER?
   S4   101107  MERGER? OR ACQUISITION? OR TAKEOVER?

?SS S4 AND SC=2834 [combine the total number of documents with the
                    SIC code for the pharmaceutical industry]

        101107  S4
   S5     1999  SC=2834
   S6      421  S4 AND SC=2834

?SS S6 AND UD=9001? [further narrow the results of the prior combination to
                    only those updates added to the database
                    during January 1990]

          421  S6
   S11    8610  UD=9001?
   S12       2  S6 AND UD=9001?

?T 12/3/1-2 [display the two documents in short form]

   12/3/1
08022918    DIALOG File 649: NEWSWIRE ASAP   *Use Format 9 for FULL TEXT*
Marion Merrell calls estimates achievable. (Marion Merrell Dow Inc.)
 Reuters R010800820 Jan 8, 1990
 SOURCE FILE: NW File 649
 AVAILABILITY: FULL TEXT Online  LINE COUNT: 00050

   12/3/2
08005800    DIALOG File 649: NEWSWIRE ASAP   *Use Format 9 for FULL TEXT*
ICC  gains   foothold  in  central  nervous  system  market  through  new
      acquisition. (includes ICI Pharmaceutical background material)
 PR Newswire 0103NY005 Jan 3, 1990
 SOURCE FILE: NW File 649
 AVAILABILITY: FULL TEXT Online  LINE COUNT: 00104
```

wire databases dedicated to business news: BUSINESSWIRE and KNIGHT-RIDDER FINANCIAL NEWS. With their emphasis on business, these files can provide much of the corporate change news found in the general wire services, plus more specialized reporting from business sources.

BUSINESSWIRE (File 610) delivers timely, full-text news stories that are simultaneously distributed to over 700 news media and more than 100 institutions and firms in the investment community. Topics include finance, business, science, labor, education, and entertainment. News sources consist of public and investor relations firms, business organizations and associations, government agencies, colleges and universities, trade associations, and legal and accounting firms. Emphasis is placed on U.S. company news, but non-U.S. company news is also provided. BUSINESSWIRE is updated continuously throughout the day.[6]

KNIGHT-RIDDER FINANCIAL NEWS (KRFN) (File 609) provides comprehensive, up-to-the-minute financial and business news reports and other market-related data on a broad range of activities. Subjects range from credit markets to the foreign exchange market, and from the stock market to the commodities and futures market. KRFN is continuously updated throughout the day. KRFN also obtains news from AP, UPI, Agence France Presse, PR NEWSWIRE, and BUSINESSWIRE, in addition to other contributors.[7]

It is possible that the wire services alone, with the large number of sources they cover, could meet monitoring needs. However, DIALOG offers several other databases that may supplement electronic news gathering. For example, wire services do not provide coverage of business news magazines and trade and industry journals that can provide further information or analysis of corporate change activity. There are three databases in particular we recommend: PTS PROMT, ABI/INFORM, and BUSINESS DATELINE.

Although there are additional databases offering coverage of business news, we find these most useful because they are updated either daily or weekly (except BUSINESS DATELINE, which is updated monthly), and offer either full text or abstracts. A database offering only article references is less useful because of the need to locate the original printed source for details. This detracts from the utility of electronic monitoring. PTS PROMT, ABI/INFORM, and BUSINESS DATELINE offer a good mix of sources: business magazines, national business newspapers, regional business newspapers, press releases, and trade and industry journals.

We do not recommend databases that duplicate news stories retrieved with newswire services. For example, both Moody's and Standard and Poor's offer corporate news databases. Yet a significant portion of the content of these databases is collected from newswire services or from the company press releases themselves.[8] Both of these sources would likely provide duplication of wire services already discussed.

PTS PROMPT (File 16 on DIALOG) is sometimes referred to as a "megafile" because of the vast number and diversity of multi-industry resources covered by this database. PROMPT abstracts items from over 1,500 sources, including newspapers, journals, annual reports, product announcements, news releases, and newsletters. The file is updated daily. The ability to search by Predicasts codes adds much versatility to PROMPT. There are product codes for thousands of products. For corporate change monitoring, searching with the event code "EC15" is useful. Articles dealing with acquisitions, mergers, divestitures, and buyouts are assigned this code. The codes are found online as well as in the Predicasts' user's manual and in the print counterpart of this database. Keywords such as "acquisition" or "merger" may also be used in searching. Another plus for PROMT is in the rapid access it gives to business articles. Publications such as *Business Week* and *Fortune* are indexed and abstracted within twenty-four hours of their receipt.

ABI/INFORM (File 15 on DIALOG) abstracts articles selected from over 600 business magazines and journals. This includes virtually all popular business magazines, as well as many academic and scholarly business journals. The latter may be useful for occasional analytical articles on M&A activity or trends in corporate change. ABI/INFORM is best known for its lengthy and authoritative abstracts. The database is also well indexed. Unlike some of the newswires, ABI/INFORM has several "descriptor" terms related to corporate change. These include "mergers & acquisitions" and "leveraged buyout." Using descriptors in a search statement can improve the relevancy of documents retrieved. This database is updated weekly.

BUSINESS DATELINE (File 635 on DIALOG) is the primary source of news and information on local and regional business developments. It provides machine-readable access to the full text of regional business newspapers. This is important when smaller firms are affected by corporate change. Often, the national business press will report minimal, if any, news on such deals. A regional business paper emphasizes events of interest to their local readership. The database is searchable by keyword and descriptor terms. BUSINESS DATELINE is also available on DJNR and the LEXIS and NEXIS Services.

DIALOG offers two databases focusing on M&A activity. They are M&A FILINGS (File 548) and IDD M&A TRANSACTIONS (File 550). How effective are they for monitoring corporate change? M&A FILINGS provides summaries of every original and amended merger and acquisition document submitted to the Securities and Exchange Commission (SEC). When an individual or company acquires a significant share of a publicly held company or launches a bid to acquire the company by tendering outstanding shares, such activities must be reported to the SEC. Therefore, M&A FILINGS, which is updated daily, can provide news on potential change.

Many individuals acquire significant blocks of stock in a company, yet have no intention of making a takeover bid. Acquisitions of private companies or subsidiaries of public companies are not reported to the SEC. Divestitures, corporate restructuring, and other nontakeover changes are not covered in this database. Consequently, M&A FILINGS is probably less useful for monitoring corporate change than a general or business newswire database. However, if you need to monitor potential takeover activity and are willing to scan the many acquisition-related documents submitted to the SEC, this database may be of interest.

IDD M&A TRANSACTIONS can be a good supplement to electronic monitoring efforts. It covers all partial or completed acquisition, merger, or divestiture transactions valued at $1 million or more, or with an undisclosed value. Updated daily, it also covers a small but informative group of publications. These include the *Wall Street Journal*, *New York Times*, newswires from Dow Jones and PR NEWSWIRE, corporate news releases, and SEC corporate acquisition documents.

The primary weakness of IDD M&A TRANSACTIONS for monitoring is the fact that it is designed to provide data on the deals, not news. Unlike newswire databases and those giving abstracts of magazine and newspaper articles, IDD M&A TRANSACTIONS provides only minimal discussion of the acquisition activity. The text portion of IDD M&A TRANSACTIONS is limited to a description of the terms of the deal, the source of funds, and fees paid to advisors. IDD M&A TRANSACTIONS will keep you alert to the players in the deals, deals in specific industries, and deals meeting specific criteria. This may include deals of a certain value, those using a specific advisor, or those involving specific financing strategies. The database has no update feature, but can be searched by the announcement date of the transaction.

Daily or weekly monitoring of the DIALOG databases we have described can provide a comprehensive monitoring strategy, but covering all the applicable databases, even with the speed of electronic searching, will require significant time. One option is to limit time spent by selecting only two or three databases to monitor. A preferable solution is to develop a current awareness service. By automating searches, the current awareness service will routinely search the databases you choose each time they are updated. DIALOG refers to this service as DIALOG ALERT.

To use DIALOG ALERT, log on to DIALOG and select the appropriate database. ALERT does not work in all databases. To find out if ALERT may be used in a particular database, type HELP ALERT at the DIALOG prompt (the ''?''). Once an applicable file is selected, type in the search statement you have formulated. When the search is complete, enter a PRINT TITLE command to assign an optional title. Then enter a second PRINT command to identify the set of documents to print and deliver each time the search is run. The default delivery option is postal service, so you are prompted for a mailing address. If you choose delivery by DIALMAIL, DIALOG's electronic mail service, use ''via DIALMAIL'' in the PRINT statement. The default address is your own in-box, but you are able to specify another party's in-box.

DIALOG will give an estimated cost of the search used to create the ALERT profile. First, use the SAVE command to save the ALERT. Some databases allow you to choose the frequency with which your search is conducted (e.g., SAVE ALERT DAY or SAVE ALERT WEEK). Some of the continuously updated files do offer a daily ALERT update, but others, such as BUSINESSWIRE, have only a weekly ALERT update available. After the ALERT is saved, enter the PRINT CANCEL command to cancel the results of the search that created the DIALOG ALERT.[9] There is a charge each time you receive an ALERT update. The fee ranges from $1.00 to $15.00. The cost of the daily update is $1.00, while the weekly update is $3.50. Again, use of the HELP ALERT command will show the ALERT fees.

DIALOG offers another option for performing your monitoring searches. If you choose to follow several databases, and you generally perform a similar search in each, you may be able to run the search simultaneously in all the files using ONESEARCH. To use ONE-SEARCH, enter the BEGIN command to select databases. Follow the BEGIN command with a list of the file numbers you want to search. The system responds by displaying the numbers and names of the requested files. Proceed by entering a search statement at the ''?'' prompt. DIA-LOG makes available ONESEARCH groups that bring together databases on a similar subject. For example, MERGEACQ is the category for M&A acquisitions databases. Fourteen databases are included. Among them are several discussed in this chapter.

Nearly all DIALOG commands work with ONESEARCH. An important caution is to check the documentation of each file being combined to verify that search variables are uniform among the files. For example, some databases may use the search prefix ''PY'' for publication year, while others may use ''PD'' for publication date. If a code is used that is not recognized in a database, the search results may be flawed. Example 3.6 shows how ONESEARCH is used to search two newswire databases simultaneously.

Just as DJNR and DIALOG have different searching procedures, the LEXIS and NEXIS Services have their own unique search system. They too offer many databases, but they are organized into clusters known as ''libraries.'' The *New York Times*, for example, is in the NEXIS library. The *Times* is considered its own database, referred to as a ''file.'' There is a MERGER library. It includes several M&A related databases, including IDD's M&A Database and the newsletter M&A News. You can specify an individual file to search or may combine files to search jointly. For example, to conduct a search of computing publications you could combine *Computer World* (file name DMPWLD), *Datamation* (file name DATAMA), *Infosystems* (file name INFSYS) and *INFOWORLD* (file name INFWLD). This custom database could be used to track corporate change in the computer/software industries. Example 3.7 illustrates this type of search.

As a user convenience, many of the files available on the NEXIS Service are divided into interest areas. These include categories such as trade and technology, finance, government and political news, and regional

Example 3.6
Use of ONESEARCH

```
?B 609,610 [user requests two files]

System:OS  - DIALOG OneSearch


    File 609:KNIGHT-RIDDER FINANCIAL NEWS - 89-90/Jan 13
            (Copr. 1990 KRFI)

    File 610:BusinessWire - 86-90/Jan 13
            (Copr. 1990 BusinessWire)

    Set  Items  Description
    ---  -----  -----------
?SS MERGER? OR ACQUISITION? OR TAKEOVER?

    S1    9333  MERGER?
    S2   22154  ACQUISITION?
    S3    2708  TAKEOVER?
    S4   29238  MERGER? OR ACQUISITION? OR TAKEOVER?

?SET DETAIL ON [user asks for detail to see
                retrieval for individual files]

DETAIL set on
?SS MERGER? OR ACQUISITION? OR TAKEOVER?


609: KNIGHT-RIDDER FINANCIAL NEWS - 89-90/Jan 13
            842  MERGER?
            974  ACQUISITION?
           1657  TAKEOVER?
           2949  MERGER? OR ACQUISITION? OR TAKEOVER?

610: BusinessWire - 86-90/Jan 13
           8491  MERGER?
          21180  ACQUISITION?
           1051  TAKEOVER?
          26289  MERGER? OR ACQUISITION? OR TAKEOVER?

TOTAL: FILES 609,610
    S5    9333  MERGER?
    S6   22154  ACQUISITION?
    S7    2708  TAKEOVER?
    S8   29238  MERGER? OR ACQUISITION? OR TAKEOVER?


?SS S8 AND PHARMACEUTICAL? [user chooses to limit by keyword]

  609: KNIGHT-RIDDER FINANCIAL NEWS - 89-90/Jan 13
           2949  S8
            204  PHARMACEUTICAL?

             69  S8 AND PHARMACEUTICAL?

610: BusinessWire - 86-90/Jan 13
          26289  S8
           2953  PHARMACEUTICAL?
            662  S8 AND PHARMACEUTICAL?

TOTAL: FILES 609,610
          29238  S8
    S11    3157  PHARMACEUTICAL?
    S12     892  S8 AND PHARMACEUTICAL?

?SS S12 AND PY=1990 [user further limits by publication year]

  609: KNIGHT-RIDDER FINANCIAL NEWS - 89-90/Jan 13
             69  S12
          12702  PY=1990
              2  S12 AND PY=1990

610: BusinessWire - 86-90/Jan 13
            662  S12
```

Example 3.6 (continued)

```
          1176   PY=1990
             3   S12 AND PY=1990

TOTAL: FILES 609,610
            892   S12
   S13   13878   PY=1990
   S14       5   S12 AND PY=1990  [final search yields 5
                                   documents]
```

Source: "This search example is reproduced courtesy of DIALOG* Information Retrieval Service (the "DIALOG Service") of Dialog Information Services, Inc. (*Servicemark Reg. U.S. Pat. & TM Off.).

Example 3.7
Use of NEXIS Service

```
NEXIS;DMPWLD,DATAMA,INFSYS,INFWLD [user asks to search the four
                                   publications in NEXIS]
```

Please type your search request then press the TRANSMIT key.
What you transmit will be Search Level 1.

HEADLINE (ACQUISITION OR MERGER OR TAKEOVER) AND DATE AFT 6/89

[user searches corporate change terms, but they must appear in
article headlines or titles, and must be published in or later
than June 1989. Note that the NEXIS Service will add plurals
automatically. The term "MERGER" will retrieve either "MERGER" or
"MERGERS"]

NEXIS is working on the displayed request.
If it is not what you intended to transmit, please press the STOP
key.

Your search request has found 24 STORIES through Level 1.
To DISPLAY these STORIES press either the KWIC, FULL, CITE or
SEGMTS key.   To MODIFY your search request, press the M key (for
MODFY) and then the TRANSMIT key.

.CI [user requests to display documents in short citation format]

                 LEVEL 1 - 24 STORIES

1. Copyright (c) 1990 IDG Communications, Inc.; InfoWorld,
January 8, 1990,
NEWS; Pg. 5, 449 words, Northgate to Offer 486 With MCA;
Executives Say They're Also Negotiating a Possible Merger with
CPT, BY LAURIE FLYNN AND PATRICK BURNSONPLYMOUTH, MN

2. Copyright (c) 1989 IDG Communications, Inc.; InfoWorld,
December 11, 1989,
INDUSTRY; Pg. 46, 207 words, Proposed Merger May Yield Super
Distributor, BY
BARBARA DARROW

3. Copyright (c) 1989 IDG Communications, Inc.; Computerworld,
December 4, 1989,Pg. 1, 617 words, Merger-weary users turn wary,
By Amy Cortese,CW Staff

.FU [user requests to display a document in full format]

             (c) 1989 Computerworld, December 4, 1989

December 4, 1989

SECTION: Pg. 1

LENGTH: 617 words
```
```

Example 3.7 (continued)

```
HEADLINE:  Merger-weary users turn wary

BYLINE: By Amy Cortese,CW Staff

BODY:
   The software industry has been caught up in its own version of
"Let's Make a Deal" that shows no signs of abating, leaving
customers wondering whether smaller firms been raised.

   The proposed merger of Management Science America, Inc. and
McCormack & DodgeCorp. is the latest and most dramatic example of
a market that is in the throes of consolidation.

   While a powerful suitor can provide the research and
development capital that small software companies need to
survive, customers see consolidation as a double-edged sword....
```

Source: Reprinted with permission of Mead Data Central, Inc., provider of LEXIS®/
NEXIS® services.

business news. Each of these categories groups together a variety of publications dealing with the subject. This simplifies the procedure of searching a larger number of publications covering the same industry.

The NEXIS Service offers several databases already mentioned in this chapter. These include AP NEWSWIRE, BUSINESS WIRE, PR NEWSWIRE, and UPI NEWS. The BUSINESS DATELINE file of regional business newspapers is also available. Like the M&A FILINGS database in DIALOG, the LEXIS Service offers SECABS, a group of files containing abstracts of documents submitted to the Securities and Exchange Commission. These files include the merger and acquisition documents known as the 13-D and 14-D series. The NEXIS Service has some wire services not available in other databases, including those from more non-U.S. countries. One difference is in the update frequency of some of the newswires. Most of the newswires carried by the NEXIS Service are updated once each twenty-four hours, with some every twenty-four to forty-eight hours. By comparison, DIALOG's PR NEWSWIRE and BUSINESSWIRE, are updated continuously. The LEXIS and NEXIS Services offer a current awareness feature, called ECLIPSE. It is similar to DIALOG'S ALERT Service.

Newsletters provide the timely, detailed information needed for corporate change monitoring. Their brief but concentrated reporting style makes newsletters quick and potent reading material. Subscribing to several special interest newsletters would be costly. In addition, if your primary interest in newsletters is monitoring corporate change, then much of the other information would be extraneous.

NEWSNET combines the advantages of newsletter information with those of electronic information retrieval. While other databanks, including both DIALOG and the LEXIS and NEXIS Services, may offer access to some full-text newsletters, only NEWSNET is exclusively dedicated to providing full-text newsletters. In NEWSNET each newsletter is a database. Newsletters may be searched individually in user-defined combinations, or by categories created by NEWSNET. "Telecommunications" and "automotive" are examples of the categories available.

NEWSNET is easy to use. It has three primary search modes: READ, SCAN, and SEARCH. All three are search commands. READ allows you to read, print, or download to disk the full text of any selected newsletter issue(s) from beginning to end. READ is used primarily for quick capture of a specific issue or multiple issues within a specified date range. Within NEWSNET some databases, mostly wire services and time series files, are updated continuously. READ is also used to find and capture specific recent updates in these files.

SCAN is a command that displays a sequentially numbered list, or menu, of headlines from a single newsletter issue. Any headline(s) from the list can be selected for full-text display of the related article. NEWS-NET databases are organized into numbered headlines. These headlines may be those given by the newsletter publisher, or if extremely short items, supplied by NEWSNET. Any selected article may be read, printed, or downloaded to disk. As with all search modes, you may select the latest issue, a particular issue, or range of issues specified by date.

READ and SCAN are useful for monitoring the latest stories in a particular newsletter without regard for specific subject content. To monitor acquisition activity within a specific industry, however, it is necessary to search on keywords related to corporate change. With its wide selection of highly industry-specific newsletters, NEWSNET is a good choice for this type of search.

The SEARCH command allows you to search by keyword, phrase, or subject string. NEWSNET offers most of the search features found in other databanks (e.g., logical search operators, proximity searching, truncation). Example 3.8 uses the newsletters HEALTH CARE COMPETITION WEEK (File HH11), HEALTH NEWS DAILY (File HH01), and INVESTEXT/HEALTH CARE (File IX15).

NEWSNET, like DIALOG and the LEXIS and NEXIS Services, has "current awareness" searching. NEWSFLASH is an electronic clipping service that monitors a specified profile of topics as information is added to databases selected for monitoring. Users create a profile of any number of keywords or phrases. Terms such as "merger," "acquisition," "buyout," or "takeover" would be examples for a NEWSFLASH profile. Enter the term FLASH at the command prompt to begin creation of a NEWSFLASH profile. Enter CREATE to create a "folder" (their term for a collection of keyword phrases). Follow successive prompts by supplying the keywords and database codes. You may create multiple NEWS-FLASH profiles so different keywords can be searched in multiple newsletters. Once the profile is established, a notice will appear at log-on if

Example 3.8
Use of NEWSNET

```
Enter command or <RETURN>

-->SEARCH

Enter service or industry code(s)

-->HH11 HH01 IX15 [user enters all three codes together]

Enter Latest for latest issue, or other date options in MM/DD/YY
format

-->LATEST [user wants latest issues only searched]

Enter keyword phrase

-->MERGERS OR ACQUISITIONS OR TAKEOVERS
!!!
     8 Occurrences

Enter HEAd for headlines; TExt for full text; Analyze for
occurrences in each
service; or <RETURN> for new keyword(s)
-->HEAD


  1)  1/22/90  HH01    HEALTH NEWS DAILY
MCKESSON CREATING NORTH AMERICAN DRUG DISTRIBUTION NETWORK WITH
$81 MIL. CASH ACQUISITION OF LARGEST CANADIAN WHOLESALER MEDIS.

  2)  1/22/90  IX15    INVESTEXT/HEALTH CARE
SURGICAL CARE AFFILIATES - COMPANY REPORT    TS=SCAF
DONALDSON, LUFKIN & JENRETTE, INC. - Hindelong, J.F., et al
11-27-89    (RN=940818)   9 Pages


3)  1/22/90  IX15    INVESTEXT/HEALTH CARE
HEALTHCARE NOTES - INDUSTRY REPORT
DREXEL BURNHAM LAMBERT INCORPORATED - Sidoti, P., et al
12-01-89    (RN=941890)   10 Pages

4)  1/22/90  IX15    INVESTEXT/HEALTH CARE
HEALTHSOUTH REHABILITATION CORPORATION - COMPANY REPORT    TS=HSRC
SMITH BARNEY, HARRIS UPHAM & CO., INC. - France, J.
12-18-89    (RN=942925)   24 Pages


5)  1/22/90  IX15    INVESTEXT/HEALTH CARE
GREENERY REHABILITATION GROUP, INC. - COMPANY REPORT    TS=GRGI
SMITH BARNEY, HARRIS UPHAM & CO., INC. - France, J.
12-18-89    (RN=943396)   2 Pages


6)  1/22/90  IX15    INVESTEXT/HEALTH CARE
HEALTHSOUTH REHABILITATION CORP. - COMPANY REPORT    TS=HSRC
SMITH BARNEY, HARRIS UPHAM & CO., INC. - France, J.
12-18-89    (RN=943397)   2 Pages


7) 12/25/89  HH11    HEALTH CARE COMPETITION WEEK
DECADE CLOSES WITH HOSPITALS "BACK AT SQUARE ONE"

8) 12/25/89  HH11    HEALTH CARE COMPETITION WEEK
ZERO IN ON CLUSTERS FOR SUCCESS

Enter headline number(s) or ALL to read; PREview; or AGain to
redisplay
headlines
-->ALL [user requests full text of documents]
```

Example 3.8 (continued)

```
Copyright
HEALTH NEWS DAILY via NewsNet
Monday     January 22, 1990

   1)
MCKESSON CREATING NORTH AMERICAN DRUG DISTRIBUTION NETWORK WITH
$81 MIL. CASH ACQUISITION OF LARGEST CANADIAN WHOLESALER MEDIS.
McKESSON's $81 MIL. ACQUISITION OF CANADIAN WHOLESALER MEDIS
Health and Pharmaceutical Services Inc. from parent Provigo Inc.
will "create the first integrated international pharmaceutical
distribution entity," McKesson Chairman Alan Seelenfreund
remarked in a Jan. 19 release announcing the proposed merger.
The move gives McKesson the volume growth so critical for
profitability in the wholesale/distribution industry at a time
when the pool of potential U.S. acquisitions is dwindling. At the
same time, it offers access to an entirely new and growing market
via an established, coast-to-coast Canadian national drug
distribution operation....
```

any items have been found in response to your NEWSFLASH profile. The items are displayed five headlines at a time. Various options are available for reading, saving, or deleting any combination of articles.

The four databanks we have discussed in this chapter represent only a fraction of the online resources available. Other prominent databanks include BRS INFORMATION TECHNOLOGIES, ORBIT, DATA-STAR, and VU/TEXT. These offer a wide range of bibliographic and full-text databases, many of which might be applicable to corporate monitoring. Other databank vendors offer highly specialized industry databases that may be useful. With over 3,000 databases now available it is difficult to predict which are the most appropriate for monitoring routines, other than those specified in this chapter.

For corporate change monitoring, databanks such as DJNR, DIALOG, the LEXIS and NEXIS Services, and NEWSNET should meet most monitoring needs. The availability of frequently updated business news databases in these databanks, many of which provide the full text of newspapers, news releases, business magazines, and industry and trade publications, will provide reports of corporate change. Which file to use may be dictated by specific needs, preference of search features, cost, or availability within the workplace.

NOTES

1. A survey by Digital Information Group as reported in *Personal Computing,* p. 202 (October 1989).

2. DIALOG Information Retrieval Service, "Newswire ASAP," *Bluesheets* (August 1987).

3. DIALOG Information Retrieval Service, "PR Newswire," *Bluesheets* (April 1989).

4. DIALOG Information Retrieval Service, "AP News," *Bluesheets* (April 1990).

5. DIALOG Information Retrieval Service, "UPI News," *Bluesheets* (June 1983).

6. DIALOG Information Retrieval Service, "BusinessWire," *Bluesheets* (June 1986).

7. DIALOG Information Retrieval Service, "Knight-Ridder," *Bluesheets* (February 1989).

8. DIALOG Information Retrieval Service, "Moody's News—U.S.," *Bluesheets* (November 1984); "Standard & Poor's News," *Bluesheets* (February 1986).

9. "Expanded DIALOG ALERT Service for Current Awareness," *DIALOG CHRONOLOG* 89:350 (September 1989).

4

Williams Act Filings:
Public Disclosure of M&A

The Williams Act may not be familiar to M&A researchers, but it is an important piece of legislation that affects their work. For researchers, the act itself is less important than the amount of deal data made public as one of its requirements. The primary objective of the Williams Act, passed in 1968 as an amendment to the Securities Exchange Act of 1934, is to provide full disclosure concerning cash tender offers and other techniques for accumulating large blocks of equity securities of publicly held companies.[1] Knowing what constitutes a "publicly held company" is essential for understanding how M&A information becomes available in primary and secondary sources.

There are thousands of M&A transactions each year. However, only a small fraction of all deals involve companies that are publicly held. During the period 1976-1988, *Mergerstat Review* identified 1,348 successful tender offers made for publicly traded target companies. In the same period, the *Review* recorded 14,699 acquisitions of privately owned companies.[2] Publicly held companies are those whose stock is publicly traded. In the United States, ownership shares are traded on the major stock exchanges or over-the-counter markets, including the NASDAQ (National Association of Securities Dealers Automated Quotations) system. The Securities and Exchange Commission (SEC) regulates the issuance and trading of public stock in the United States. To protect the interests of potential public investors, SEC regulations require public companies to disclose virtually all aspects of business operations. Similarly, to protect current investors in public companies that become acquisition targets, any block purchase of stock exceeding 5 percent of all outstanding shares, or any offer to "tender" (buy) the shares of those stockholders must be publicly disclosed in a filing to the SEC.

The amount of information available on planned or completed transactions is often determined by the target's status as a public or private company. Deals involving private companies are not subject to the scrutiny of the SEC. Consequently, the details of such deals are usually kept secret. Fearing other offers from competitors for their target, acquirers prefer to conduct their transactions in private. The Williams Act exposes a bid for a public company to the target, the stockholders, and the media. This publicity increases the amount of information available about the impending deal.

WILLIAMS ACT FILINGS

The Williams Act filings related to mergers and acquisitions are:

- 13D (report of 5 percent or more equity ownership)
- 13E-3 (going privaté through stock repurchase)
- 13E-4 (issuer purchase of securities)
- 14D-1 (tender offer)
- 14D-9 (management response to tender offer)

Thousands of filings related to M&A acquisitions are filed annually with the SEC. We wanted to learn more about the numbers of filings submitted for each of the individual filings listed above. M&A FILINGS (DIALOG File 548) is a database that compiles the filings as they are submitted to the SEC. Filings dating back to 1985 are in the database. In M&A FILINGS each filing is searchable by the code "FL." For example, to find all the 13D filings we typed the search statement:

S FL = 13D

Table 4.1 gives the number of each filing in the database.

13Ds AND PROXY FIGHTS

Any individual or group accumulating 5 percent or more of a public company's outstanding shares must submit a 13D. A new 13D is filed each time an owner adds to or reduces holdings. However, the 13D's impact on merger and acquisition activity is less than the numbers might imply. Although 13D filings may indicate stock accumulations that could lead to a corporate acquisition, this is usually not the case. Stock accu-

Table 4.1
Total M&A Filings since 1985

Filings	1985	1986	1987	1988	1989
13D	6,885	7,965	8,653	9,439	10,005
13E-3	232	526	524	756	532
13E-4	272	465	573	458	485
14D-1	576	1,286	1,070	2,123	1,672
14D-9	270	620	598	1,284	1,038
ANNUAL FILINGS	8,235	10,592	11,418	14,060	13,732
TOTAL FILINGS	58,037				

mulations may lead to a proxy battle. In a proxy battle, instead of trying to buy up a majority of the company's stock, an acquirer holds a smaller stake and seeks to engineer a coup by enlisting the support of other stockholders. The acquirer urges other stockholders to vote out the current board of directors and vote in a roster of directors loyal to the acquirer.[3]

This technique was used by Coniston Partners to pressure UAL to submit to a purchase by the company employees. Coniston owned 11.8 percent of UAL and threatened a proxy battle. Although the proxy battle has regained some popularity, most 13D filings will not lead to corporate takeovers. Because it is required by the Williams Act, the 13D filing is considered a merger and acquisition document, and important enough to warrant regular monitoring for indicators of potential corporate change. You will find the following types of information in a 13D filing:

- name of issuer (company whose securities have been acquired)
- class of stock
- number of shares acquired and percent of outstanding shares
- identity and background of the reporting party (stock acquirer)
- source and amount of funds or other considerations for making the stock purchases
- purpose of the transaction, including, but not limited to, passive investment, a future tender offer, seeking representation on board of directors, or involvement in a joint venture
- extent of interest in the securities of the issuer
- any contracts, arrangements, or relationships between the issuer and the reporting party

The 13G is a form that is related to the 13D. Like the 13D, it is filed by parties acquiring 5 percent or more of a class of securities. However, the 13G is an abbreviated version of Schedule 13D. It is filed annually, usually by a limited category of reporting parties. This includes banks, stock brokers, insurance companies, and other large institutional investors. Because the 13G is filed in the ordinary course of business and is unrelated to influencing or changing control of the issuer, it is largely ignored for M&A research purposes.

GOING PRIVATE AND CORPORATE RESTRUCTURING

The self-tender acquisition strategy that requires 13E filings can change the structure of a publicly held company. The company can go private or reduce its outstanding shares. Schedule 13E-3 is often associated with transactions in which a public company is "going private." The goal of the transaction is to decrease the number of shareholders to the point where the company need not report to the SEC.

The 13E-3 is also the filing normally submitted in a going-private leveraged buyout (LBO) transaction involving a corporation registered with the SEC. Private companies and subsidiaries of public companies can also conduct an LBO, but in these transactions the 13E-3 is generally not required because the firm is not registered with the SEC. The intention of the buyout is to buy back sufficient outstanding shares to take the company from public to private status. The term "leveraged" refers to the financing techniques being used. The acquirer is financing the deal primarily through debt instruments. LBO deals are also routinely characterized by a tender offer price that is significantly higher than the current market price of the tendered security. Despite the declining numbers of heavily debt financed buyouts, companies continue to use the LBO to go private.

For example, LPL Technologies, a company traded over the counter, filed a 13E-3 in April 1990. The deal was valued at $158 million, not a large amount by megadeal standards. The deal involved an offer by the company's chair and president to purchase for cash all the company's Class A common shares. The stated purpose of the deal was to acquire the entire interest in the issuer in order to facilitate the going private transaction of the issuer. In the LPL Technologies deal the cash offer price was only $.63 more per share than the closing sale price on the day of the filing.

You will find the following types of information in the Schedule 13E-3:

- name of stock issuer and class of security
- identity and background of the reporting party
- terms of the transaction
- plans related to activities after the transaction
- source and amount of funds used in the transaction

- statement on alternatives to, reasons for, and effects of the transaction
- any interest in the securities of the issuer by the reporting party
- descriptions of any contracts, arrangements, or understandings between the issuer and reporting party
- certain financial statements of the issuer

There are times when it is strategically necessary for companies to reduce the amount of outstanding shares of certain classes of securities. It may be that the company is reorganizing and wants to change its capitalization. Shareholders may be offered bonds in exchange for their shares, which is known as a leveraged recapitalization. This has the effect of increasing corporate debt and reducing equity. Reducing outstanding shares may be an avenue to boosting per share market value. Taking shares out of the public market can serve as a takeover defense; the more shares the issuer holds, the fewer can fall into the hands of a raider. Whatever the strategy may be, when an issuer makes a tender offer for its own securities it must file the Schedule 13E-4.

Like the 13E-3, Schedule 13E-4 involves a company buying its own stock. Here the intention is different. The primary objective in these transactions is to raise shareholder value, not to take the company private. For example, in August 1989, Figgie International Inc. filed a 13E-4 with the SEC in which they proposed to purchase up to 437,811 shares of their Class A stock and up to 162,189 shares of their Class B stock. The stated purpose of the tender was to offset the dilution to primary earnings per share during the past year resulting from issuance of issuer shares in connection with employee benefit programs. Figgie sought to increase each share's earnings by decreasing the number of outstanding shares.

Here is some of the information usually found within a 13E-4 filing:

- amount and class of securities sought
- source and amount of funds or other considerations to be used
- purpose of the tender offer
- plans or proposals of the issuer
- transactions or other activity pertinent to the issuer's securities
- certain financial information about the issuer

TENDER OFFERS

Among the Williams Act filings, the 14D is the most indicative of actual takeover or merger activity. Unlike the 13E filings, which technically represent tender offers, the 14D is a bid for shares by an outside acquirer. Because there are many variations on how publicly held corporations may be acquired, the tender offer is a complex subject. A definitive definition of tender offer is elusive. While the conventional meaning is well established as an open cash offer to all shareholders to buy their securities, the Williams Act does not define a tender offer.[4] Nor has the SEC adopted a rule defining a tender offer. In a 1979 notice issued in the *Federal Register*, the SEC stated that the term "includes a request or invitation for tenders, and means one or more offers to purchase or solicitation of offers to sell securities of a single class, whether or not all or any portion of the securities sought are purchased."[5] However, the definition was never adopted.

As previously stated, the section on tender offers was adopted to provide adequate disclosure in connection with takeover bids. Disclosure helps ensure that shareholders have sufficient information to make informed decisions in determining whether to tender their shares.[6]

The lack of a specific definition of tender offer may point to congressional and administrative uncertainty about what constitutes an offer to buy, since many strategies are used in the effort to obtain the securities of shareholders. In one case, the court stated "that the failure of Congress and the SEC to define 'tender offer' was not inadvertent . . . it appears the full meaning of the term was intentionally left to be developed on a case-by-case basis."[7]

Since the Williams Act became law in 1968, takeover practices in the United States have undergone fundamental changes. In the first five years of the act, there was an average of only 54 tender offers per year.[8] The tender offer's development as an acquisition technique was enhanced by the availability of widespread financing that makes huge cash tender offers feasible. The hostile takeover is said to have originated in 1974 when Morgan Stanley & Co. represented International Nickel Co. of Canada in its successful offer for ESB, Inc. Since 1974, there have been an average of 131 tender offers per year.[9] In 1988, there were 46 contested or "hostile" tender offers for public companies. This represented 21 percent of all tender offers, and was the highest number of hostile offers ever recorded.[10]

Section 14(d) of the Williams Act requires that on the day a bidder begins the drive to acquire control of a public company by tendering outstanding shares, the bidder must file a Schedule 14D-1 with the SEC. Section 14(d) defines what events shall be considered the commencement of a tender offer. In almost all cases the tender offer is started by the use of the summary advertisement, the type so often seen in the financial pages of the *Wall Street Journal*. The date of the advertisement is important because it begins the twenty business days that the tender offer must remain open. Purchases of stockholder shares other than through the offer are prohibited once the offer is commenced. On the day the tender offer commences, the bidder must file the Schedule 14D-1 with the SEC, and deliver copies to the target and to the exchanges where the target's stock is traded.[11]

The following types of information are provided in the Schedule 14D-1:

- name and address of the target company
- class and exact amount of stocks being sought and the consideration being offered for them
- information about the market for the stocks and their current market value
- identity and background of the bidder
- description of any business transactions between the bidder and target for any of the preceding three fiscal years of the target
- source and amount of funds or other considerations for the offer, and any loan arrangements if the funds are borrowed
- purpose of the tender offer, and any plans the bidder has to sell or trade assets of the target or change the corporate structure of the target
- amount of target company's stock owned by the bidder and any transactions involving the target's stock made by the bidder in the previous sixty days
- identities of any persons retained by or on behalf of the bidder to make solicitations or recommendations in connection with the tender offer
- financial statements of the bidder (not always required)

The Schedule 14D-9 communicates the response of the target company's management. In the 14D-9, officially known as the "Solicitation/ Recommendation Statement," management may either recommend that shareholders accept or reject the offer, or may state that it remains neutral to the offer. Management must provide sufficient disclosure on any stand that it takes in the 14D-9. The 14D-9 may also transmit information regarding any action the target plans in response to the bid. Such plans may include a reorganization, sales of assets, or possibly a plan to merge with a company other than the bidder.[12]

The SEC also requires that if any material change occurs in the information contained in a Schedule 14D-1, the bidder must file an amendment to the original document. Likewise, a change in management's position would be disclosed in an amendment to the original 14D-9. A change in the cash price being offered to stockholders for their shares would require the filing of an amendment. Tender offers that develop into lengthy takeover battles may result in dozens, sometimes hundreds of amendments being submitted to the SEC. For example, during Georgia-Pacific's bid for Great Northern Neekoosa, Georgia-Pacific filed forty-seven amendments to its original 14D-1 between January 1989 and March 1990. In the same period, Northern Neekoosa filed thirty-three amendments to its original form 14D-9.

OTHER FILINGS

In addition to the filings required by the SEC that can provide significant acquisition and merger information to researchers, documents may
be available at the state level. Since the enactment of the Williams Act in
1968, many states have adopted antitakeover statutes that require companies involved in tender offer activity to submit filings at the state level.
The M&A researcher may find it difficult to identify and locate a state
filing because there are no sources outside the state regulatory agencies
themselves that routinely report the filing of state takeover documents.
Although it provides no direct access to state filings, the *Blue Sky Law
Reporter* published by Commerce Clearing House may be of help in
researching them. It provides the name and address of the appropriate
state agency that collects the filings, and provides details on each state's
M&A filing requirements. The *Blue Sky Law Reporter* is available online
through both WESTLAW and the LEXIS Service.

There are other public documents that contain information of potential
use to M&A researchers. For example, in some friendly mergers, before
the actual tender offer, the shareholders of both companies may receive
a proxy statement providing details of the proposed transaction. The 8K
filing, which companies use to report significant events to the SEC, may
have acquisition or merger information. However, deals reported in 8Ks
are often those in which a public parent acquires or divests one of its
holdings.

Because acquisitions of public companies are complex, there are a
number of ways to complete the deals, which may involve any number
of different federal and state regulatory filings. Many of these filings are
not retrievable through any secondary sources.

INFORMATION SOURCES FOR TENDER OFFERS

There are several reasons why the public documents of M&A are
sought out for their information. The following types of research could
require access to or knowledge of the filings:

- monitoring of ongoing acquisition activity (who is bidding for whom)
- exploration of how other deals were financed
- research on specific deals or deals in certain industries
- identification of deals involving certain types of tender offer techniques (e.g.,
  one-step versus two-step)
- identification of deals meeting specific financial criteria
- identification or study of takeover defense techniques
- confirmation of rumors or investment decisions based on disclosures of corporations and investors

- planning of investment moves by predicting stock trading based on M&A activity
- industry studies for market analysis

Research of this kind requires more than simple access to a filings collection. An ability to search the text of the documents to locate those fulfilling the search requirements is needed. This can usually be accomplished with an electronic filings database. Online databases are but one format in which SEC filings are found. They are also available in paper, microform, and laser disk formats. These other formats, however, serve primarily as an archive of SEC filings at best. Usually, online electronic databases offer superior capability for researching M&A filings. We will examine availability of resources for each format.

There are only a few print sources for monitoring or researching SEC filings. Corporate stockholders do not receive copies of the Williams Act filings, and few individuals have the luxury of spending all their time at a SEC library reviewing the filings as they are submitted. One source for monitoring is the *SEC News Digest*, a daily publication of the SEC. In addition to reporting agency announcements, proceedings, and other news items, it provides a complete listing of Williams Act filings submitted to the SEC. The only information provided is the name of stock issuer and the purchaser, the class of security purchased, the form filed (e.g., 13D, 14D-1), the transaction date, number of shares acquired and percent owned, prior percent owned, and filing status (e.g., new, update, or revision).

This source would be useful for monitoring acquisition activity, although the majority of the transactions listed are 13D filings to report 5 percent purchases or additions to existing 5 percent holdings. The limitations of *SEC News Digest* are that it is useful only for monitoring filings and that it lacks detailed information about the nature of the transaction reported. No index to the *Digest* is compiled, so it is virtually impossible to use this publication for retrospective research. Because it is a government publication, *SEC News Digest* has low subscription rates. Users of the LEXIS Service can access an electronic version of the *SEC News Digest*. The name of the database is SECNEW, and it is in the COMPNY library.

Commercial document delivery services will allow you to obtain copies of filings as they are needed. This is a good strategy for the researcher who only needs to review specific filings, and does so only occasionally. For organizations that need to collect the full text of all Williams Act filings, microform is an option. There are several companies that obtain all the filings and make them available on microfiche. Microfiche are four inch by six inch cards that contain ninety-six pages of text. A special reader is required to view and print the microfiche. Filings microfiche are usually available from commercial vendors, such as Disclosure Inc., on a subscription basis. A subscriber may receive all available filings or specify a certain class of documents. For example, a subscriber may only want to receive 14D-1 and 14D-9 filings.

The advantage of microfiche is its compactness. A room full of paper filings in microformat can fit into a single filing cabinet. When a filing is needed, it can be located quickly and a paper copy made. While microfiche filings could be used as an M&A acquisition monitoring tool, there is a time lag of several weeks before they are received. This may be too late to act on information provided in the filings. As a practical matter it would be too time-consuming to read the many filings that are received.

There are some disadvantages to microfiche. The most frequent complaint from those who use this format is the difficulty in reading the cards. Paper is certainly more legible. The thousands of filings must be organized and filed as they are received, and refiled after use. The subscriptions to microfiche collections are expensive (about $1.00 per document). Even if you were to collect all the filings on microfiche, there still would be no direct way to locate a filing on a particular subject. Also, at least two parties are always involved in a M&A filing. The fiche may be organized by only one company name, usually the stock issuer. Thus, it would be difficult, if not impossible, to locate all the filings in which a certain company or individiual was the party submitting the form to the SEC.

The latest option in acquiring and researching the contents of SEC filings is the laser disc or compact disc (CD-ROM) format. This format offers many advantages over paper or microform. The CD-ROM medium offers compact storage similar to that of microfiche, as thousands of pages of text can be stored on one compact disc. Retrieval of documents is much easier. Generally, documents are searched by company name or ticker symbol. Other advantages of CD-ROM are:

- rapid retrieval of a specific document
- higher quality print output (usually from laser printers)
- ability to locate filings by either stock issuer or filing party
- virtually maintenance free
- fixed cost retrieval of documents

Currently, Disclosure Inc. offers SEC documents on CD-ROM. Called LASERd, the product offers a variety of filings, and plans to offer most Williams Act filings. If you are considering a purchase of this product, consider not only the completeness of documents offered and timeliness of the discs, but also searchability. Despite its being an electronic database, the text of the documents is not now searchable. Cost is another consideration. Subscriptions to LASERd can run from $15,000 to $50,000 depending on the organizational affiliation (e.g., academic institution or commercial bank) and type of subscription. Finally, there is some minimal time lag between the actual filing and the availability of new CD-ROM discs. Monitoring filings would not be a useful application for CD-ROM databases.

For actual searching of Williams Act filings, electronic time-sharing databases offer the greatest practical advantage. Examples of applications for filings databases include:

- finding filings submitted by either stock issuer (target) or reporting person (acquirer)
- searching the abstracts of filings to identify specific financing or defensive techniques
- identifying deals meeting specific criteria such as deal value, industry, or time period

These applications are difficult, if not impossible, in print, microform, and CD-ROM versions of Williams Act filings.

There are several time-sharing databases providing access to the filings. At present, none offers full text of the filings. Online availability is limited to abstracts in all files. The primary filings databases available on popular commercial databanks are ACQUIS, M&A FILINGS, FED-FILES and Disclosure's SEC FILINGS INDEX.

ACQUIS provides abstracts of all 13 and 14 series filings with the exception of the 13F. This database is available only through Mead Data's LEXIS Service. It is found in the COMPNY library under a file called ACQUIS. This database is produced by States News Service, a Washington, D.C. wire service specializing in reporting news from Congress and federal agencies. All amendments to the filings are included. In addition to information drawn from the filings, stories from major newspapers supplement the abstracts. Abstracted records of the 13D, 14D-1, and 14D-9 are usually available within forty-eight hours of the filing date. The 13E-3, 13E-4, and 13G filings are usually available within three weeks of public availability from the SEC. Database coverage of filings extends back to 1987.

The entire database record may be searched with any terms. However, the record is structured into "segments." This allows for greater search flexibility. For example, filings may be retrieved by issuer or filing party. Other segments are filing date, number of shares owned, purpose of transaction, and abstract. While it could be possible to locate deals of a specific value by searching for the value, ACQUIS is limited in terms of search parameters. It is certainly a better database for obtaining information by name of issuer or reporting party than by other screening criteria, such as deal value.

Example 4.1 shows a search in the ACQUIS database. We want to locate the 14D-9 that Time Inc. submitted in response to a hostile tender offer from Paramount Communications. Time was attempting to merge with Warner. Paramount's strategy was to prevent Time from acquiring Warner by taking over Time. The search is fairly easy in the LEXIS Service.

M&A FILINGS, mentioned previously, is the best of existing online time-sharing databases for researching Williams Act filings. It offers the most informative abstracts and the most search variables. Produced by Charles E. Simon & Company, who collects the filings made with the SEC, M&A FILINGS contains detailed abstracts of every original and amended merger and acquisition document released by the SEC. Coverage extends back to early 1985. The database is updated daily, usually within twenty-four hours of filing at the SEC.

Each record in the database is composed of about thirty searchable fields. Some examples of variables are company name (the stock issuer), reporting person (filing party), purpose of transaction, deal manager, source of funding, and shareholdings. The abstracts range from fewer than a hundred words to a page or two for complex original filings. Two unique features of M&A FILINGS are the event name and event code fields. Typical event names include tender offer, cash offer, and employee agreement. There are over a hundred events classified in the database. This makes it much easier to identify filings discussing particular strategies, financing techniques, or events. For example, to identify deals involving the "white knight" takeover defense, the searcher would use the statement S EV=WHITE KNIGHT; in this statement "EV" is the search prefix for event name.

Example 4.2 shows a search illustrating M&A FILINGS. We perform the same search for the original 140-9 submitted by Time Inc. in response to Paramount. Searches in filings databases often retrieve many records because of amendments to the original filing. The original filing usually contains the most deal information. M&A FILINGS offers an easy technique to limit retrieval to only original filings. The search statement AM=ORIG when used alone or when combined with other search statements will retrieve only original filings. Example 4.3 illustrates how M&A FILINGS is screened to identify documents meeting specific criteria. We want to identify tender offers for firms in the pharmaceutical industry where the value of the deal exceeded $30 million and the amount of stock being tendered was 50 percent of outstanding shares for the transaction to occur. You should note that our

Example 4.1
A Search in the ACQUIS Database

FORM (14D-9) AND NAME-OF-ISSUER (TIME) [**FORM is the segment used to search by filing type, and NAME-OF-ISSUER is the segment for the company whose stock is being acquired**]

NEXIS is working on the displayed request.
If it is not what you intended to transmit, please press the STOP key.

Your search request has found 14 REPORTS through Level 1.
To DISPLAY these REPORTS press either the KWIC, FULL, CITE or SEGMTS key. To MODIFY your search request, press the M key (for MODFY) and then the TRANSMIT key.

.CI [**First we examine the documents in "CITE" format**]

LEVEL 1 - 14 REPORTS

1. Schedule 14D-9, amendment no. 11, FILING-DATE: July 18, 1989, NAME-OF-ISSUER:Time Inc., FILING-PERSON: Time Inc.

2. Schedule 14D-9, amendment no. 10, FILING-DATE: July 17, 1989, NAME-OF-ISSUER:Time Incorporated, FILING-PERSON: Time Incorporated

3. Schedule 14D-9, amendment no. 9, FILING-DATE: July 14, 1989, NAME-OF-ISSUER: Time Inc., FILING-PERSON: Time Inc.
.
.
.

13. Schedule 14D-9, FILING-DATE: June 19, 1989 (States News Service Receipt Date-Filing Date Unknown), NAME-OF-ISSUER: Time Inc., FILING-PERSON: Time Inc.

14. Schedule 14D-9, amendment no. 1, FILING-DATE: June 19, 1989, NAME-OF-ISSUER:Time Inc., FILING-PERSON: Time Inc.

.FU;13 [**Look at document 13 in full format, with abstract**]

LEVEL 1 - 13 OF 14 REPORTS

Copyright (c) 1989 Mead Data Central, Inc.; prepared by States News Service
SEC Abstracted Filings

Schedule 14D-9

FILING-DATE: June 19, 1989
(States News Service Receipt Date-Filing Date Unknown)

NAME-OF-ISSUER: Time Inc.

TITLE OF SECURITIES: common

FILING-PERSON: Time Inc.

CUSIP NO.: 88722410

ABSTRACT:
This Statement relates to the tender offer disclosed in a Schedule 14D-1 dated June 7, 1989, by KDS Acquisition Corp., an indirect wholly owned subsidiary of Paramount Communications Inc., to purchase all outstanding shares for $175 per share. At the June 15-16 meeting, after lengthy review, Time's board of directors unanimously voted against the tender offer, determining that it was inadequate and not in the best interests of Time, its stockholders and its other constituencies.
The board further decided to begin a tender offer for Warner Communications.

Example 4.1 (continued)

```
EXHIBIT-INDEX: 1 -- Excerpts from Proxy Statement/Prospectus
dated May 22, 1989 of Time Inc.

2 -- Letter to Stockholders of Time Inc. dated June 16, 1989

3 -- Press Release issued on June 16, 1989

4 -- Opinion of Wasserstein Perella and Co. Inc., dated June 16,
1989, relating to the PCI Offer.

5 -- Opinion of Shearson Lehman Hutton Inc. dated June 16, 1989,
relating to the PCI Offer.

6 -- Agreement and Plan of Merger dated as of March 3, 1989, as
amended and restated as of May 19, 1989 and as of June 16, 1989,
between Time Inc. and Warner Communications Inc.

7 -- Offer to purchase dated June 16, 1989, of Time Inc.

8 -- Letter of transmittal

9 -- Opinion of Wasserstein Perella and Co., Inc., dated June 16,
1989, relating to the Offer and the Merger.

10 -- Opinion of Shearson Lehman Hutton Inc. dated June 16, 1989,
relating to the Offer and the Merger.

11 -- Amendment No. 3 to Rights Agreement dated as of April 29,
1986, as amended,between Time and First Chicago Trust Co. of New
York, as Rights Agent.
```

Source: Reprinted with the permission of Mead Data Central, Inc., provider of the LEXIS®/ NEXIS® services.

search will only identify a stock issuer (acquisition target) in this industry. There is no way to screen acquirers by industry code.

Our search identified seven deals in the database that met all the criteria of our search. If we examine the abstract of document 7 (above), Kodak's bid for Sterling Drug, you can see where the phrase "50% of the shares" occurs. It is possible that our search could have retrieved an abstract with the phrase "$50 per share" referring to the cash price of the shares being tendered. This unintentional retrieval is sometimes called a "false drop." Although the search was for tender offers, several filings retrieved were actually 13D filings, which usually are filed when 5 percent or more of securities have been acquired. A search strategy for 14D filings would have been more precise, but fewer documents would have been retrieved. M&A FILINGS, because of its many searchable fields, allows for screening techniques that would be impossible in the other filings databases.

A recent addition to the SEC filings database market is found on DOW JONES NEWS/RETRIEVAL. Called FEDFILES, the database is produced by Federal Filings Inc., a Washington, D.C. subsidiary of Dow Jones. There are several differences between FEDFILES and other filings data-

Example 4.2
A Search in the M&A FILINGS Database

```
?SS FL=14D9 AND TIME/CO [requesting any documents that are a 14D-
                          9 submitted by Time Inc.  FL is the
                          search prefix for filings and /CO
                          the search suffix for issuer]

      S4   4006  FL=14D9  (MANAGEMENT RESPONSE TO
                A TENDER OFFER) [4006 documents are 14D-9s]
      S5     82  TIME/CO   [82 documents with Time as issuer]
      S6     12  FL=14D9 AND TIME/CO [a total of 12 documents
                          where Time filed a 14D-9]
```

?3/3/ALL [display all documents in short format]

3/3/1
0058864
TIME INC

14D9 Amendment Number 11 Filed on 07/18/89
Number of Pages: 4

Reporting Person: Time Inc

Synopsis Sentence:
  Reports litigation or similar matters.

3/3/2
0058807
TIME INC

14D9 Amendment Number 10 Filed on 07/17/89
Number of Pages: 4

Reporting Person: Time Inc

Synopsis Sentence:
  Reports litigation or similar matters.
  .
  .
  .
3/3/11
0057603
TIME INC

14D9 Amendment Number Orig Filed on 06/16/89
Number of Pages: 12

Reporting Person: Time Inc

Synopsis Sentence:
  Reports management's rejection of the offer.

3/3/12
0057589
TIME INC

14D9 Amendment Number 1 Filed on 06/19/89
Number of Pages: 1

Reporting Person: Time Inc

Synopsis Sentence:
  Reports the Reporting Person's intention to include certain
information as exhibit material not filed previously.

?T3/5/11 [display document number 11 in full format]

Example 4.2 (continued)

```
3/5/11
0057603
TIME INC
```

```
Ticker Symbol: TL          Exchange:  NYS
CUSIP No: 88722410
SIC Codes: 2721
State of Incorporation: DE
Headquarters Location:  New York NY
```

```
14D9 Amendment Number Orig Filed on 06/16/89
Number of Pages: 12
```

```
Reporting Person:   Time Inc
Reporting Location: New York  NY  USA
```

Date of Event Requiring Filing: 06/16/89

This statement relates to the tender offer of KDS Acquisition Corp

Synopsis Sentence:
  Reports management's rejection of the offer.
Management Opinion: Disapprove
Fairness Opinion By: Wasserstein Perella & Co Inc and Shearson Lehman
Hutton Inc

Summary Abstract:
  Summary:
  Statement relates to an offer to purchase all outstanding shares of Time Inc. Common Stock (including associated Preferred Stock Purchase Rights) at $175 per share by KDS Acquisition Corp., a wholly-owned subsidiary of Paramount Communications Inc.
    Item 4.   The Solicitation or Recommendation:
  Reports that Time's Board of Directors, at meetings held on 6-15-89 and 6-16-89, unanimously determined that the Offer is inadequate and not in the best interests of Time or its stockholders.
    Item 5.   Persons Retained, Employed or to be Compensated:
  Reports that Time has retained Wasserstein Perella & Co., Inc. (WP) and Shearson Lehman Hutton Inc. to act as financial advisors to Time in connection with the Offer. Time has paid each of WP and Shearson $6 million for acting as financial advisors. Furthermore, Time has agreed to pay each of WP and Shearson an additional fee of $10 million, if by 2-14-90 (i) the Merger is consummated or (ii) no business combination transactions between Time and any party is consummated.
    Item 9.   Material to be Filed as Exhibits:
  Excerpts from Proxy Statement-Prospectus dated 3-22-89 of Time. Letter to Time stockholders dated 6-16-89.
  Press Release dated 6-16-89.
  Fairness Opinions of WP dated 6-16-89.
  Fairness Opinions of Shearson dated 6-16-89.
  Agreement and Plan of Merger, dated 6-16-89, between Time, TW Sub Inc.
and Warner Communications.
  Offer to Purchase dated 6-16-89.
  Amendment No. 3 to Rights Agreement dated 4-29-89, as amended between
Time and First Chicago Trust Co. of New York, as Rights Agent.

Event Name(s) and Code(s):
  TENDER OFFER (51)
  HOSTILE (26)

Example 4.3
Screening with M&A FILINGS

```
?SS SC=2834 [search for issuers whose SIC code is 2834]

    S1      568   SC=2834 [there are 568 filings]

?SS S1 AND DV>30,000,000 [limit search set 1 to those where the
                          deal value is greater than $30 million.
                          DV is the search prefix for deal value]


    S1      568   S1
    S2     1336   DV>30,000,000
    S3       23   S10 AND DV>30,000,000 [23 documents meet the
                          deal value criteria]

?SS S3 AND EC=51 [limit search set 3 to those where a tender
                  offer was made.  EC is the search prefix for
                  event code and 51 is the code for tender offer]

    S3       23   S12
    S4     4688   EC=51   (TENDER OFFER)
    S5       15   S12 AND EC=51 [15 documents are tender offers]

?SS S5 AND 50(3N)SHARE/AB  [limit search set 5 to those filings
                            where the term "50" is within 3
                            words of the term "share", and those
                            terms must be in the filing
                            abstract]

    S5       15   S14
    S6     7483   50/AB
    S7    32499   SHARE/AB
    S8     5121   50/AB(3N)SHARE/AB
    S9        7   S14 AND 50(3N)SHARE/AB [7 documents have the
                            term 50 within three of share in the
                            abstract]

?T9/3/ALL [display all 7 documents in short format]


9/3/1
0060952
CONNAUGHT BIOSCIENCES INC

13D Amendment Number Orig Filed on 09/15/89
Number of Pages: 7

Reporting Person:    JV Vax Inc
                     JV Vax Holdings Inc
                     CIBA-GEIGY Ltd
                     Chiron Corp

Synopsis Sentence:
  Reports the original filing of a tender offer.


23/3/2
0060951
CONNAUGHT BIOSCIENCES INC

14D1 Amendment Number Orig Filed on 09/15/89
Number of Pages: 7

Reporting Person:    JV Vax Inc
                     JV Vax Holdings Inc
                     CIBA-GEIGY Ltd
                     Chiron Corp
```

Example 4.3 (continued)

```
Synopsis Sentence:
  Reports the original filing of a tender offer.
  .

  .

  .

23/3/6
0037037
STERLING DRUG INC

13D Amendment Number Orig Filed on 01/25/88
Number of Pages: 7

Reporting Person:    Eastman Kodak Co

Synopsis Sentence:
  Reports the original filing of a tender offer.

23/3/7
0037036
STERLING DRUG INC

14D1 Amendment Number Orig Filed on 01/25/88
Number of Pages: 7

Reporting Person:    Eastman Kodak Co

Synopsis Sentence:
  Reports the original filing of a tender offer.


Summary Abstract:

  Summary:
  Statement reports an offer to purchase all outstanding shares
  of Sterling Drug, Inc.  Common  Stock  at  $89.50  per  share by
  KRH Holdings, Inc., a wholly-owned subsidiary of Eastman Kodak
  Co.
    Item 5. Purpose of the Tender Offer and Plans or Proposals of
  the Bidder:  The  Offer  is  being  made  pursuant to an
  Agreement and Plan of Merger, dated  1-22-88,   between Kodak, the
  Purchaser and Sterling Drug. The Merger Agreement  provides  that
  as  soon  as practicable after completion of the Offer,  the
  Purchaser will be merged with and into Sterling Drug, and each
  outstanding  Common  Share (other than shares owned by Kodak, the
  Purchaser or  their affiliates) will be converted into the right
  to receive $89.50 in cash.
    Sterling  Drug's  Board  of Directors has unanimously
  determined that the Offer  and  the  Merger are fair and in the
  best interests of Sterling Drug and  its  shareholders,  and
  further recommend that shareholders accept the Offer and tender
  their shares.
    The Offer, which will expire on 2-22-88, is conditioned upon a
  minimum of 50% of the shares outstanding being validly tendered.
```

bases. Most important, this is a real time newswire service. That is, filings released to the public at the SEC are reported on FEDFILES as quickly as possible throughout the day. FEDFILES also includes SEC filings other than 13 and 14 Schedule filings. Registrations for debt and equity securities (S-1, S-2, S-3, S-4), 8-Ks, and M&A information from proxy statements are also found in this database. The other key difference is that information is stored on the database for only ninety days.

As with other DJNR menus databases, FEDFILES is searchable only by name or ticker symbols of publicly held companies or DJNR news codes.

Although keyword text searching is not possible, it is easy to retrieve news stories on a variety of topics with the use of codes. Codes include news subjects (e.g., bankruptcies, corporate changes, buyouts), industries (e.g., aerospace, computers), and document types (e.g., 13D, 14D-1, original filings only, amended filings only).

In the following examples, we illustrate two applications for FED-FILES. In Example 4.4, the code for 14D-1 is searched. This retrieves a list of stories about all 14D-1 filings submitted to the SEC within the last ninety days, a strategy appropriate for quick monitoring of tender offer activity. Example 4.5 shows the retrieval of information about a specific public company. This technique could be used to confirm rumors about deals, to obtain details about current deals involving specific firms, or to keep up to date on deals in process.

The abstract for the document in Example 4.5 is five screens long, a considerable amount for a filings abstract.

Disclosure's SEC FILINGS INDEX, as the name suggests, is different from the other three databases. It is the only database that provides no abstract. Available on the NEWSNET system, SEC FILINGS INDEX is produced by Disclosure, Inc. Disclosure is the SEC's contractor for making filings available for public purchase. Although not a real-time file like FEDFILES, the SEC FILINGS INDEX is still updated frequently. The producer states the update frequency is three to six times daily. Like FEDFILES, the INDEX includes all types of SEC filings. It is not restricted to Williams Act filings. The database contains only the last fifty-one weeks of filings. The cost of this file is $252 per connect hour, making it the most expensive file to search. The file name on NEWSNET is IV97T.

As discussed in the previous chapter, NEWSNET offers three modes of searching, READ, SCAN, and SEARCH. For research that is limited to Williams Act filings, SEARCH is the preferable mode. READ and SCAN allow you to view all filings submitted during a specific time. This means the user must browse through 10K and 10Q filings as well as many other SEC filings to find those related to M&A. SEARCH allows keyword searching. This makes it possible to specify the type of filing, as well as issuer or reporting party. Example 4.6 provides a full record from Disclosure's FILINGS INDEX.

As this example shows, there is limited data available for each filing. Additionally, unlike M&A FILINGS, ACQUIS, or FEDFILES there are no searchable fields or codes to help identify filings meeting specific criteria. Still, this database can be searched to quickly identify what filings were submitted by whom and with regard to what issuer. In fact, it is possible to conduct a search similar to that done in the other databases to identify filings related to the Paramount Communications hostile bid for Time Inc. (see Example 4.7).

Example 4.4

A Search Using FEDFILES

```
.N/14D1 [type the Dow Jones code for 14D-1 filings. The ".N"
            indicates that we want to see a list of all headlines
            for the last 90 days. Without the ".N" the stories
            would be displayed in full format one at a time.]

      14D-1 TENDER OFFERINGS            HEADLINE PAGE   1 OF   8

      [there are 8 screens of headlines. The stories run from
       EY to AA. We will look at the full format for story EV]


   EY 04/27 Sikes Offer - Projections/Termination Fees - 4 -
   EX 04/27 Sikes Offer - Additional Background -3-
   EW 04/27 Sikes Offer - Funds/Legal Matters -2-
   EV 04/27 Sikes Offer - Premark Bid Was Best Received
    .

    .
   EI 04/23 MGM/UA Offer - Financing Arrangements -3-
   EH 04/23 MGM/UA Offer- HSR Approval
------------------------------------------------------------------
ENTER STORY IDENTIFIER, OR ENTER A PERIOD (.) AND A NEW CODE.

   EV

      14D-1 TENDER OFFER FILINGS            STORY   EV

PAGE  1 OF  2

04/27 Sikes Offer - Premark Bid Was Best Received

                    MAJOR SHAREHOLDER ALERT
                   Based upon 14D-1 Original
ISSUER: SIKES CORP. CL A
SYMBOL: SK.A
FILER: PREMARK INTERNATIONAL INC.
CLASS: COMMON
SHARES OWNED: N/A            N/A%       AGGREGATE AVG PRICE: $N/A
TRANS: NONE
NARRATIVE DESCRIPTION:
        BACKGROUND:  Following its oral indication of interest
in a possible purchase of the Sikes for $190-$200 million,
Norcros told Sikes it wished to privately negotiate an
acquisition, and was not interested in pursuing a hostile
takeover or participating in a competitive auction to acquire
Sikes.
        In accordance with its position, Norcros declined to
participate in a review by Sikes of additional expressions of
acquisition interest by those
parties which had proposed the highest acquisition values to
Sikes as part of Sikes review of interest received.
        Norcros was contacted by Sikes' advisor Lazard Freres on
two occasions to inquire whether Norcros intended to make a
further offer for Sikes.    Although Norcros expressed continuing
interest in acquiring Sikes in a privately negotiated
transaction, Norcros did not make any further offer in response
to invitations to do so.
        In a preliminary indication of interest received from a
group including Nicolas Gargour, the Gargour group proposed a
merger in which all Sikes stock would be acquired for $150-$175
million, or alternatively, an unspecified combination of cash and
securities.  Sikes subsequently notified Gargour on 3/1/90 that
further consideration of the proposal would not be productive.
        On 4/18/90, Premark made its proposal to acquire Sikes
at $201 million.  On 4/19/90, Premark was informed by Sikes'
board that its proposal was the best received.
04/27/90 15:46
```

Example 4.5
Information Retrieval Using FEDFILES

```
.TTT 01 [search for any filings by or for the firm Telecom.
         The "01" indicates we want to display a list of
         story headlines only]

STOCK SYMBOL: TTT                              HEADLINE PAGE
1 OF   1

  AD 04/12 Updated 8K Filings
  AC 04/12 Latest 8K Filings
  AB 04/12 Updated List For 9:00
  AA 04/12 Telecom/MCI Merger- Legal Matters/Termination Fees
---------------------------------------------------------------
ENTER STORY IDENTIFIER, OR ENTER A PERIOD (.) AND A NEW CODE.

MORE, OR ENTER A PERIOD (.) AND A NEW CODE.

  AA [enter the code AA to see the story on the Telecom/MCI
      merger]

STOCK SYMBOL: TTT                               STORY   AA

PAGE  1 OF  5


04/12 Telecom/MCI Merger- Legal Matters/Termination Fees

                    MAJOR SHAREHOLDER ALERT
                    Based upon 13D Amend #1
ISSUER: TELECOM USA
SYMBOL: TTT
FILER: Telecom Partners et al
Contact Edward C. Roberts at (803) 748-3516.
CLASS: COMMON
SHARES OWNED: 5,788,319      21.77%    AGGREGATE AVG PRICE: $N/A

TRANS: NONE
NARRATIVE DESCRIPTION:
        On 4/8/90, MCI Communications Corp. and the issuer
entered into a merger agreement pursuant to which MCI will
acquire the issuer at $42 per share in cash.  The filing exhibits
the 4/8/90 merger agreement.
        STOCKHOLDER AGREEMENT:  In order to induce MCI to enter
into the merger agreement, the filers entered into a stockholders
agreement with MCI....
```

The one occurrence refers to a grouping of filings in which Time Inc. is the issuer. In the transaction involving Time, Warner, and Paramount Communications, KDS Acquisition Corp. was the acquisition corporation created by Paramount to acquire Time. The search in FILINGS INDEX retrieved slightly fewer filings related to this deal than did our similar searches in M&A FILINGS and ACQUIS. FEDFILES, remember, retains filings for only ninety days, so it would not be useful for a retrospective search such as this. While FILINGS INDEX may be used to search for Williams Act filings, by design it is intended primarily for current monitoring of filings submitted to the SEC. It also lacks much of the information, such as the abstract, provided by other online filings databases. Its value is questionable given its high search cost.

There are other databases that can be used to identify companies that have submitted significant filings to the SEC. For example, newswire

Example 4.6
A Full Record from the SEC FILINGS INDEX

```
TIME WARNER INC
-------------------
SCA 13DA          TENDERS AND ACQUISITIONS - ACT 1934
DOC CTL #: 89162262
                  FILED BY: WARNER COMMUNICATIONS INC
                  EXCH: NYSE        SEC RCPT: 08/25/89
```

databases often report tender offers if the reporting party issues a press release. A significant tender offer also would be reported in the business news databases. Still, these sources may not provide the actual text from the filing. The DISCLOSURE database (DIALOG, BRS, DJNR), in addition to providing financial information from a public company's 10K report, also lists any filings the company has submitted to the SEC. However, this is only a list and provides no further information about the filing.

Williams Act filings are an important source of M&A information. Besides identifying potential, proposed, and ongoing transactions, they can provide insight into the structure of many different types of deals. The challenge lies in identifying filings, their content, and how to obtain them. We have examined several ways to meet these challenges. Let us summarize some of the strengths and weaknesss of these multiple access methods.

Maintaining paper collections of Williams Act filings is difficult since it requires large amounts of space and human labor for organizing the documents. Paper collections fail to provide a method to search their contents.

Microfiche is a preferable format to paper for maintaining an archive of Williams Act filings. Fiche may be acquired selectively, or may be subscribed to through commercial vendors. Although they require less storage space, they demand extensive filing and refiling, and by themselves provide no methods for searching their contents. Microfiche will require special machines for reading and producing paper copies.

Laser disk products provide the most convenient fixed cost method for maintaining an in-house archival collection of Williams Act filings. They are space-saving and require little or no collection maintenance. Document retrieval is fast, and laser printing technology produces high quality paper output. The drawbacks to CD-ROMs include high cost and inability to selectively collect filings (all filings are provided through a subscription). There is still some time lag in receiving the filings.

Time-sharing databases, although expensive, provide the best method for identifying and locating Williams Act filings. They are probably the best option for those who only need to obtain filings selectively (i.e.,

Example 4.7
A Search Using SEC FILINGS INDEX

Enter command or <RETURN>

-->SEARCH [**enter the command to search by keywords**]

Enter service or industry code(s)

-->IV97T [**enter the code for Disclosure's SEC FILING INDEX**]

Enter Latest for latest issue, or other date options in MM/DD/YY

format

-->01/01/89-12/31/89 [**specify the year 1989**]

Enter keyword phrase

-->14D9 AND TIME

     1 Occurrences [**one record includes both Time and a
               14D-9 filing**]

Enter HEAd for headlines; TExt for full text; Analyze for
occurrences in each service; or <RETURN> for new keyword(s)

-->TEXT

Copyright
Disclosure SEC FILINGS INDEX via NewsNet
WEDNESDAY JUNE 21, 1989

TIME INC /DE/

SC 14D1A   TENDERS AND ACQUISITIONS - ACT 1934   DOC CTL
#: 89142334
               FILED BY: PARAMOUNT COMMUNICATIONS INC
               EXCH: NYSE   SEC RCPT: 06/15/89

SC 14D1A   TENDERS AND ACQUISITIONS - ACT 1934   DOC CTL
#: 89150560
               FILED BY: KDS ACQUISITION CORP ET AL
               EXCH: NYSE   SEC RCPT: 06/19/89

SC 14D1A   TENDERS AND ACQUISITIONS - ACT 1934   DOC CTL
#: 89150558
               FILED BY: KDS ACQUISITION CORP ET AL
               EXCH: NYSE   SEC RCPT: 06/19/89

SC 14D9   **TENDERS AND ACQUISITIONS - ACT 1934**   **DOC CTL**
#: 89150565
               FILED BY: TIME INC

               EXCH: NYSE   SEC RCPT: 06/16/89

SC 14D9A   TENDERS AND ACQUISITIONS - ACT 1934   DOC CTL
#: 89150559
               FILED BY: TIME INC
               EXCH: NYSE   SEC RCPT: 06/19/89

SC 14D1A   TENDERS AND ACQUISITIONS - ACT 1934   DOC CTL
#: 89142356
               FILED BY: KDS ACQUISITION CORP ET AL
               EXCH: NYSE   SEC RCPT: 06/15/89

SC 14D1A   TENDERS AND ACQUISITIONS - ACT 1934   DOC CTL
#: 89150621
               FILED BY: KDS ACQUISITION CORP ET AL
               EXCH: NYSE   SEC RCPT: 06/19/89

search for filings by criteria and then order them on paper or fiche from document delivery services). The strength of these files, depending on which is chosen, is either timeliness of the file content or the ability to identify filings by a range of search criteria. At present, no full-text filings databases are available.

SEC FILING INDEX and FEDFILES are preferable for routine monitoring of M&A filings submitted to the SEC. Both lack field searching and are limited in their retrospective coverage of filings. ACQUIS and M&A FILINGS are better files for retrospective searching. Both offer field searching for greater access by multiple search criteria, but M&A, FILINGS is superior to ACQUIS in this respect. At present, there are no databases available for identifying, locating, or obtaining state level M&A filings.

Researching Williams Act filings is hampered by a division between the source documents (the text of the filings on paper, microfiche, or compact disk) and finding tools (principally the online databases of filing abstracts). The source documents provide all the detail that is available, but severely limit the ability to search content. The finding tools often allow us to screen on scores of variables but give us at most an abstract of the document.

The split between source documents and finding tools will be lessened in the next few years as the SEC's database EDGAR is implemented. EDGAR (Electronic Data Gathering Analysis and Retrieval) is designed to capture all filings of all public companies in electronic form. Companies will file the forms electronically with the SEC. The SEC will make all filings available in full-text searchable form through EDGAR shortly after their release. Access to EDGAR is likely to be available on the LEXIS and NEXIS Services. The introduction of EDGAR will certainly affect techniques for researching and retrieving Williams Act filings.

NOTES

1. U.S. Senate Committee on Banking, Housing and Urban Affairs, *Securities and Exchange Commission Report on Tender Offer Laws* (Washington, D.C.: U.S. Government Printing Office, 1980), p. 47.

2. W. T. Grimm & Co., *Mergerstat Review 1988* (Schaumburg, Ill.: Merrill Lynch Business Brokerage & Valuation, 1989).

3. Thomas McCarroll and William McWhirter, "The Proxy Punchout," *Time* 135(16):40-41 (1990).

4. Nathaniel B. Smith, "Defining 'Tender Offer' under the Williams Act," *Brooklyn Law Review* 53:189-203 (Winter 1987).

5. Securities Exchange Act Release No. 16385, November 29, 1979. 44 FR 70349.

6. Marc I. Steinberg, ed., *Tender Offers: Developments and Commentaries* (Westport, Conn.: Quorum, 1985), p. 286.

7. Smith, "Defining 'Tender Offer,'" p. 195.

8. Steinberg, *Tender Offers*, p. 10.

9. Ibid.

10. *Mergerstat Review: 1988*, p. 84.

11. Stanley F. Reed and Lane and Edson, *The Art of M & A: A Merger, Acquisition, Buyout Guide* (Homewood, Ill.: Dow Jones-Irwin, 1989), p. 729.

12. Browne & Co., *Regulations 14D, 14E and Rule 14F1: Tender Offers under the Securities and Exchange Act of 1934* (New York: Browne, 1987), p. 35.

M&A Transaction Databases

The intense coverage of merger activity and its instant availability in electronic form can sometimes overwhelm the researcher. The larger and more complex an M&A transaction is, the more will be written about it. "Billion-dollar" transactions generate hundreds, even thousands of articles and reports. As a result, we often cannot easily find the central facts concerning a transaction because of a welter of detail. In contrast, small transactions have little coverage in the financial press. Here, the problem is finding any information at all.

There are several databases that bring together the central facts concerning individual M&A transactions. These databases take information about M&A activity from newswire stories, the financial press, and official SEC reports. We refer to this group of databases as "transaction databases." The filings databases" (discussed in Chapter 4) consist of reports and report abstracts of filings by companies with the U.S. Security and Exchange Commission (SEC) that relate to M&A. There are important differences between transaction and filings databases:

Filings databases organize their records around individual M&A-related reports that a company files with the SEC. Transaction databases organize their records by individual M&A transactions. For example, a search for information about Philip Morris' acquisition of Kraft in a filings database would retrieve more than twenty individual filings concerning the transaction. A search for information about the acquisition of Kraft by Philip Morris in a transaction database would retrieve one record.

There is no direct indication in a filings database about the outcome of an individual transaction. For example, the Philip Morris Company's acquisition of Kraft in 1988 required several SEC filings. There is no

direct way of determining from the filings what the outcome of the transaction was. A search of a transaction database would indicate that Philip
Morris did complete the acquisition of Kraft.

Only transactions involving U.S. public companies (typically companies that trade stock on national exchanges) require SEC filings. Consequently, transactions involving private companies or foreign companies that do not trade in the United States will not be included in
filings databases. Private company and non-U.S. M&A transactions are
frequently reported in transaction databases.

Filing databases tend to give more information about the target than
the acquirer. This is a consequence of the information required by the
SEC filings. Transaction databases give equal information about both
target and acquirer.

In this chapter, we describe transaction databases and give examples
of how these databases are searched and the information they provide.

IDD's M&A TRANSACTIONS

IDD's M&A TRANSACTIONS file is available online from IDD, DIA-
LOG (File 550), and DATA-STAR (File BYZZ). It is also available in compact disk format from both DIALOG and LOTUS/ONESOURCE. Our description is based on the DIALOG online file version. DIALOG's online
version of the file will be more up-to-date than the database on compact
disk and will have a wider audience than IDD's own version.

IDD's M&A TRANSACTIONS includes data on partial or completed
merger, acquisition, or divestiture transactions valued at $1 million or
more, or with an undisclosed value. These transactions include stock repurchases, self-tenders, spinoffs, and exchange offers. Up to 175 data
items per transaction are available. M&A TRANSACTIONS contains
detailed descriptive data on target and acquirer companies, terms of the
transactions, and advisor and fee information (including company name,
ticker symbol, exchange, public status, state, and country). Other information includes transaction amount, financial data, pricing and
premiums, status of transaction, attitude, and transaction. Defensive
techniques are included with related transaction information and
changes in offer. Sources for information in M&A TRANSACTIONS
include the *Wall Street Journal*, *New York Times*, DOW JONES NEWS-
WIRE, PR NEWSWIRE, corporate proxy statements, and SEC documents, including the 14D-1 (Tender Offer), 14D-9 (Management
Responses to Tender Offer), 13E-3 (Leveraged Buyout), and 13E-4 (Self-
Tender). The file covers the period from January 1984 to the present and
is updated weekly.[1]

Example 5.1 shows a brief record describing the acquisition of Kraft by
Philip Morris.

Example 5.1
Philip Morris' Acquisition of Kraft

```
Target Company:
---------------
Kraft Inc

Acquirer Company:
-----------------
Philip Morris Companies Inc

Deal Specifics:
---------------
Announcement Date:    10/17/88    Deal Value ($MIL):   13,443.98
Effective Date:       12/08/88    Price/Share:      $106.00

Transaction Type:     Acquisition
Status:               Completed
Attitude:             Hostile
```

Sources: Wall Street Journal; *New York Times;* DOW JONES NEWS SERVICE; PR NEWS-
WIRE; 14D-1 Tender Offer.

A full record from DIALOG for Philip Morris' acquisition of Kraft
indicates the comprehensiveness of the reporting (Example 5.2)

ADP's M&A DATA BASE

Another comprehensive source of the latest information on mergers,
acquisitions, divestitures, leveraged buyouts, tender offers, and partial
acquisitions is ADP's M&A DATA BASE. Available through the ADP
Online System, M&A provides information on transactions valued at $1
million or more in cash, market value of capital stock exchanged, debt
securities, or other considerations involving both public and private
companies. Partial acquisitions of 5 percent or more of a company's
capital stock are covered if the $1-million threshold is met.

The M&A DATA BASE covers the period from 1979 to the present and
is updated daily. Pending transaction records are updated until the deal
is completed or unsuccessfully terminated. The database reports M&A
activity of U.S. firms, takeovers of U.S. companies by foreign companies, and acquisitions of foreign companies by U.S. corporations. Real
property M&A activity is not reported. Sources include DOW JONES
NEWS SERVICE, the *Wall Street Journal,* Standard & Poor's *Corporation
Records Daily News,* and the *SEC News Digest.* Additional information
about the terms of each transaction and the companies involved is compiled from government documents, business information publications,
and directories of company information.

A typical record includes SIC codes, type of transaction, company
name, sales volume, status of transaction, value of deal, location of company, date of transaction, mode of payment, and other criteria. M&A
DATA BASE offers several report formats, including a "customized"

Example 5.2
DIALOG Record of Philip Morris' Acquisition of Kraft

```
Target Company:
---------------
Kraft Inc
Glenview, IL 60025
USA

Exchange: NYS
Ticker Symbol: KRA
State of Incorporation: DE
DUNS Number: 00-132-6255
CUSIP Number: 500902

Company is Public

Target Business Description
---------------------------
Primary SIC Code:     2022
Secondary SIC Codes:  2035; 2079; 2033; 2023; 3691

Description of Business:
  Mnfr & whl dairy products cheeses frozen desserts and processed
    foods

Acquirer Company:
-----------------
Philip Morris Companies Inc
New York, NY 10017
USA

Exchange: NYS
Ticker Symbol: MO
State of Incorporation: VA
DUNS Number: 14-462-8310
CUSIP Number: 718154

Company is Public

Acquirer Business Description
-----------------------------
Primary SIC Code:     2111
Secondary SIC Codes:  2082; 2086; 3079; 2754; 6552
Description of Business:
  Mnfr Cigarettes Malt beverages soft drinks & specialty papers
    packaging materials & tissue & Land development - - - -


Deal Specifics:
---------------
Announcement Date:    10/17/88   Deal Value ($MIL):   13,443.98
Effective Date:       12/08/88   Price/Share:     $106.00

Transaction Type:     Acquisition
Status:               Completed
Attitude:             Hostile

Target Advisors:
  Financial -         Goldman, Sachs
                      Lazard Freres
  Legal -             Wachtell Lipton Rosen & Katz
  Fairness Op -       Goldman, Sachs
                      Lazard Freres

Acquirer Advisors:
  Financial -         Wasserstein, Perella
  Legal -             Arnold Porter
                      Fried Frank Harris

Dealer Manager:       Wasserstein, Perella
Depositary:           The Chase Manhattan Bank, NA
```

Example 5.2 (continued)

```
Deal Terms:
-----------
        Philip Morris Cos Inc completed its tender offer to acquire
Kraft Inc for a sweetened $106 per share, or $13.4 bil. Kraft had
rejected a previous offer of $90 a share, and proposed a
restructuring valued at $110 a share. Kraft, a consumer foods
giant, remained willing to talk with a bidder offering at least
$110 a share before accepting the $106 a share offer. 98% of the
shares outstanding were tendered and accepted. A merger followed
in which shares still outstanding were converted into the right
to receive $106.

Techniques:
    Tender Offer; Tender Merger; Recapitalization
    Defensive Tactics: Poison Pill; White Knight
    Regulatory Agencies:  Securities & Exchange Commission
                          Federal Trade Commission
                          Non-US Government
Tombstones:               TARGET (01/10/89), (01/10/89)

              Consideration ($MIL)

------------------------------------------------------------
Cash:                                        13,443.98
------------------------------------------------------------
Total Dollar Value of Transaction:           13,443.98

Consideration Includes:
  $106 Cash Sh com

Common Share Information
------------------------
Offer Price/Share:                    $        106.00
Shares Outstanding Prior to Transaction:   126,830,096
Shares Acquired in Transaction:            126,830,096

Percentage of Total Shares Acquired:          100.00%

Shares Tendered:                              117,000
Shares Accepted:                              117,000

Related Deals
-------------

Announcement  Target   Acquirer
    Date      CUSIP     CUSIP     Related Deals ID
------------  ------   --------   -------------------
   10/18/88   500902   50023I     221988292500902000

Target Financials
-----------------

Date of Financials               12/26/87
Total Assets ($MIL)              5,547.00
Current Assets ($MIL)            2,302.80
Intangible Assets ($MIL)           888.30
Current Liabilities ($MIL)       2,166.40
Total Liabilities ($MIL)         3,648.60
Net Worth ($MIL)                 1,898.40
Total Revenue ($MIL)            10,717.80
Net Income ($MIL)                  390.30
EBIT ($MIL)                        846.80

Shares Outstanding           131,183,136

Source of Financial Data: Disclosure

Acquirer Financials
-------------------
Date of Financials               12/31/87
Total Assets ($MIL)             21,437.00
Total Revenue ($MIL)            28,183.00
Net Income ($MIL)                1,842.00
Debt/Capitalization                   .41
```

Example 5.2 (continued)

```
Source of Financial Data: Disclosure

Stock Prices (4 Weeks Prior to Announcement)
---------------------------------------------
Target Stock Price                      57.75
Acquirer Stock Price                    95.25

% Change in Stock Price
(4 Weeks Prior to Announcement)
---------------------------------------------
Target Premium                         83.54%
Acquirer % Change                       3.54%

Stock Prices (1 Day Prior to Announcement)
---------------------------------------------
Target Stock Price                      59.50
Acquirer Stock Price                    98.63


% Change in Stock Price
 (1 Day Prior to Announcement)
---------------------------------------------
Target Premium                         78.15%
```

Sources:Wall Street Journal; New York Times; DOW JONES NEWS SERVICE; PR NEWS-WIRE; 14D-1 Tender Offer.

report option that allows the searcher to report any combination of 400 variables. The "Comprehensive Deal Summary Report" is the most complete preformatted report. Example 5.3 shows this report format for the Kraft–Philip Morris acquisition.

SDC's MERGERS AND CORPORATE TRANSACTIONS

The final transaction database we will describe is MERGERS AND CORPORATE TRANSACTIONS produced by Securities Data Company, Inc. (SDC). This database provides descriptive information on worldwide corporate M&A. Updated daily, the database goes back to 1981. Its information is compiled primarily from SEC documents and business publications. All M&A activity valued at $1 million or more, or with an undisclosed value, or involving purchases resulting in 5 percent or more ownership is included.

The database has up to 550 record items for each transaction, including target's and acquirer's financial positions; managers and fees; transaction specifics; price tracking; and geographical locations of target and acquirer.

MERGERS AND CORPORATE TRANSACTIONS is primarily a menu-driven system (although it has a limited command mode option). The user chooses options from menu screens. The system has several standard reports and special reports. In addition, users can create their own report. We have chosen a "multiples report," a special report that gives several ratios for the target company that relate the value of the company to its sales, income, and cash flow. Example 5.4 shows menu options for SDC reports.

Example 5.3
M&A DATA BASE Report of the Kraft–Philip Morris Acquisition

COMPREHENSIVE DEAL SUMMARY
(in $ Mil except per share amounts)

Acquirer Philip Morris Cos. Inc.
Target Kraft Inc.

Type:	Acquisit	Total Val	12644.22
First Bid	10/17	Mode of P	
Announcem	10/17	Price/Com	106
Closing D	12/07	Price/Prf	
Status:	Comple		
LBO?			
Hostile?	Initia		
Deal ID:	0340		

```
-------- Acquirer Data ---------       --------- Target Data --------
New York, NY, USA                       Glenview, IL, USA
Public:                                 Public:
Ticker:                                 Ticker:
Primary S     2082                      Primary S      2022
Other SIC Codes:                        Other SIC Codes:
  2011 2013 2015                          2024 2026 2033
  2024 2111 2037                          2035 2079 2899
  2043 2052 2095
LTM Prima     9.58                      LTM Ful D     3.19
```

Financial	6/30	Financial	6/30
Fincl Dat	Cmpst	Fincl Dat	Cmpst
Sales:	6244	Sales:	10563.6
Net Incom	1957	EBITDA:	1076.6
Total Ass	3805	Depr & Am	164.9
		EBIT:	911.7
		Interest	138.6
		Pretax In	773.1
		Inc Bef E	419.7
		Extraordn	708.3
		Net Incom	1128
		Cash Flow	584.6
		Cash & ST	1159.7
		Total Ass	5998
		Total Lia	3699.6
		Total LT	861
		Total Com	2298.4
		Common Sh	124444

```
------------------------ Deal Value Summary --------------------
```

Total Val	12644.22	Debt:	
Cash:	12644.22	Other:	
Common:		Liabs Ass	
Preferred		Composite	12644.22 *17

```
------------------------------ Multiples -----------------------
```

Purchase	33.229 *10	Cash Flow	21.628	
P/E 1 Mo.	18.103 *10	Comp. Val	1.197	*17
Book Mult	5.501 *14	Comp. Val	11.209	*17
Mkt/Bk 1	3.199 *14	Comp. Val	13.869	*17

```
----------------------- Premiums & Market Values ---------------
```

Premium 1	78.151	Mkt Val	17353.188
Premium 1	74.486	Mkt Val	17507.667
Premium 1	83.55	Mkt Val	17136.918
Premium 2	93.166	Mkt Val	26781.617

Example 5.3 (continued)

```
------------------------- Financing Summary -------------------

Bridge:                     Subordina
Revolver:     12000         Mezzanine
Senior:      488.68         Equity:
Senior Su                   Permanent12488.68


------------------------- Tender Offer Summary ------------------

Tender Of     10/18         Withdrawa    11/15
Expiratio     11/15         Extension    12/02

Minimum %    53.163         Minimum #    63415
Common %       100          Common #    119285
Common %       100          Common #    119285

---- % Change in Holdings -----   -- Actual Change in Holdings ---
Pre:  % C        0          Pre:   # C        0
Post: % C       100         Post:  # C   119285
```

```
------------------------------ Terms -------------------------
```
    Philip Morris submitted an unsolicited offer to acquire all
of the outstanding common stock of Kraft in a transaction valued
at $10.7 billion. Subsidiary Corp., a unit of Philip Morris,
began a $90-per-share cash tender offer for all of the
outstanding common stock of Kraft, including the associated
common stock purchase rights. Kraft requested that its
shareholders defer any decision until Kraft board members
considered and made a recommendation. Philip Morris filed suit
against Kraft and certain of its directors alleging breach of
fiduciary duties. The suit also sought to block Kraft's poison
pill. The FTC began a formal review of the transaction. Kraft
rejected the offer as inadequate and developed a recapitalization
plan with a value of at least $110 per share. Shareholders were
to receive a cash dividend of $84 per share and securities that
Kraft valued at $14 per share. Morris filed suit to block
restructuring. Kraft accepted an increased offer
from Morris and was acquired for $106 per share, or $12.64
billion.
    Morris intended to use $12 billion in bank loans and $1.1
billion of its cash. The FTC requested additional information.
Morris held 98 percent of Kraft as a result of the tender offer
and purchased the remainder through a cash merger. The FTC raised
no objections to the transaction.
    It was accounted for on a purchase basis.

```
-------------------- Acquirer Description -------------------
```

    Philip Morris is the largest U.S. tobacco company. Product
brands include Marlboro and Virginia Slim cigarettes, Lite beer,
and Post cereals. Its Miller Brewing Co. unit is the
second-largest brewer in the world. It is also involved in
financing and real estate development. Its General Foods Corp.
unit is a major U.S. food processor that owns Maxwell House,
Jell-O, and KoolAid. It makes cereals, coffee, fresh-baked foods,
processed meats, and rice. Philip Morris has about 113,000
employees.

```
----------------------- Target Description --------------------
```

    Kraft is an independent consumer foods and food services
company. Product brands include Miracle Whip salad dressing,
Velveeta cheese, Parkay margarine, Breyers and Sealtest ice
cream, Polly-O, Cheez Whiz, Budget Gourmet, Breakstone's, Frusen
Gladje, Light 'n' Lively, Lender's bagels, and Seven Seas salad
dressings. It specializes in cheese, margarine, mayonnaise, salad
dressings, sour cream, yogurt, and frozen bagels. It employs
about 46,500 people.

Example 5.3 (continued)

```
-------------------- Acquirer Advisers----------------------

     Wasserstein, Perella & Co. Inc.; Kissel-Blake Inc.; Chase
Manhattan Bank NA; Citibank NA; Manufacturers Hanover Trust Co.;
Simpson Thacher & Bartlett; Fried, Frank, Harris, Shriver &
Jacobson; Hunton & Williams; Arnold & Porter; Jenner & Block;
Richards, Layton & Finger


-------------------- Target Advisers----------------------

     Goldman, Sachs & Co.; Wachtell, Lipton, Rosen & Katz; Lazard
Freres & Co.; Sidley & Austin; Potter Anderson & Corroon


-------------------- Adviser Fee Summary--------------------

Acq. Advi      12          Trgt Advi     5.5


     Codes for Mode   M=Cash,  C=Common Stock,  P=Preferred Stock,
D=Debt of Payments:  T=Convertible Debt,  V=Convertible Preferred
Stock  X=Other (Warrants, Contingent Payments)

*10 P/E ratio based on latest 12 month, fully diluted earnings.

*11 Book multiple based on common equity.

*17 Composite value is the total value of the deal including
     disclosed liabilities assumed.
```

Source: ©Copyright ADP BISG Data Services/MLR Publishing. The ADP/MLR M&A Data Base is jointly researched and updated by ADP BISG Data Services and MLR Publishing. The M&A Data Base is easily accessed through a window-driven PC interface, InQuery℠, which also provides push-button access to historical stock price and foreign exchange data, as well as corporate and banking fundamentals. For more information, call 1-800-ADP-DATA.

SCREENING TRANSACTION DATABASES

ADP's M&A DATA BASE

The most powerful feature of transaction databases is their ability to screen thousands of transactions to find only those that fit a certain profile. Example 5.5 presents a search of the M&A DATA BASE to answer the following question: Find the names of U.S. public companies who were merged or acquired between 1979 and 1989 and who were in the industries with any of the following SIC codes:

- 2082 (beer and other malt beverages)
- 2084 (wine)
- 2085 (distilled liquor)

For each target company list such financial and stock-related variables as net sales, assets, and their stock price one day and one month before the transaction was announced.

Example 5.4
Menu Options for SDC Reports

```
-------------------------------------------------------------------------
SDC Standard Reports (Short)           Special Reports
   1.  Brief Summary Report              8.  Stock Premiums Report
   2.  Brief Financials Report           9.  Source of Funds Report
   3.  Brief Advisors/Fees Report       10.  Tender Offer Report
                                        11.  Leveraged Buyout Report
                                        12.  Multiples Report
SDC Standard Reports (Long)            80.  80 Character Standard Reports
   4.  Comprehensive Summary Report
   5.  Comprehensive Financials Report  Saved Reports
   6.  Comprehensive Advisors/Fees Report  COMP  Your Company's Reports
   7.  Merger/Corporate Transaction Report MINE  Your Personal Reports

   R.  Design New Report    A.  Advisor Rank/Data Analysis   H.  Help
   Q.  Query Further        F.  File Management               X.  Exit

   Enter a report choice

-------------------------------------------------------------------------
> 80   [WE CHOOSE AN 80 COLUMN REPORT]

SDC Standard Reports (Short)           Special Reports
   1.  Brief Summary Report              8.  Stock Premiums Report
   2.  Brief Financials Report           9.  Source of Funds Report
   3.  Brief Advisors/Fees Report       10.  Tender Offer Report
                                        11.  Leveraged Buyout Report
                                        12.  Multiples Report
SDC Standard Reports (Long)
   4.  Comprehensive Summary Report
   5.  Comprehensive Financials Report  Saved Reports
   6.  Comprehensive Advisors/Fees Report  COMP  Your Company's Reports
   7.  Merger/Corporate Transaction Report MINE  Your Personal Reports

   R.  Design New Report    A.  Advisor Rank/Data Analysis   H.  Help
   Q.  Query Further        F.  File Management               X.  Exit

   Enter a report choice
> 12       [MENU CHOICE FOR "MULTIPLES REPORT"]

Your report is ready to print
Choose one of the below          [THE MENU GIVES ADDITIONAL OPTIONS BEFORE
                                  PRINTING REPORT]

   1 - Add TITLES to report
   2 - SORT report
   3 - SAVE report text to a file
   4 - Change default print settings

   L - DOWNLOAD to Lotus

   R - RUN report

   X - Exit

> R
Report is ready.  Align paper and hit return.
```

Date Announced	Target Name		Equity Value	Sales
Date Effective	Acquiror Name		Enterprise Value	Net Income
Date Financial	Form		Target Market Value	Ebit
Status	Offer Price Per Share		Debt/Capitalization	CashFlow
10/17/88	Kraft Inc		13,444.0	10,856.7
12/07/88	Philip Morris Inc		13,256.4	451.2
09/24/88	Merger		7,324.4	922.9
Completed	106.00		0.23	1,090.7

Example 5.4 (continued)

Value/Sales Value/NI Value/Ebit Value/CF	Entval/Sales Entval/NI Entval/Ebit Entval/CF	EPS Book Value Price/Earnings Price/Book	Stock Premiums One Day One Week Four Weeks
1.2	1.2	3.54	+78.2
29.8	29.4	17.630	+74.5
14.6	14.4	29.9	+83.5
12.3	12.2	6.0	

Consideration: $106 cash/sh com
Investor(s)

Footnotes:
EQUITY VALUE AND EQUITY VALUE MULTIPLES DO NOT INCLUDE ASSUMED LIABILITIES
ENTERPRISE VALUE= (OFFER PRICE*ACTUAL COMMON SHS) + COST TO RETIRE
    IN-THE-MONEY OPTIONS + STRAIGHT DEBT + CONVERTIBLE DEBT
    + SHORT-TERM DEBT + PREFERRED EQUITY - CASH AND MARKETABLE
    SECURITIES
MARKET VALUE BASED ON CLOSING PRICE FOUR WEEKS PRIOR TO ANNOUNCEMENT

Source: From Securities Data Company's "Merger and Corporate Transactions Database," copyright 1991. Reprinted with permission of Securities Data Company.

Example 5.5
M&A DATA BASE Search

SCREEN -- Version 15.0

Enter Data Base -- MAC   ["MAC" IS THE MNEMONIC FOR THE M & A

                            DATABASE]

M&A Data Base

Copyright 1989, MLR Publishing Company and Automatic Data
Processing Inc. All rights reserved.

38949 TRANSACTIONS found in subset # 1 [THE DATABASE CONTAINS OVER 38,000
                                           TRANSACTIONS]
Enter your commands:

* CREATE ON TSIC ["TSIC" IS THE M & A DATABASE CODE FOR "TARGET SIC NUMBER"]

Enter TRANSACTIONS identifiers (terminate with DONE) [THE SYSTEM PROMPTS THE
                                                       USER FOR THE SIC NUMBER]

TSIC 1: 2082   [WE ENTER THE SIC NUMBER FOR BEER]
TSIC 2: DONE   [AND INDICATE THAT NO MORE NUMBERS WILL BE ENTERED]

37 TRANSACTIONS stored in subset # 2   [THERE WERE 37 "DEALS" IN THE
            DATABASE IN WHICH THE PRIMARY INDUSTRY OF THE TARGET WAS
            THE MANUFACTURE OF BEER OR OTHER MALT BEVERAGES]

* FIN TPUB EQ 'Y' ["TPUB" IS THE SYSTEM CODE FOR "TARGET'S PUBLIC STATUS"]
                   [WE WANT TO INCLUDE ONLY TARGETS THAT WERE PUBLIC
                    COMPANIES]

Example 5.5 (continued)

```
23 TRANSACTIONS found in subset #3   [THERE WERE 23 TRANSACTIONS THAT INVOLVED
                                     PUBLIC COMPANY TARGETS WHOSE PRIMARY SIC CODE
                                     WAS 2082]

* FIN CLOSIN BT 1/1/84-12/12/89   [WE WANT TO INCLUDE DEALS THAT WERE
                                  COMPLETED BETWEEN JAN 1, 1984 AND DECEMBER 12, 1989]

9 TRANSACTIONS found in subset # 4   [OF THE 23 TRANSACTIONS IN SUBSET #3,
                                     ONLY 9 WERE COMPLETED DURING THE TIME WE SPECIFIED]

* FIN TYPE EQ 'A' OR TYPE EQ 'M'   [WE ARE FURTHER LIMITING THE SET TO
                                   DEALS THAT WERE EITHER ACQUISITIONS OR MERGERS]

4 TRANSACTIONS found in subset # 5   [ONLY 4 TRANSACTIONS MEET ALL OF OUR
                                     CRITERIA]

* REPORT [THIS IS A REQUEST TO PRINT SELECTED CHARACTERISTICS OF THE 4 DEALS
WHICH          WE HAVE RETRIEVED]

Enter your report titles (terminate with DONE). [WE ARE PROMPTED FOR A TITLE]

Title 1: U.S. PUBLIC BEER COMPANIES AS M & A TARGETS
Title 2: 1984 - 1989
Title 3: DONE

Enter column definitions (terminate with DONE). [WE ARE PROMPTED TO INDICATE
              THE VARIABLES WE WISH TO HAVE IN THE REPORT.  THESE ARE THE
MNEMONICS FOR THE VARIABLES WE WISH TO SEE.]

Item 1: TNAME    ["TNAME" STANDS FOR "TARGET NAME"]
Item 2: ANAME    ["ANAME" STANDS FOR "ACQUIRER NAME"]
Item 3: VALTOT   ["VALTOT" STANDS FOR TOTAL VALUE OF DEAL]
Item 4: CLOSIN   ["CLOSIN" STANDS FOR DATE THE DEAL WAS COMPLETED]
Item 5: DONE

Enter output file name ( or terminal ): TTY [WE INDICATE THAT WE WANT THE
                                            REPORT TO BE PRINTED AT THE
                                            TERMINAL]

        Data cost per record:    $    0.85
        Number of records:       x      4
        Estimated total cost:    $    3.40    [THE SYSTEM TELLS US HOW
                                              MUCH THE PRINTING OF THIS
                                              REPORT WILL COST (cost does
                                              include connect rate or
                                              CPUs)]

        Do you still wish to produce this report? (Y/N): Y

[WE INDICATE THAT WE WANT THE REPORT TO BE PRINTED - IF WE ANSWER "N" TO THIS
QUESTION, THE REPORT WILL NOT BE PRINTED, AND WE WILL NOT BE CHARGED FOR THE
REPORT]

Turn to top of form and press RETURN KEY ...
```

TNAME	ANAME	CLOSIN	VALTOT
Falstaff Brewing Corp.	Paul Kalmanovitz Testamentary	5/16/89	27.649
G. Heileman Brewing Co.	Bond Corp. Holdings Ltd.	3/03/88	1296.016
Pittsburgh Brewing Co.	Bond Corp. Holdings Ltd.	4/30/86	23.985
Pabst Brewing Co.	S&P Co.	3/04/85	50.860

Source: ©Copyright ADP BISG Data Services/MLR Publishing. The ADP/MLR M&A Data Base is jointly researched and updated by ADP BISG Data Services and MLR Publishing. The M&A Data Base is easily accessed through a window-driven PC interface, InQuery℠, which also provides push-button access to historical stock price and foreign exchange data, as well as corporate and banking fundamentals. For more information, call 1-800-ADP-DATA.

Example 5.5 presents the search done on the M&A DATA BASE. Our comments are in parentheses. We have used the ADP's command language to search the database. As you will see, it is rather cryptic. Searchers of the M&A DATA BASE can also use ADP's software "front-end" menu system (called INQUERY), which simplifies the mechanics of retrieval.

IDD's M&A TRANSACTIONS

Example 5.6 shows a search on the DIALOG version of IDD's M&A TRANSACTIONS. We want a list of major acquisitions by Japanese companies of U.S. public companies. DIALOG uses prefix codes to refer to parts of a record. The searcher can obtain a list of the codes either online or from printed documentation. The system allows the searcher to screen the database in one step.

SDC's MERGER AND CORPORATE TRANSACTIONS

SDC's system is menu-driven and consequently is easy to screen. Example 5.7 shows a screening of the database for all U.S. deals announced in the first half of 1990 that involved "poison pill defenses." (A poison pill defense is the term given to techniques that targets of take-overs use to make acquisitions unprofitable for acquirers.)

RETRIEVAL DIFFERENCES AMONG THE DATABASES

Screening all three databases for the same characteristics frequently produces different results. For example, if, in addition to M&A TRANS-ACTIONS we had screened M&A DATA BASE and MERGERS AND CORPORATE TRANSACTIONS for Japanese acquirers of U.S. public companies, we would have produced three similar but not identical lists. It should not be a surprise that there are differences in the results of the searches. To screen three distinct files containing millions of data items on several characteristics and to expect them to produce identical results is asking the impossible. There are several reasons for differences.

First, the three databases give different definitions to terms. For example, ADP would consider a U.S. subsidiary of a Japanese company to be a "Japanese" acquirer; IDD would consider the subsidiary to be a "U.S." acquirer.

Second, SIC codes give the appearance of great precision—they are numbers after all. But there is a surprising lack of agreement among databases as to what SIC codes a given company should have. In a study done in 1983, one of the authors compared SIC numbers that were assigned to five major U.S. companies by four databases. A total of eighty-five different primary and secondary SIC numbers were assigned

Example 5.6
A Search on the DIALOG Version of IDD's M&A TRANSACTIONS

```
SS   DS=C
OMPLETED AND TR=(ACQUISITION? OR MERGER) AND TY=PUBLIC AND AR=JAPAN
AND CN=USA AND DV>100M
```

In the search statement above:

"SS" STANDS FOR "SELECT STEPS". THIS SEARCH COMMANDS ALLOWS US TO RETRIEVE
    SETS FOR THE INDIVIDUAL COMPONENTS OF OUR SEARCH

"DS" STANDS FOR "DEAL STATUS" - IN THE CASE WE WANT ONLY COMPLETED DEALS

"TR" STANDS FOR "TRANSACTION TYPE" - WE WANT EITHER MERGERS OR ACQUISITIONS

"TY" STANDS FOR "TYPE OF TARGET" - IN THIS CASE PUBLIC COMPANIES

"AR" STANDS FOR "AQUIRER COUNTRY" - (JAPAN)

"CN" STANDS FOR "TARGET COUNTRY" -   (USA)

"DV" STANDS FOR "DEAL VALUE" - WE REQUESTED DEALS GREATER THAN $100 MILLION

Set	Items	Description
S1	33443	DS=COMPLETED
S3	48715	TR=ACQUISITION? OR TR=MERGER
S4	17815	TY=PUBLIC
S5	428	AR=JAPAN
S6	33325	CN=USA
S7	5489	DV > 100M
S8	16	DS=COMPLETED AND TR=(ACQUISITION? OR MERGER) AND TY=PUBLIC ..

[THE DIALOG SYSTEM RESPONDS TO OUR SEARCH QUESTION WITH A LIST OF "SETS" FOR
EACH PART OF THE SCREEN. IN THE ENTIRE DATABASE, THERE WERE:
- 33,443 COMPLETED TRANSACTIONS.
- 48,715 DEALS THAT WERE EITHER ACQUISITIONS OR MERGERS.
- 17,815 DEALS INVOLVING TARGETS THAT WERE PUBLIC COMPANIES.
- 428 DEALS INVOLVING JAPANESE COMPANIES AS ACQUIRERS.
- 33,325 DEALS INVOLVING U.S. COMPANIES AS TARGETS.
- 5,489 DEALS VALUED AT OVER 100 MILLION DOLLARS.
THERE WERE 16 DEALS THAT HAD ALL CHARACTERISTICS.]

[WE NEXT REQUEST A PRINTOUT OF EACH OF THE 16 DEALS SHOWING THE ACQUIRER,
THE TARGET, THE VALUE OF THE DEAL AND THE EFFECTIVE DATE OF THE TRANSACTION.]

REPORT 8/AC,TG,DV,TD/ALL   [THIS IS A REQUEST FOR A "REPORT" ON THE THREE
DEALS. "8" REFERS TO SET 8. THE CODES AC,TG,DV,AND TD REPRESENT THE NAME OF
THE ACQUIRER, THE TARGET COMPANY, THE VALUE OF THE DEAL AND THE EFFECTIVE
DATE. THE COMMAND "ALL" REQUESTS THAT ALL 16 OF THE DEALS BE REPORTED.]

Align paper; press ENTER

Acquirer Company	Target Company	Value ($MIL)	Effective Date
Sony Corp	Columbia Pictures Entertainment	3,406.00	11/07/89
Bridgestone Corp	Firestone Tire & Rubber Co	2,651.86	05/05/88
Nippon Mining Co Ltd	Gould Inc	1,047.08	11/01/88
Kyocera Corp	AVX Corp	618.46	01/18/90
Dainippon Ink & Chemicals	Reichhold Chemicals Inc	540.70	09/28/87
Nippon Life Insurance Co	Shearson Lehman Brothers Inc	530.00	04/15/87
Yamanouchi Pharmaceutical	Shaklee Corp	392.00	05/18/89
Nippon Kokan KK	National Steel Corp	322.00	09/01/84
Yasuda Mutual Life Insur	PaineWebber Group Inc	300.00	12/17/87
Mitsubishi Bank Ltd	Ban Col Tri State Corp	282.00	06/18/84
Sony Corp	Guber Peters Entertainment Co	273.97	11/10/89
TDK Corp	Silicon Systems Inc	226.00	05/23/89
Orix Corp	Commercial Alliance Corp	190.00	09/20/89
Fujitsu Ltd	Amdahl Corp	189.20	04/19/84
Sunstar Inc	John O Butler Co	164.35	08/17/88
NKK Corp	National Steel Corp	146.60	06/26/90

Example 5.7
SDC Screening

```
Choose one of the following

    1.  Domestic Merger and Corporate Transactions    (US Targets)

    2.  International Merger and Corporate Transactions (Non-US Targets)

    3.  Combined Domestic and International           (All Targets)

> 1 [WE CHOOSE DOMESTIC MERGERS]

Specify start date, end date for announcement date range    (e.g. 1/1/88,

6/30/88)

> 1/1/90,6/30/90

Company Information              Transaction Information

1.  Industry/SIC Codes          12.  Transaction Type
2.  Specific Deal/Company/Investor  13.  Transaction Value
3.  Location                    14.  Acquisition Techniques
4.  Financial Information        15.  Defensive Tactics
5.  Public Status               16.  Consideration Offered/Sought
6.  Financial Advisors           17.  Percent Acquired Advisor
7.  Financial Advisor Assignments  18.  Attitude
8.  Legal Advisors              19.  Source of Funds
9.  Fee Information             20.  Effective/Unconditional Date
10. Depositaries/Registrars      21.  Announcement Date
11. Information Agents           22.  Challenged Bids
                                23.  Regulatory Agencies
                                24.  Status


A.  All deals in date range     R.  Report/Rank    U.  Utilities
O.  Screen any other data item  Q.  Quick Display  X.  Exit

Enter a search item, LIST to display selections, MORE for more selections,
R to print reports, or X to exit

> 15  [WE CHOOSE "DEFENSIVE TACTICS"]

Select defensive tactic(s), separated by semicolons  (e.g. 11;12)

1.  Lockup              9.  Self-Tender
2.  Asset Lockup       10.  Shareholder Rights Plan (Poison Pill)
3.  Stock Lockup       11.  Back-end Shareholder Rights Plan
4.  Pacman             12.  Flip-over Shareholder Rights Plan
5.  Recapitalization   13.  Voting Plan Shareholder Rights Plan
6.  Repurchase(s)      14.  White Knight
7.  Greenmail          15.  Any Defensive Tactic
8.  Scorched Earth

> 10

Query begins.

10 deals selected from Merger/Corporate Transactions deal table.
0 deals selected from Original SDC Mergers, 1979-84 deal table.
Total deals selected:   10.

The current query number is 1.

> R [WE WANT THE INFORMATION ON THE DEALS DISPLAYED AS A CUSTOMIZED REPORT]

Enter one data item at each prompt (:)  Press RETURN at prompt when finished
with current page

1:  TN    [TARGET NAME]
2:  AN    [ACQUIRER NAME]
3:  VAL   [VALUE OF DEAL]
4:  DA    [ANNOUNCEMENT DATE]
```

Example 5.7 (continued)

```
The current column is : 78.   Enter 1 - Add another page
2 - Start entire report over    3 - Add more data items to page
4 - Preview column headings    R - Finished entering data items    X - EXIT

> R

Your report is ready to print

Choose one of the below
1 - Add TITLES to report 2 - SORT report 3 - SAVE report text to a file
4 - Change default print settings L - DOWNLOAD to Lotus R - RUN report X - Exit

> 2   [WE CHOOSE TO SORT THE REPORT BY DEAL VALUE]

Specify the sorting criterion
TN   Target Name   AN   Acquiror Name   VAL  Dollar Value   DA    Announcement
Date (Default Sort Criterion)   A     Any Data Item

> `VAL

Do you want to sort in    A. Ascending order    D. Descending order

> D [WE WANT THE LARGEST DEALS LISTED FIRST]
```

Acquiror Name	Target Name	Value (mils$)	Date Announced
Norton Co	BTR PLC	1,666.0	03/16/90
National Intergroup Inc	Centaur Partners	77.4	01/29/90
National Savings Bank,Albany	TrustCo Bank Corp	44.3	01/03/90
Hershey Oil Corp	Bellwether Exploration Co	1.1	01/25/90
Healthco International Inc	Gemini Partners LP	-	05/03/90
Lockheed Corp	Investor Group	-	02/02/90
Lancaster Colony Corp	Newell Co	-	04/10/90
Anacomp Inc	The Cooper Cos Inc	-	02/05/90

Source: From Securities Data Company's "Mergers and Corporate Transactions Database," copyright 1991. Reprinted with permission of Securities Data Company.

to the companies. The databases' agreement on which SIC numbers to assign varied for a low of 22 percent to a high of only 52 percent.[2] There are several reasons for the lack of agreement among databases in the assignment of codes. It is difficult to pigeonhole the activities of a large, diversified company into the categories allowed by the SIC classification. In addition, there is no incentive for one database to be consistent with a competing database in the assignment of codes. A further complication is that online databases often use the SIC numbers assigned to companies by third-party publishers. For example, ADP gets its SIC codes from Standard & Poors COMPUSTAT Service. IDD gets its codes from Disclosure (which in turn gets them from Dun & Bradstreet). Most companies, especially large companies, are involved in several lines of work. Assigning one four-digit SIC number that represents a company's primary industry is often a matter of judgment.

Finally, databases contain mistakes and omissions. M&A transactions data is often complex and confusing. In reading and interpreting the mass of material published in newspapers, press releases, and SEC filings, its not surprising that occasional errors are made.

We have examined three major sources of M&A transactions: IDD's M&A TRANSACTIONS, ADP's M&A DATA BASE, and SDC's MERGER & CORPORATE TRANSACTIONS database. All three databases will allow you to retrieve much information about individual M&A deals. If the deal involves a U.S. public company, you can be confident that information will be available. In summary, you will want to use a machine-readable M&A database (online or on compact disk) when:

- the speed and completeness of retrieval are more important than cost
- the deal occurred within the last decade. The oldest file begins in 1979. Most of the databases begin coverage in 1985.
- you are interested in screening many M&A deals to find only those that have a set of attributes. The more detailed the set of characteristics you are searching for, the more you will need a machine-readable merger database.

NOTES

1. DIALOG Information Retrieval Service, "IDD M&A Transactions," *Bluesheets* (May 1990).

2. Ruth Pagell and Michael Halperin, "SIC Codes: The SIC Confusion in Comparing Codes," *Online* 7(6):49-55 (November 1983).

6

Finding Acquisition Candidates

One way of finding acquisition candidates is to hire an expert to do it for you. This is the role of merger "finders" and "brokers," professionals who specialize in bringing together acquirers and targets. An example of a directory that contains names and descriptions of merger "intermediaries" is *Buyouts: Directory of Intermediaries.*[1]

Buyouts lists approximately 450 U.S. and Canadian merger intermediary firms. The description of each firm includes the type of services offered (e.g., "Matching Buyers and Sellers of Businesses"), industry preferences, type of firms, and fees. The volume is indexed by name of firm, location, area of industry concentration, and specific overseas markets. In addition, several articles by industry experts are included to provide an overview of the M&A market.

Another list of business intermediary firms is included in *The Corporate Finance Sourcebook.* The *Sourcebook* includes descriptions of about 200 U.S. firms. These descriptions include contact persons, size of deals, and areas of service specialty.

The names and descriptions of M&A intermediary firms can also be retrieved online from D&B—DUN'S MARKET IDENTIFIERS (DIALOG File 516). Described in detail later in this chapter, D&B—DUN'S MARKET IDENTIFIERS has a unique classification number (87320106) for companies doing merger, acquisition, and reorganization research. To retrieve the names of the companies with this classification do the following search:

S PC = 8732106   ["PC" stands for "Product Code"]

This search will retrieve the records of about 400 firms.

There is surprisingly little overlap among the firms listed in *Buyouts*, *The Corporate Finance Sourcebook*, and D&B—DUN'S MARKET IDEN-TIFIERS. For example, of the forty largest "merger" companies listed in D&B—DUN'S MARKET IDENTIFIERS (ranked by sales), only four were listed in *Buyouts*.

Another method of discovering acquisition candidates is through net-working. Companies that are interested in selling all or part of their business often make their wishes known by informing potential acquirers or by publishing their intention to sell. *World M & A Network*[2] is a quarterly publication that lists companies for sale, merger candidates, and willing buyers. A typical listing is a 100-word description of a busi-ness, the terms of the deal, and an asking price. The companies' names are not given. Leads are organized by company size, geographic region, and SIC codes. Although primarily a source of U.S. opportunities for American sellers and investors, *World M & A Network* does include non-U.S. offers.

If you wish to do a general search for companies that have certain char-acteristics, you must examine company directories. Printed directories such as *Thomas Register of U.S. Manufacturers* and Dun and Bradstreet's *Million Dollar Directory* include only a small fraction of the millions of existing U.S. corporations. By relying exclusively on printed directories you will automatically exclude most companies from your search. In addition, printed sources are difficult to search when you are looking for more than one characteristic of a company. The method that we recommend for researching M&A candidates relies on machine-readable databases (online or ondisk). For any but the simplest directory ques-tions, machine-readable databases are superior to printed sources in both scope and speed of retrieval. In addition, online databases will allow you to "download" your searches (i.e., capture information on your own disk). Downloading gives you great flexibility in the way you present retrieved information. Although we emphasize commercially available online (time-sharing) databases in this chapter, compact disk (CD-ROM) databases are often a good alternative source. Several of the online databases we discuss are available on compact disk. Typically, compact disk databases are purchased by annual subscription. Their main advantage compared to commercial time-sharing systems is fixed cost. The more they are searched, the lower the per search cost. Their main disadvantage is that they are not as up to date as their online counterparts.

As Table 6.1 indicates, many of the standard business directories have machine-readable counterparts, but the largest computer-readable direc-tories have no printed equivalent. Thus, you can search Dun and Brad-street's *Million Dollar Directory* either in print, online, or on compact disk, but D&B—DUN'S MARKET IDENTIFIERS database exists only in

Table 6.1
Standard Business Directories in Print, Online, and in CD-ROM

Name	Number of Records	Format
D&B Million Dollar Directory	150,000	Print, Online, CD-ROM
D&B MARKET IDENTIFIERS	6 million	Online
DUN'S BUSINESS DIRECTORY	8.4 million	Online, CD-ROM
Thomas Register	90,000	Print, Online, CD-ROM
TRINET U.S. BUSINESSES	7.5 million	Online, CD-ROM

machine-readable form. For your search to be comprehensive, you must use computer files.

SEARCHING FOR COMPANY CHARACTERISTICS

The greatest advantage that machine-readable databases have over print is the ability they give searchers to combine concepts, to search for the mix of characteristics desired. These characteristics range from the simple (where the company is located) to the complex (how much the company is worth). The ability of databases to select companies on the basis of one or more characteristics is often called "screening." We refer to the collection of directory, financial, and other databases that are useful in retrieving information about acquisition candidates as "screening databases."

Company characteristics we may be searching for in potential acquisition targets include:

- location
- size
- product/industry
- share of market
- patents/trademarks owned
- lines of business
- value of business
- organization of business

Screening for Industry, Location, and Size

Initially we may be interested in only those companies that fit a profile defined by three characteristics: industrial group, company size, and location.

An industrial group is often defined by one or more standard industrial classification codes but may also be given a general description. Company size is measured by sales, share of market, number of employees, or other financial or market characteristics. Location is determined by geography (cities, counties, states, and nations). In *How to Do a Leveraged Buyout*, J. Terrence Greve gives an example of a "Target Company Profile" to illustrate potential targets. The criteria below are adopted from his list of characteristics.[3]

1. Company size—annual sales 5 to 10 million
2. Company location—U.S. Southwest
3. Type of business—manufacturing
4. Types of products—industrial valves

We will use two large directory files on the DIALOG system to answer this question. Most of the examples in this chapter will be from the DIALOG system. Of all online systems, DIALOG has the greatest range of business directory databases. It is important to note that our initial use of these files will be to search for establishments (individual places of business) rather than for companies (which may include more than one establishment).

D&B—DUN'S MARKET IDENTIFIERS

The first file we will examine is D&B—DUN'S MARKET IDENTIFIERS (DMI) file. The version of the file available on the DIALOG system (File 516) gives detailed information on more than 6 million U.S. business establishments that have five or more employees or companies with $1 million or more in sales. DMI contains current address, product, and financial and marketing information for each company. Both public and private companies are included as well as all types of commercial and industrial establishments and all product areas.

The DMI file is extracted by Dun & Bradstreet for their data on more than 9 million U.S. businesses. These data are collected and maintained by a staff of business analysts through daily in-person interviews with business owners and officers, and are supplemented by large-volume mailings and phone interviews. DMI was created from Dun & Bradstreet records updated within the last twelve months. We can easily translate the characteristics of our profile into DIALOG commands.

We begin by defining "U.S. Southwest" as simply the states of Texas and Oklahoma. In practice, we could use any combination of zip codes or city, county, and state names to define a geographic region. We use the prefix "ST" for state and the standard two-letter abbreviations for Texas and Oklahoma. We use the word "or" between the two abbreviations because we are interested in retrieving company records from either state. The letter "S" at the beginning of the commands means "Select."

S ST = (TX or OK)

The system will respond by indicating the number of businesses in the database located in Texas or Oklahoma:

465522 ST = TX
98430   ST = OK
S1 563952 ST = (TX OR OK)

"S1" stands for "Set 1." The database has records for more than 500,000 establishments in Texas or Oklahoma. We could search for the phrase "Industrial Valves" as text, but it is more precise to use the Standard Industrial Code (SIC) for the manufacture of industrial valves. This number (3491) is available from the *U.S. Standard Industrial Classification Manual*.[4] For the DIALOG command we use the prefix "PC," which stands for "primary SIC code." Dun & Bradstreet assigns primary SIC codes to designate a company's principal business. Here we "select" records for companies whose main business is manufacturing industrial valves:

S PC = 3491

The system responds by noting the number of company records indicating "industrial valves" as the main product line.

S2   319 PC = 3491 (Industrial valves)

The DIALOG tag for annual sales is "SA." We select companies with sales ranging between $5 and 10 million with the following comand:

S   SA = 5M:10M

There are over 120,000 companies in the database with this sales range.

S3 120413   SA = 5M:10M

We then combine the sets we have created for location, industry, and size.

C 1 AND 2 AND 3

The result is a set (Set 4) of seven companies that have the criteria we want.

S4   7 1 AND 2 AND 3

One option that we have of displaying the companies is in a report format. Often we want to sort the report by some criterion, such as sales or employee size. The DIALOG command requests that the seven records we created be sorted by sales (SA) in descending order. The company with the largest sales will be listed first.

SORT 4/ALL/SA,D
S5   7   Sort 5/ALL/SA,D

We then request that the names of the companies be listed together with their sales, the state in which they are located, their SIC code, and their telephone number.

REPORT 5/CO,SA,ST,PC,TE/ALL

The resulting report is shown in Table 6.2

The report format is useful for displaying a few facts about many companies. If you want more detail, display individual company records. Example 6.1 is a record is for Barton Industries. The record gives some historical sales and employee figures as well as the names of the principal company officers.

TRINET U.S. BUSINESSES

The second file we will search is TRINET U.S. BUSINESSES, a directory file produced by TRINET, Inc. Like DIALOG File 531 this database contains the current address, telephone number, annual sales, employment data, and corporate linkages for about 7.5 million U.S. business establishments. Both public and private U.S. companies are included. Industries are identified by four-digit SIC codes. The database attempts to include every business location with one or more employees throughout the United States. Each record lists the number of employees, the

Table 6.2
Industrial Valve Manufacturers in D&B—DUNS MARKET IDENTIFIERS

Company	Sales (in dollars)	State	Primary SIC	Telephone Number
Barton Industries	10,041,731	OK	3491	405-273-7660
American Energy Valve	6,400,000	TX	3491	713-681-7553
Oil Capital Valve Co	6,054,946	OK	3491	918-627-1942
Atlas Fluid Controls Corp	6,038,364	TX	3491	713-666-2190
Coastal Industries	5,704,108	TX	3491	713-869-0791
Hindle Hamer	5,000,000	TX	3491	713-937-3447
Mc Iver & Smith Fabricators	5,000,000	TX	3491	713-682-3633

Example 6.1
Barton Industries Record

```
Barton Industries, In
2401 N Hwy 177
Shawnee, OK  74801-9760

TELEPHONE: 405-273-7660
COUNTY: Pottawatomie       SMSA: 427  (Oklahoma City,Okla)
BUSINESS:  Mfg  Flow  Control  Valves  &  Gray  Iron  Casting Foundry & Mfg
    Oilfield equipment

PRIMARY SIC:
  3491     Industrial valves, nsk
  34919905   Pressure valves and regulators, industrial
SECONDARY SIC(S):
  3321     Gray and ductile iron foundries
  33219903   Gray iron castings, nec
  3533     Oil and gas field machinery, nsk
  35339903   Oil field machinery and equipment

LATEST YEAR ORGANIZED: 1981  OWNER CHANGE DATE:          NA
STATE OF INCORPORATION:  OK   DATE OF INCORPORATION: 08/23/1967
ANNUAL SALES REVISION DATE: NA
                         LATEST          TREND          BASE
                         YEAR            YEAR           YEAR
                                        (1987)         (1984)
SALES         $     10,041,731  $    10,500,000  $    6,680,000
EMPLOYEES TOTAL:           170             110             118
EMPLOYEES HERE:            100
  SALES GROWTH:   57 %  NET WORTH: $     7,678,052
  EMPLOYMENT GROWTH:  -7 %
SQUARE FOOTAGE: 89,000  OWNED
SALES TERRITORY: U.S.,CANADA          NUMBER OF ACCOUNTS: 500
ACCOUNTING FIRM: Peat Marwick Main & Co
BANK: Harris Trust & Savings Bank

THIS IS:
    A   MANUFACTURING LOCATION
    A   HEADQUARTERS LOCATION
    AN  ULTIMATE LOCATION
    A   CORPORATION
    AN  EXPORTER
    A   PUBLIC COMPANY
    A   MILLION DOLLAR DIRECTORY COMPANY

DUNS NUMBER:            04-260-6780
CORPORATE FAMILY DUNS:  04-260-6780

CHAIRMAN:                 Inda, John P  /Chb
PRESIDENT:                Johnson, C W  /Pres & Ceo
VICE PRESIDENT:           Joyce, Victor L  /V Pres & Cfo
SECRETARY:                Day, Bruce W  /Sec
TREASURER:                Cook, Don E  /Tr
FINANCE:                  Joyce, Victor L  /V Pres & Cfo
CHIEF EXECUTIVE OFFICER:  Johnson, C W  /Pres & Ceo
CHIEF FINANCIAL OFFICER:  Joyce, Victor L  /V Pres & Cfo
FINANCE VP:               Joyce, Victor L  /V Pres & Cfo
```

primary business activity, and sales and share of market. Full company profiles are available for businesses with two or more locations. The TRINET U.S. BUSINESSES database is also available on the LEXIS Service (as the TRIEST File).

The form of the search in TRINET U.S. BUSINESSES is the same as in D&B—DUN'S MARKET IDENTIFIERS File. We combine the codes for state locations, SIC numbers, and annual sales. However, the results of the search are quite different (see Table 6.3). At the time the search was run there was only one company the two lists had in common (Barton Industries). The differences in retrieval of TRINET U.S. BUSINESSES and the D&B DMI File are the results of three facts: (1) the TRINET database is larger than the DIALOG D&B database (7.5 million companies compared to 6 million companies); (2) company sales figures that are used in both databases are either self-reported or are estimates made by the database producer and (3) SIC numbers are assigned differently by the two database producers.

The lack of agreement among databases concerning individual company sales and industry affiliation is, unfortunately, very common. The important point to remember in this context is not to depend on one online directory to produce a comprehensive list of companies. Using more than one file will allow you to cross-check information and to fill in gaps in company coverage. Keep in mind that discrepancies and inaccuracies in the coverage of directory databases are usually not the result of outright coding mistakes on the part of database producers, but of inconsistencies in data reporting from the companies, lack of standardization in classifying the companies into detailed industry groups, and a failure to update the information in a timely way. For example, the companies in the D&B list are also included in the TRINET database. They did not appear on the TRINET report either because they had been assigned different SIC numbers or because they had sales outside the $5 to $10 million range.

An individual company record from TRINET U.S. BUSINESSES gives less detail than a similar record from D&B—DUNS MARKET IDENTIFIERS. For example, it gives no other sales figures than those from the current year. It does have one piece of information missing from the D&B files: "share of market." The share of market given for Aitken Inc. is .0829 percent of the entire U.S. market for industrial valves. The market share calculation in TRINET allows us to prepare share of

Table 6.3
Industrial Valve Manufacturers in TRINET U.S. BUSINESSES

Company	Sales	State	SIC Number	Telephone Number
AIKEN IN	8,400,000	TX	3491	713-692-3340
AEROPARTS MFG CO	8,400,000	OK	3491	918-627-2474
HOERBIGER EJ MITCHELL IN	8,400,000	TX	3491	713-681-4681
BALON CORPORATION	8,400,000	OK	3491	307-266-1267
E I M CO IN	8,400,000	TX	3491	713-499-1561
FLO VALVE CO IN	8,200,000	TX	3491	713-776-9196
P M I INDUSTRIES	8,000,000	TX	3491	713-781-3733
BARTON INDUSTRIES IN	7,800,000	OK	3491	405-273-7660
RAM FORGE & STEEL CO	7,000,000	TX	3491	409-825-6501
ALLOY CARBIDE CO	7,000,000	TX	3491	713-923-2708
ENPRO SYSTEMS IN	7,000,000	TX	3491	713-452-5865

Example 6.2
TRINET U.S. BUSINESSES Record

```
AITKEN IN
4920 AIRLINE DR
HOUSTON, TX  77022-3021
Telephone: 713-692-3340
County: HARRIS
MSA: 3360   (HOUSTON, TEXAS)

Primary SIC:
  3491  (INDUSTRIAL VALVES)
Secondary SIC(s):
  3569  (GENERAL INDUSTL MACHINERY NEC)
Number of employees:        60
Estimated location sales:   $8,400,000
Share of market (SIC 3491): 0.08920 %

THIS IS:
  a(n) SINGLE location of a PRIVATE company
TRINET location number: 307070029
General Management:        JOE RICE / PRESIDENT
```

market reports for many product lines. Example 6.2 shows a TRINET U.S. BUSINESSES record.

DUN'S ELECTRONIC BUSINESS DIRECTORY

There are other useful electronic directories that can be used to screen for acquisition candidates. The largest of these files is D&B—DUN's ELECTRONIC BUSINESS DIRECTORY (DUN'S EBD). It is DIALOG File 515. Formerly called D&B—DUN'S ELECTRONIC YELLOW PAGES, the file provides online directory information for over 8 million businesses and professionals throughout the United States. A full directory listing is provided for each entry, including address, telephone number, SIC codes and descriptions, and employee size range. DUN'S EBD covers both public and private U.S. companies of all sizes and types. DUN'S EBD is not intended to be a reflection of information contained in the printed yellow pages.

When we run our search on industrial valve manufacturers in D&B— DUN'S ELECTRONIC BUSINESS DIRECTORY, we can no longer search for a range of annual sales figures. The database does not have this information. However, we can use an alternative measure of company size, namely, the number of employees. In DUN'S EBD, employee size is grouped by categories ranging from "B" (which stands for companies with between 1 and 4 employees) to "I" (companies with between 500 and 999 employees). Category "A" indicates that employee figures are not available. As Table 6.4 indicates, most establishments are small (between 1 and 9 employees).

Table 6.5 shows the results of our search on DUN'S EBD for industrial valve manufacturers in the Southwest. We have selected only companies with an employee category of between 5 and 9.

Table 6.4

Employee Size Classes in DUN'S ELECTRONIC BUSINESS DIRECTORY

Number of Records	Category	Number of Employees
882,738	A	NOT AVAILABLE
4,656,160	B	1-4
1,307,824	C	5-9
667,539	D	10-19
439,486	E	20-49
152,007	F	50-99
85,151	G	100-249
23,169	H	250-499
9,752	I	500-999
5,126	J	1,000-2,499
1,118	K	2,500-4,999
333	L	5,000-9,999
90	M	10,000 and over

TOTAL   8,230,493

Table 6.5

Industrial Valve Manufacturers in DUN'S ELECTRONIC BUSINESS DIRECTORY

Company	Employee Total	State	SIC Code	Telephone Number
CONTROL VALVE SERVICE	C (5-9)	TX	3491	713-473-1001
PHOENIX SUPPLY	C (5-9)	TX	3491	713-941-7542
BTR IN	C (5-9)	TX	3491	713-222-0205
HESS VALVE CO IN	C (5-9)	TX	3491	713-674-8735
AMERICAN MACHINE & TOOL CO	C (5-9)	OK	3491	405-794-9820
APPLIED HYDRAULICS IN	C (5-9)	TX	3491	512-629-9145
CONTROLS INTERNATIONAL IN	C (5-9)	TX	3491	214-343-9980
CLEVELAND MACHINE CO IN	C (5-9)	TX	3491	713-592-6549
COASTAL INDUSTRIES IN	C (5-9)	TX	3491	713-869-0791
CAREY MACHINE COMPANY IN	C (5-9)	OK	3491	405-677-7721
LINE FLOW EQUIPMENT MFR CO	C (5-9)	TX	3491	713-681-1666
DAKO TECHNOLOGIES IN	C (5-9)	TX	3491	817-473-0221
BAKER OIL	C (5-9)	OK	3491	405-476-3762
WALTER LATHAM IN	C (5-9)	TX	3491	713-681-4490

We can print individual records (see Example 6.3) from D&B—DUN'S ELECTRONIC BUSINESS DIRECTORY just as we could from D&B—DUN'S MARKET IDENTIFIERS and TRINET U.S. BUSINESSES. Note that the D&B—DUN'S ELECTRONIC BUSINESS DIRECTORY record tells when a record for the company is available in D&B—DUN'S MARKET IDENTIFIERS with the notation "DMI Record Available in File 516."

All of the directory databases that we have discussed are useful for creating mailing labels. We can request that just the name and the address of the companies be printed. Another option on the DIALOG system is to have the mailing labels printed at the DIALOG office in Palo Alto, and sent to you via U.S. mail or electronic mail.

Example 6.3
Record from DUN'S EBD

```
08087616                    DMI RECORD AVAILABLE IN FILE 516


CONTROL VALVE SERVICE
1616 S RICHEY       PASADENA, TX    77502
TELEPHONE: 713-473-1001    COUNTY: HARRIS
SMSA: 247   (HOUSTON,TEXAS)

INDUSTRY GROUP: MANUFACTURING            PRIMARY SIC:  3491
THIS IS A(N):  FIRM        SINGLE LOCATION
D-U-N-S NUMBER: 60-448-9872    NUMBER OF EMPLOYEES:    C (5-9)
CITY POPULATION: 7 (100,000-249,999)
```

Expanded SIC Codes

Both D&B—DUN'S MARKET IDENTIFIERS and D&B—DUN'S ELEC-TRONIC BUSINESS DIRECTORY use an expanded Standard Industrial Classification Code to describe a company's business. The four-digit U.S. Industrial Classification Codes for establishments are not sufficiently detailed to describe products and services. For example, the SIC code 3491 describes businesses primarily engaged in manufacturing industrial valves. Dun & Bradstreet's expands this number to eight digits for increased precision in describing a company's products. Listed below are the eight-digit codes for industrial valves:

3491 9901	Boiler Gauge Cocks
3491 9902	Compressed Gas Cylinder Valves
3491 9903	Fire Hydrant Valves
3491 9909	Nuclear Valves

In D&B—DUN'S MARKET IDENTIFIERS and in D&B—DUN'S ELEC-TRONIC BUSINESS DIRECTORY, using the statement "S PC= 34919903" would retrieve only those companies in the database that manufactured fire hydrant valves. Using the statement "S PC=3491" would retrieve all companies whose business was manufacturing indus-trial valves, including those who manufactured fire hydrant valves, nuclear valves, or any type of valve described by the general SIC number.

Screening for Service Companies

We have been using the retrieval of manufacturing establishments as our example in describing online directories. It is important to keep in mind that the directories include the entire range of economic activity: agriculture, mining construction, transportation, wholesale and retail trade, finance, and services. We can use D&B—DUN'S ELECTRONIC

BUSINESS DIRECTORY to search for the names of companies in the Philadelphia area that plan parties and rent facilities. D&B has a specific SIC code (7299 05 02) for party planning service and a more general number (7299 05) for both catering and party planning. To retrieve companies that are involved in facility rental and party planning, we enter the following statements:

S PC = 729905

S1   718 PC = 729905 (facility rental and party planning)

There are 718 companies in the database that rent facilities and plan parties. When we limit our search to Philadelphia area companies and sort the list by employee size, we can create the list shown in Table 6.6.

Screening for Financial Variables

Often we are interested in screening on more detailed financial information than sales. If we are willing to limit our search to the approximately 12,000 U.S. public companies, there are hundreds of potential financial variables we can use. For example, assume that we are searching for billion-dollar public companies with adequate returns on sales and assets and relatively low debt. We can define these characteristics in terms of standard ratios:

Net income/net sales > 5%

Net income/total assets > 9%

Long-term debt/equity < 50%

Current ratio > 2

Net sales > $1 billion

Table 6.6
Philadelphia Area Facility Rental and Party-Planning Companies from DUN'S ELECTRONIC BUSINESS DIRECTORY

Company	Employee Total	SIC Code	Telephone Number
SPRINGFIELD FOODS CORP	G (100-249)	7299	215-544-1230
MC MANUS & DENT ENTERPRISES	D (10-19)	7299	215-228-0969
CELEBRATION	C (5-9)	7299	215-947-0169
BEST PARTY SERVICES	B (1-4)	7299	NA
ULTIMATE WEDDING EXTRAVAGANZA	B (1-4)	7299	609-985-1138
GORDON CAROLE POWERS ENTPS	B (1-4)	7299	215-664-4369
ANGEL ENTERPRISES	B (1-4)	7299	215-622-2300
NEW RIVERIA HALL & CATERERS	B (1-4)	7299	609-547-3030
HALL KENSINGTON CORPORATION	B (1-4)	7299	215-634-8965
ADDIE'S BRIDAL	B (1-4)	7299	NA
PERSONALLY YOURS BY	B (1-4)	7299	609-547-1692

The DISCLOSURE database (File 100) on DIALOG is an excellent database for this type of search. DISCLOSURE contains extensive extracts from reports that companies file with the U.S. Securities and Exchange Commission. A search of DISCLOSURE on the criteria above would retrieve the companies having these characteristics in a few seconds. A report, sorted by sales, could be used to list the companies (see Table 6.7).

We can display individual records from DISCLOSURE, but they are quite long (thirty pages on average). Often it is more econmical to print individual company records listing only the variables we are interested in. Example 6.4 shows a record of Digital Equipment Corporation that gives the variables on which we screened.

Although the DIALOG version of DISCLOSURE is a powrful and flexible database, it has two important limitations for financial screening. The file contains only the most current five years of company financial data. If you want to know Eastman Kodak's annual sales for the past ten years, you will not find the information on DISCLOSURE. The second limitation is the inability to calculate new variables on the DISCLOSURE database. An example should make this clear. In his book *Mergers and Acquisitions: A Financial Approach*, James W. Jenkins discusses "financial screens" as a way of searching for merger candidates.[5] Here are some examples of his screens:

- a ratio of current assets to current liabilities that is greater than or equal to 2.0
- a ratio of total debt to stockholders' equity that is less than or equal to 1.0
- a price earnings ratio that is less than or equal to 30 percent of the average highs of the stock in the last three years
- a growth in earnings per share that is at least 10 percent compounded annually over the past decade

Table 6.7
Screening Report from DISCLOSURE

Company Name	Ticker Symbol	Primary SIC	5 Year Sales Growth	Net Sales ($000s)
DIGITAL EQUIPMENT CORP	DEC	3573	13.7	12,741,956
MINNESOTA MINING & MANUFACTURI	MMM	2641	7.7	10,581,000
ALCAN ALUMINIUM LTD	AL	3350	9.3	8,529,000
ARCHER DANIELS MIDLAND CO	ADM	2075	10.8	7,928,836
MELVILLE CORP	MES	5651	9.7	6,780,359
BRISTOL MYERS CO	D.BYO	2834	7.3	5,972,500
.				
.				
COMPAQ COMPUTER CORP	CPQ	3573	44.3	2,065,562
ASARCO IN	AR	1021	8.4	1,988,087
ILLINOIS TOOL WORKS IN	ITW	3643	26.6	1,929,805
GENERAL CINEMA CORP	GCN	7832	40.9	1,913,804

Example 6.4
Digital Equipment Corporation Record

```
                         ANNUAL INCOME (000$)

    FISCAL YEAR ENDING        07/01/89     07/02/88     06/27/87

    NET SALES             12,741,956    11,475,446    9,389,444

                    KEY ANNUAL FINANCIAL RATIOS

    FISCAL YEAR ENDING           07/01/89   07/02/88   06/27/87

    CURRENT RATIO                   2.88       2.87       3.40

    LONG TERM DEBT/EQUITY           0.02       0.02       0.04

    NET INCOME/NET SALES            0.08       0.11       0.12

    NET INCOME/TOTAL ASSETS         0.10       0.13       0.14
```

DISCLOSURE is capable of screening on the first two criteria (the current ratio and debt to equity ratio), but it cannot do the calculations required by Screens 3 and 4. Screen 3 requires the database to calculate and average three years of annual stock price highs and to compare this number to the current price earnings ratio. Screen 4 requires the database to calculate a compound growth rate over ten years for all companies in the database and to eliminate those that have grown less than 10 percent.

A database that can perform the calculations required by Screens 3 and 4 is the COMPUSTAT Industrial file. The COMPUSTAT Industrial database contains information on more than 7,000 U.S. public companies. In addition, it has information on 5,000 companies that have been delisted because of bankruptcy, mergers, or privatization. The file contains up to twenty years of detailed financial information on each company. COMPUSTAT can be searched online (through the ADP system, for example) or can be purchased as a CD-ROM database. COMPUSTAT is frequently mounted as a private online database by business schools for the use of their faculty and students.

On the CD-ROM version of COMPUSTAT (called PC-PLUS), we can calculate the compound growth rate for the previous ten years with the following expression:

@CGR (EPSFI, Y80,Y90)

"@CGR" asks for the compound growth rate to be calculated for the expression in parentheses. "EPSFI" stands for "earnings per share fiscal year." "Y80,"Y90" refers to the period on which the growth rate is to be calculated. We can then screen the database for companies that have a 10 percent or greater growth rate and present the information as a report (see Table 6.8).

Table 6.8
COMPUSTAT Report on U.S. Companies with High EPS Growth Rates

Company	Earnings per Share	Annual Sales	Growth Rate
MAYFAIR SUPER MKTS -CL A	1.64	573.767	85.9
ACTION INDUSTRIES INC	0.78	154.711	50.2
ECC INTERNATIONAL INC	1.136	44.226	49.8
ROYAL PALM BEACH COLONY -LP	1.05	12.122	38.6
SUNLITE INC	0.67	2.249	36.4
WILLIAMS INDUSTRIES INC	0.79	90.609	36.4
PRIME MOTOR INNS INC	2.01	298.003	36.3
DBA SYSTEMS INC	1.5	61.871	35.2
HOLLY CORP	2.76	385.897	34.4
UNIFI INC	2.34	298.346	34.4
ENTWISTLE CO	6.68	43.182	33.6
FIRST REPUBLIC CP -CL A	17.16	73.766	32.0

The only source of extensive financial information about U.S. private companies is from Dun & Bradstreet. D&B—DUNS FINANCIAL REC-ORDS PLUS (DFR) is File 519 on DIALOG. It provides up to three years of comprehensive financial statements for more than 1.8 million private companies. The records have most of the information contained in a Dun and Bradstreet credit report. The database provides extensive information, including balance sheet, income statements, and ratios for measuring solvency, efficiency, and profitability. In addition, a company's financial position may be compared to others in the same industry as determined by industry norm percentages.

DFR also contains company identification data, such as company name, address, primary and secondary SIC codes (1987 version), D-U-N-S number, and number of employees. Textual paragraphs cover the history and operational background of a firm. Example 6.5 shows a full record from DFR. We have excluded a lengthy financial statement found with this record.

The file has several drawbacks:

1. The online record from DIALOG does not include the credit raitng, payment history, or legal filings.
2. Complete financial information is often not available for a company.
3. The information is often self-reported and unaudited.
4. The database is expensive. Individual reports cost $96 plus $147 an hour connect cost.

If you need information on credit ratings, payment history, or legal filings, or if you do extensive analysis of private companies, you should

Example 6.5
A Full DFR Record

```
          Sample Reports From DUNS FINANCIAL RECORDS PLUS (sm)
                                ---
                    (Sample reports do not contain real data.)
   Sample Financial Records Report
   Name & Address:

      Harrison Pharmacy Inc
      13 Main Street
      FALLS, CA 00000
      Telephone: 000-000-0000
      DUNS Number: 00-000-0000
      Line of Business: DRUGSTORE, GIFT SHOP
      Primary SIC Code:  5912
      Secondary SIC Code:  5947
      Year Started: 1945                  (12/31/86)  FISCAL
      Employees Total:        28          Sales:  888,066
      Employees Here:         25          Net Worth: 161,349


      HISTORY
      10/27/86
      CHARLES HARRISON, PRES              KAREN LAWSON, V PRES
      DORIS HARRISON, SEC/TRES
      DIRECTOR(S): THE OFFICER(S)
            Incorporated California Sep 1 1976. Authorized capital
            consists of 7,600 shares common stock, $10 par value.
            Business started 1945 by Charles and Doris Harrison as a
            partnership. 100% of capital stock is owned by officers
            equally.
            This has been a family-owned corporation since 1945. C
            Harrison has controlling interest with balance held by
            Harrison family members.

   C HARRISON born 1918 married. 1935-45 Tings Pharmacy, Escondido,
   CA, pharmacist. 1945-present active here.

   K LAWSON born 1946. Daughter of C Harrison. Completed education
   in 1969 when she received pharmacist degree from University of
   Arizona. Has been active here since 1962. Started operating here
   as a pharmacist in 1969.

   D HARRISON born 1920 married, not active here. Active as a
   homemaker. 1941-present wife of Charles.

   Retail drug store (60%) and Hallmark gift shop (40%). Sells for
   cash 70% balance net 30 days. Has 500-700 accounts. Sells to
   general public. Price range competitive. Territory :Local.
   Nonseasonal.

            EMPLOYEES: 28 including officers and 1 part-time. 25
   employed here.

            FACILITIES: Leases 6,480 sq. ft. in one story concrete
   block building in good condition. Premises owned individually by
   the Harrisons.

            LOCATION: Central business section on main street.

            BRANCHES: Harrison's Hallmark Shop, 211 Powers St, Brook,
   CA,
      leases 2,800 sq ft. Operates as gift shop.
      12/31/86 FISCAL
      (Figures are as stated)

      FINANCIALS (not included here)
```

order reports directly from Dun & Bradstreet. Dun & Bradstreet will require a minimum order of 100 reports per year. D&B will either send the report by mail or allow you to print it online through their DunsPrint online service. Individual reports will cost about $25 each. If information about a company is not available or is too old, D&B will prepare a report as part of the service contract.[6]

Screening for Share of Market

A company's market share is the ratio of its sales to industry sales for a given period of time, usually a year. Market share is an important measure of a company's value. As we noted earlier, the TRINET U.S. BUSINESSES file gives share of market information by four-digit SIC number for over 7 million U.S. establishments. In addition, you can create "Share of Market Reports" that rank up to fifty companies in an industry according to their share of market in the United States. In Table 6.9 we give the first few entries from a market share report for the U.S. industrial valve industry. In addition to share of market information, the

Table 6.9
TRINET Share of Market Report

```
                    SHARE OF MARKET REPORT
                 INDUSTRY ANALYSIS BY COMPANY

                    3491 INDUSTRIAL VALVES
```

RANK	TRINET NUMBER	COMPANY NAME	SALES ($MIL)	SHARE OF MKT	CUMUL SHARE	NO OF ESTAB
1	006432835	AMERICAN CAST IRON PIPE COM 2930 16TH ST N BIRMINGHAM, AL 35207	$ 234.8	4.037	4.037	2
2	007511793	DRESSER INDUSTRIES INC 1600 PACIFIC AV DALLAS, TX 75201	$ 195.7	3.365	7.402	4
3	007532013	ROCKWELL INTERNATIONAL 600 GRANT ST PITTSBURGH, PA 15219	$ 179.5	3.086	10.488	4
4	007537897	TYCO LABORATORIES INC 1 TYCO PA EXETER, NH 03833	$ 175.8	3.023	13.511	2
5	007528615	PARKER HANNIFIN CORP 17325 EUCLID AV CLEVELAND, OH 44112	$ 155.1	2.666	16.178	8

```
Cumulative Sales              $2,217.6

Industry Sales               $5,771.5
```

report gives the number of establishments the company has producing the product, the sales for the company, and the total estimated sales for the industry in the United States.

Another way of examining market share on the TRINET U.S. BUSI-NESSES database is through a "Line of Business Report." This report gives a corporate family's lines of business by SIC code ranked by sales, as well as figures for sales, percentage of total company sales, share of market, and number of establishments engaged in that line of business. Table 6.10 gives a Line of Business Report for the Monsanto Corporation.

Some information concerning a public company's lines of business is required to be reported to the U.S. Security and Exchange Commission. "Segment Data," as it is sometimes called, is reported in a company's 10K report for lines of business that constitute 10 percent or more of sales or income. The information is available online through several sources, including the DISCLOSURE database and the STANDARD AND POOR'S ONLINE file on DJNR. Here is the line of business information for Monsanto Company as reported in STANDARD & POOR'S ONLINE file:

Table 6.10
TRINET Line of Business Report

```
                        SUMMARY OF SALES BY INDUSTRY
                                    FOR
                        MONSANTO  (TU=007525207)
```

SIC CODE	SIC DESCRIPTION	SALES ($MIL)	PERCENT CO SALES	SHARE OF MKT	NO OF ESTAB
2824	ORGANIC FIBERS, EXC CELLULOSIC	$2182.0	26.32	17.20410	4
2869	INDUSTRL ORGANIC CHEMICALS NEC	$1128.8	13.62	3.18970	7
2821	PLASTICS MATERIALS & RESINS	$931.6	11.24	2.34790	3
3861	PHOTOGRAPHIC EQUIPT & SUPPLIES	$912.0	11.00	7.42150	1
2819	INDUST INORGANIC CHEMICALS NEC	$601.4	7.25	2.39820	9
2834	PHARMACEUTICAL PREPARATIONS	$471.2	5.68	1.03060	1
2873	NITROGENOUS FERTILIZERS	$313.7	3.78	5.14240	1
2892	EXPLOSIVES	$286.7	3.46	29.33290	1
3087	CUSTM CMPNDG, PRCH PLAST RESIN	$200.6	2.42	18.97100	1
8731	COMML PHYSICL, BIOLOG RESEARCH	$134.5	1.62	1.06770	5
3491	INDUSTRIAL VALVES	$125.2	1.51	2.15280	2
5169	CHEMICALS, ALLIED PRODUCTS NEC	$124.2	1.50	0.57800	15
5153	GRAIN & FIELD BEANS	$103.2	1.24	0.10970	1
.					
.					
.					
5083	FARM & GARDEN MACHINERY	$ 5.6	0.07	0.06160	4
1382	OIL & GAS EXPLORATION SERVICES	$ 4.1	0.05	0.05640	2
3559	SPECIAL INDUSTRY MACHINERY NEC	$ 2.0	0.02	0.03000	1

```
US Mfg. Sales (This Report)            $7,393.7
US NonMfg. Sales (This Report)           $896.3
       Total US Sales (This Report)    $8,290.0

US Manufacturing Sales (All SIC's)     $7,393.7    89.19
US Nonmanufacturing Sales (All SIC's)    $896.3    10.81

Total US Sales                         $8,290.0
```

1988	Sales	Op.Inc.
Chemicals	48%	486M
Agriculture chemicals	19%	424M
Fisher, electronics	12%	40M
Nutrasweet	9%	154M
Pharmaceuticals, other	12%	109M

The final source for market share information that we will consider is the PROMT database from Predicasts Corporation. PROMT is available on DIALOG as File 16 as well as on other time-sharing systems. PROMT contains abstracts and full text from over 1,000 newspapers, trade publications, and reports. The database allows you to search with any combination of SIC numbers, products, event names, and geographic locations. A useful feature of the database is the ability to retrieve only those records that give tabular data. Example 6.6 shows a search for tabular data giving market share for cold cereals, and an example of one of the records retrieved

SEARCHING FOR PATENTS

Patents are legal documents that give the holder the exclusive right to produce, sell, or use an invention. Patents held by corporations may be an important part of their assets. In addition, patents may indicate a company's type and degree of technological innovation. Inventors often assign their patent rights to corporations, but there are exceptions. Inventors who found a company may keep patents in their name rather than assigning it to their company.[7] We can search for companies with patents in a particular subject area. We can use the words used to describe patents to retrieve the names of the companies owning them. A more precise way to retrieve groups of patents on a particular subject is to search by U.S. patent classification code.

Example 6.6
A PROMT Search

```
          S COLD()CEREAL AND SF=TABLE AND MARKET(5N)SHARE?


        Market shares for major US cold cereal manufacturers (%)

                               1990*      1987
            Kellogg            38.0       41.2
            General Mills      24.1       21.2
            General Foods      11.1       13.2
            Quaker Oats         7.4        7.5
            Ralston Purina      6.2        5.6

        *Share for year ended October 1
```

Source: Goldman Sachs & Company; *New York Times* (National Edition), November 18, 1990, p. f5.

In summary, patent literature may be used in two ways for M&A research: as a way to evaluate individual companies, or as a method of discovering companies with expertise in a particular field. We will give examples of both types of searches.

Patent Databases

There are several online patent databases. By far the least expensive patent database and one that is perfectly adequate for many types of company patent searching is the PATDATA database on the BRS system. PATDATA has abstracts of all U.S. patents from 1975 to date. Example 6.7 shows a search for all patents that have been assigned to the Eastman Kodak Company since 1975.

If we were interested in discovering the names of companies that have inventions similar to the Eastman Kodak Company's spectrometer, we could search the PATS database by patent classification or by using words and phrases such as "spectrometer" and "image scanner." An alternative is to use the U.S. Patent Classification Code. These codes can be found in the *Manual for Classification* issued by the U.S. Patent and Trademark Office. The complete text of the classification manual is available online on the LEXPAT file in the LEXIS Service.

Here are the first few entries we retrieved when searching PATS with the original U.S. classification code 356/328 assigned to the Eastman Kodak invention:

```
PN US 4896963.
PD JAN 30, 1990.
TI Automatic analyzer.
AS Olympus Optical Co.  Ltd.

PN US 4875773.
PD OCT 24, 1989.
TI Optical system for a multidetector array spectrograph.
AS Milton Roy Company.

PN US 4867563.
PD SEP 19, 1989.
TI Spectroradio-meter and spectrophotometer.
AS Li-Cor Inc.

PN US 4856898.
PD AUG 15, 1989.
TI Adjustable echelle spectrometer arrangement and method for its
   adjustment.
AS Jenoptik Jena GmbH.
```

Another option for patent screening is the LEXPAT file available on the LEXIS and NEXIS Service. The LEXPAT file contains the full text of U.S. patents issued since 1975, the *U.S. Patent and Trademark Office Manual of Classification*, and the *Index to U.S. Patent Classification*. The approximately 1,500 patents added to the library each week appear online within four days of their issue. This is faster, by about a month, than the BRS database. In LEXPAT, to search for Eastman Kodak as the assignee in patents issued after January 1, 1990 we would enter:

Example 6.7
A PATS Search

```
EASTMAN KODAK.AS.    [THE TAG "AS" MEANS "PATENT ASSIGNEE"]

SAMPLE RECORD FROM BRS PATS DATABASE

PN US 4898467. [U.S. PATENT NUMBER]
PD FEB 06, 1990. [DATE OF PATENT]
TI Spectrometer apparatus for self-calibrating color imaging
   apparatus. [TITLE OF PATENT]
IV Milch-James-R. [INVENTOR]
IA Pittsford NY. [INVENTOR'S ADDRESS]
AS Eastman Kodak Company. [ASSIGNEE]
AP 267596 NOV 07, 1988. [APPLICATION DATE]R 356/328. [ORIGINAL
U.S. CLASSIFICATION CODE]
XR 356/404.   358/75. [CROSS REFERENCE U.S. CLASSIFICATION CODES]
IC G01J 3/28. H04N 1/46. EDITION 4. [INTERNATIONAL PATENT CODES]

RU 4544269, OCT 1985.   4595290, JUN 1986.   4650988, MAR 1987.
   4695892, SEP 1987. [PATENT CITATIONS]
AB Spectrometer apparatus, for self-calibrating a color image
scanner of the line scanner or area scanner type, comprises a
member, having an optical slit, movable into position on an
optical axis of the scanner between its polychromatic light
source and its focusable lens in a plane occupied by a color
image when it is scanned....
```

ASSIGNEE (EASTMAN KODAK) AND DATE > 1/1/90

We would retrieve records containing the full text of the patents. The only missing element would be the illustrations. Example 6.8 shows the first page of an Eastman Kodak patent as it appears on LEXPAT.

SEARCHING TRADEMARKS

Trademarks, like patents, are an indication of company value. Trademarks are not very useful for discovering companies active in a particular field. Unlike patents, trademark files have only general descriptions of the product they depict. TRADEMARKSCAN-FEDERAL (DIALOG File 226) contains records of over 1 million currently active federal trademark applications and registrations covering all active applications and trademarks registered in the U.S. Patent and Trademark Office (USPTO). The file covers the period from 1884 to the present. Coverage in this file includes the serial number or registration number, the trademark, the U.S. classification of goods and services, the owner's name, and other pertinent information. The database uses data obtained directly from the U.S. Patent and Trademark Office or indirectly from the *Official Gazette* (Trademark Section) of the U.S. Patent and Trademark Office. TRADEMARKSCAN is one of the few online database that allows the transmission of images.

A companion file TRADEMARKSCAN—STATE (File 246) contains information on trademarks registered with the secretaries of state of all

Example 6.8
A LEXPAT Record

```
                              4,908,724
                             Mar. 13, 1990

                  Dual gap cross-field magnetic recording head with
          single gap  signal excitation

          INVENTOR: Jeffers, Frederick J., Escondido, California
          ASSIGNEE:  Eastman Kodak  Company, Rochester, New York (02)
          APPL-NO: 254,760
          FILED: Oct. 7, 1988
          INT-CL: [4] G11B 5#17; G11B 5#265
          US-CL: 360#123; 360#121
          CL: 360
          SEARCH-FLD: 360#123, 110, 118, 119, 121
          REF-CITED:
                              U.S. PATENT DOCUMENTS
          4,787,002         11/1988   *   Isozaki          360#123
                              FOREIGN PATENT DOCUMENTS
          1055840            4/1952   *  Fed Repub of Germany   360#121
          0029828            3/1981   *  Japan                  360#121
          0098124            6/1982   *  Japan                  360#121
          PRIM-EXMR: Hecker, Stuart N.
          ASST-EXMR: Severin, David J.
          LEGAL-REP: Robbins; Daniel

      ABST:
              In a recording system utilizing a cross-field head, rather
      than  excite both the field gap and the recording gap with signal
      and bias excitation as taught in the prior art, the present
      invention teaches applying bias excitation to both the field gap
      and the recording gap (as known in the prior art), but
      applying....
```

Source: Reprinted with the permission of Mead Data Central, Inc., provider of the LEXIS® / NEXIS® services.

fifty U.S. states and Puerto Rico. Each record contains the trademark, state of registration, U.S. class number, international class number, a description of the goods and services, registration number, current status, and owner. Marks are included for every type of product or service marketed commercially in the United States and Puerto Rico.

A search for "Tootsie Roll" as a trademark would retrieve the record shown in Example 6.9.

THE VALUE OF A BUSINESS

Many of the databases and retrieval techniques we have discussed are useful in establishing the value of a business. However, the valuation of a merger candidate usually takes place after a suitable candidate has been found. The valuation is made to determine what price the buyer should offer the stockholders of the target company.

Several sophisticated financial techniques are used to estimate the value of a business. They include:

- discounted cash flow modeling
- acquisition precedents

Example 6.9
A TRADEMARKSCAN Search

```
TOOTSIE ROLL      and Design
          US CLASS   : 046 (Foods and Ingredients of Foods)
          INTL CLASS : 030 (Staple Foods)
          STATUS : Registered   REG. NO. : 1468554
          REG. DATE : December 08, 1987
          PUBLISHED : September 15, 1987
          GOODS/SERVICES : CANDY
          SERIES CODE : 73   SERIAL NO. : 656212
          FILED : April 20, 1987
          DATE OF FIRST USE  : March 31, 1983
          ORIGINAL OWNER : TOOTSIE ROLL INDUSTRIES, INC. (VA.
CORPORATION); CHICAGO,IL
          CLAIMS : THE DRAWING IS LINED FOR THE COLORS ORANGE AND
     BROWN.
```

- price paid as a multiple of earnings
- premium over market trading value
- liquidation value
- replacement value

Except for the method using acquisition precedents, the data for valuation (when it is publicly available) can often be found in financial databases. The "acquisition precedents" technique requires examination of comparable M&A deals in an industry. Finding precedents is best done using one of the M&A transaction databases discussed in Chapter 5.

SCREENING FOR NON-U.S. COMPANIES

The techniques we have discussed for searching online directories, financial, patent, and trademark files for U.S. companies work equally well for non-U.S. companies. Two large Dun & Bradstreet Files of non-U.S. companies are available on DIALOG (D&B—EUROPEAN DUN'S MARKET IDENTIFIERS and D&B—INTERNATIONAL DUN'S MARKET IDENTIFIERS). In addition, there are many specific country directories online. Detailed financial information is available for many non-U.S. public companies. Non-U.S. patents are well covered in several databases, including WORLD PATENT INDEX, INPADOC, and JAPIO (Japanese Patents). Descriptions of UK trademarks are now available in a file called UKTM. We will discuss screening for non-U.S. companies in Chapter 8.

OTHER SCREENING DATABASES

THOMAS REGISTER ONLINE (DIALOG File 555) covers 130,000 U.S. manufacturers with 50,000 product classifications. In addition, the file contains more than 100,000 brand names. The file is most useful for searching on brand names and detailed product descriptions. The descriptions do not include sales figures, but give an indication of asset size. Be careful in displaying full records from THOMAS REGISTER ON-LINE; a large company may have hundreds of product listings. The *Thomas Register* is also available as a printed directory and on CD-ROM.

CORPTECH is a detailed source of company information on 33,000 U.S. manufacturers and developers of high-tech products. Ninety percent of the entries are private or are subsidiaries of public corporations. The most useful feature of the file is its detailed subject listing descriptions of high technology products. CORPTECH is available from ORBIT Search Services. CORPTECH is available as a printed directory (*Corporate Technology Directory*) and on CD-ROM.

PTS NEW PRODUCT ANNOUNCEMENTS/PLUS (DIALOG File 621) contains the full text of press releases from all industries covering announcements related to products, with a focus on new products and services. In addition to product descriptions, press releases generally contain key details about new products and technologies, including technical specifications, availability, uses, licensing agreements, distribution channels, and prices. Company contacts and phone numbers are provided to allow followup by interested parties. The press releases contained in the PTS NPA/PLUS database are obtained directly from the product manufacturer, distributor, or an authorized marketing representative. Use PTS NPA/PLUS as a supplement to the patent files.

INVESTEXT (DIALOG file 545) provides full-text financial research reports from about sixty of the leading investment banking firms in the United States, Europe, Canada, and Japan. These primary research reports contain independent sales and earnings forecasts, market share projections, research and development expenditures, and related data. INVESTEXT includes reports on approximately 8,500 of the largest publicly traded U.S. corporations, and on 2,500 smaller, emerging companies. Non-U.S. participants provide research on some 1,000 large firms listed on stock exchanges in Japan, West Germany, Britain, France, Italy, Holland, Belgium, Switzerland, Sweden, Canada, and Australia.

NOTES

1. Steven P. Galante and John A. Chippinelli, eds., *Buyouts: Directory of Intermediaries* (Needham, Mass.: Venture Economics, 1989).

2. *World M & A Network* (Washington, D.C.: International Executive Reports, 1990).

3. J. Terrence Greve, *How to Do a Leveraged Buyout for Yourself, Your Corporation, or Your Client* 3d ed. (San Diego: Business Publications, 1987).

4. *Standard Industrial Classification Manual* (Washington, D.C.: Executive Office of the President, Office of Management and Budget, 1987).

5. James W. Jenkins, *Mergers and Acquisitions: A Financial Approach* (New York: American Management Association Extension Institute, 1986), p. 44.

6. Melissa B. Mickey, "Dun & Bradstreet," *Business Information Alert* (1):3 (January 1990).

7. Marydee Ojala, "A Patently Obvious Source for Competitor Intelligence: The Patent Literature," *Database* 12(4):46 (August 1989).

7

The Muddled
Corporate Identity

In a *Forbes* cartoon, a boss speaking to his secretary says, "What a marvelous fiscal year—mergers, acquisitions, divestitures, deregulation, restructuring. . . . Refresh my memory—what business are we in?"[1] Corporate change can be marvelous for companies but usually causes headaches for business researchers trying to determine the makeup of corporations. In this chapter we will discuss techniques that can be used to discover the network of subsidiaries, divisions, affiliates, and establishments that make up the typical corporation, and to learn how a corporation has changed over time.

Over 17 million businesses in the United States file returns with the IRS. Most of the businesses filing (about 12 million) are sole proprietorships, the simplest form of business organization. The owner of the business is the proprietor and receives any profits. Most sole proprietorships are small, but there is no limit to the size a sole proprietorship may take.[2] Another 1.7 million businesses that file in the United States are partnerships. Partnerships are formed when two or more persons agree to be coowners of a business.

The most important form of business organization in the United States (as determined by the size of the companies it represents) is the corporation. The 3.3 million U.S. corporations control most of the business assets in the country. Ranging from single-person companies to the largest business combinations in the world, corporations are considered by law to be a "person" separate from their owners, the shareholders. Corporations have other characteristics of people: they are "born" (become incorporated), "die" (go bankrupt or are liquidated), "marry" (form joint ventures), and get "adopted" (are acquired by parent companies).

Corporations often have family trees that are every bit as complicated as human family trees. As corporate genealogists, we are often called on to trace the connections among a corporation's ancestors and in-laws. In M&A research, this information is useful both as a method for discovering acquisition candidates and as an answer to the question of how the company is organized. In addition, an awareness of how the company has changed over time gives important clues regarding management strategy.

An important part of understanding corporate relationships is summed up in the phrase "who owns whom." The question "who owns whom" often has a host of related questions:

- When, and from whom, were the subsidiaries that now make up the corporation acquired?
- What is the formal organization of the company?
- What is the history and status of the corporation?
- Who are the principal stockholders of the corporation and how much stock do they own?

Let us begin with what seems to be a simple question: What is the name of the company? Like people, corporations have "identities." In business literature, "corporate identity" refers to the quality and style of a business, its personality. "Name awareness" (the ability of the public to recognize a company's name and product) is an important part of corporate identity. Corporations spend much energy and expense in attempting to create names and logos that will project an image and build customer trust. As an example of the importance of name recognition, consider the Sohio company's name change. Sohio was the twenty-fourth largest company in the United States but was perceived as a local company. "Sohio," with its reference to the state name "Ohio," made the public think of the company as attached to a single state. To change this perception, the company began using its old name, the Standard Oil Company. The name change resulted in a new prestigious identity for the company.[3] Mergers sometimes result in name changes. When Burroughs and Sperry Corporation merged in 1986, they chose the name UNISYS for their combined company. A joke on Wall Street was that a merger of Fairchild and Honeywell never took place because the new combination would have been called "Farewell Honeychild."[4]

In a merger or acquisition, the acquiring company often will create a new corporation whose purpose is to acquire a target company. After the acquisition has been completed, the parent company will acquire the new company. Complex transactions such as this often create a jumble of related names. For example, here is a list of some of the names used by RJR Nabisco in its leveraged buyout by KHL.

RJR HOLDINGS CAPITAL CORP
RJR HOLDINGS CORP
RJR HOLDINGS GROUP INC.
RJR HOLDINGS CAPITAL CORP.
RJR HOLDINGS ACQUISITION CORP.
RJR NABISCO HOLDINGS CAPITAL CORP
RJR NABISCO HOLDINGS GROUP INC.

Usually the first step in disentangling corporate relationships and company names is to answer the question of "who owns whom"—that is, to discover the hierarchy of subsidiaries, divisions, and affiliations that make up a corporation. Some definitions will help us sort out corporate relationships.

- A *parent company* is one that operates and controls other separately chartered businesses called subsidiaries. Ralston Purina Company is an example of a parent company.
- A *subsidiary* is a company that, although separately chartered, is at least 50 percent owned or controlled by another company. Eveready Battery Company is one subsidiary of Ralston Purina.
- A *division*, by contrast, is a functional area or activity within the company, not a separately chartered business. The Purina Grocery Products Group is an example of a division within the Ralston Purina Company.
- An *establishment* is a single geographic location where the company's business is performed.
- A *plant* is an establishment devoted to manufacturing.

Corporate hierarchies are often made complex when subsidiaries have their own subsidiaries. Below we list some of the subsidiaries of IBM. The asterisks show the level of control. For example, the parent company IBM owns IBM World Trade Corporation, which in turn owns IBM Americas/Far East Systems Corporation. IBM Americas/Far East Systems Corporation owns both IBM Korea Systems Corporation and Thai Systems Corporation Ltd.

  IBM WORLD TRADE CORP.
 *IBM AMERICAS/FAR EAST SYSTEMS CORP.
**IBM KOREA SYSTEMS CORP.
**THAI SYSTEMS CORP. LTD.
 *IBM CHINA/HONG KONG CORP.
 *IBM INTERNATIONAL CORP.
 *IBM WORLD TRADE ASIA CORP.

*WTC INSURANCE CORP., LTD.
*IBM WORLD TRADE EUROPE/MIDDLE EAST/AFRICA CORP.
**IBM UNITED KINGDOM HOLDINGS, LTD.

This information is from the ONLINE DISCLOSURE database. The database contains extensive extracts from reports that public companies in the United States file with the Securities and Exchange Commission. (DISCLOSURE is described in Chapter 6.) With the DIALOG system, subsidiary listings can be retrieved from DISCLOSURE by selecting the parent company name, and then printing the subsidiary listing. For example, to retrieve the listing of subsidiaries for Eastman Kodak, do the following:

S CO=EASTMAN KODAK   ["CO" STANDS FOR "COMPANY NAME"]

S1 1   EASTMAN KODAK   [THERE IS ONE COMPANY RECORD]

TYPE 1/CO,SB/1   [TYPES THE PARENT COMPANY ("CO") AND
                 SUBSIDIARIES ("SB") FOR SET 1]

DISCLOSURE can be used to find the name of a parent company when you know the name of a subsidiary. For example, to find who owns Thai Systems Corporation, use the following search statements in DIALOG:

S SB=THAI SYSTEMS?   "SB" INDICATES A SUBSIDIARY COMPANY
                     THE ? WILL SEARCH FOR ANY ADDITIONAL
                     CHARACTERS AFTER "SYSTEMS"]

S1 1 [THERE IS ONE COMPANY THAT HAS THAI SYSTEMS AS A
       SUBSIDIARY]

TYPE 1/CO,SB/1   [TO TYPE THE PARENT COMPANY NAME AND LISTING]

The DISCLOSURE database obtains its information on subsidiaries principally from 10K reports (public company annual reports filed with the Securities and Exchange Commission). These reports, in paper, on microfiche, or in full-text machine-readable form, are the primary source for subsidiary listings. Older reports are also a key source for historical research on individual companies. Although companies are required to report subsidiaries in the 10K, they sometimes simply refer to another report (such as the company annual report) in which subsidiaries are listed.

As an example of an online search for the subsidiaries of IBM as listed in the complete text of their 10K report, we will search the COMPNY Library of the LEXIS Service. The COMPNY Library includes reports from all New York and American Stock Exchange companies, plus about 200 reports from NASDAQ companies. To search for subsidiaries, first display the index page to find where the subsidiaries are listed. Then display the complete text of the report listing the subsidiaries. The search statement combines the segments "Ticker-Symbol" and "Index." Segments are referred to as "fields" by most other databanks.

TICKER-SYMBOL(IBM) AND INDEX(SUBSIDIARIES)

The search will retrieve the index page for each 10K report of the company in the database. When you learn on which page the subsidiaries listing begins, display the page in full format:

• FU;P*19 [FU IS THE COMMAND FOR FULL DISPLAY FORMAT]

The 10K listing gives the state of incorporation and percent of ownership of the subsidiaries—information not available in DISCLOSURE ONLINE.

	State or country of incorporation or organization	Percentage of voting securities owned by its immediate parent
Registrant:		
International Business Machines Corporation	New York	
Subsidiaries:		
IBM Credit Corporation	Delaware	100
—	—	—
—	—	—
IBM World Trade Corporation	Delaware	100
IBM Americas/Far East Systems	Delaware	100
IBM Korea System Corp.	Korea (South)	100
Thai Systems Corp.	Thailand	100
IBM China/Hong Kong	Delaware	100
IBM International	Delaware	100
IBM World Trade Asia	Delaware	100
WTC Insurance Corporation	Bermuda	100
—		

CORPORATE AFFILIATION FILES

10Ks and other corporation reports provide comprehensive lists of subsidiaries for U.S. public companies, but they have limitations:

- They do not include private companies
- They give little information about the subsidiaries' location
- They give no information about foreign parent companies that do not trade in the United States

An online directory that overcomes some of these limitations is DIA-LOG's CORPORATE AFFILIATIONS (File 513). The online file combines the information from two printed directories: the *Directory of Corporate Affiliations*[5] and the *International Directory of Corporate Affiliations.*[6] The file includes 70,000 parent companies and their affiliates. The online version has two types of records. The first (the parent company record) contains the complete corporate family tree. The second (the affiliate company record) contains the portion of the corporate family tree in which a particular company fits. For example, to retrieve the parent company record for the Ralston Purina Company, select the parent company name using the prefix "CO."

S1   1   CO = RALSTON PURINA COMPANY

Then type the record in format 5.

T   1/5/1

As the Example 7.1 indicates, the information includes (in addition to a list of subsidiaries) the parent company name, address, and telephone number; ticker symbol and stock exchange; up to twenty Standard Industrial Classification (SIC) codes and descriptions; the number of employees, total assets, sales, and net worth; names of executives and members of the board of directors. The record also includes an NRPC (National Register Parent Company) number that can be used to retrieve all related companies, regardless of name.

More information can be found on individual subsidiaries and plants by searching directly by subsidiary name. For example, to retrieve the following information about Beech-Nut Nutrition Corporation, search for that company name:

Beech-Nut Nutrition Corporation
Checkerboard Square
St. Louis, MO 63164
Telephone: 314-982-3619
NRPC Number: 008858032
Business: Infant Foods

Example 7.1
A CORPORATE AFFILIATIONS Record

```
1967157
Ralston Purina Company
Checkerboard Square
St Louis,  MO  63164

Telephone: 314-982-1000
State of Incorporation: MO

NRPC Number: 008858000
Ticker Symbol: RAL    Stock Exchange: NYSE,PS,Bo,MW,Ph

Number of US Affiliates: 9

Business: Mfr of Cereals, Pet Foods,  Operates Ski Resort;
Wholesale Baker of Bread & Snack Cakes; Maker of Dry Cell
Battery & Lighting Prods

SIC Codes:
    2043    Cereal breakfast foods
    2047    Dog & cat food
    2051    Bread & other bakery products, except cookies &
            crackers
    2048    Prepared feeds & feed ingredients for animals &
            fowls, except dogs & cats
    2099    Food preparations, NEC
    3692    Primary batteries, dry & wet
    3645    Residential electric lighting fixtures
    3646    Commercial, industrial & institutional electric
            lighting fixtures
    3648    Lighting equipment, NEC
    7011    Hotels & motels

Number of Employees: 56,229


Sales: $6,658,300,000
Total Assets: $4,044,400,000
Net Worth: $1,089,900,000
Total Liabilities: $2,954,500,000

This is a(n) Parent, US, Public Company

Executives:
Top Officer
    William P Stiritz/Chm Bd Pres & Chief Exec Officer
      Corporate Officer (VP)
    William H Lacey/VP Chm & Chief Exec Officer-Grocery Prods
      Grp
  .
  .
  .

Marketing
    Franklin J Cornwell Jr/VP & Dir-Bus Devel
Chief Financial Officer
    James R Elsesser/VP & Chief Fin Officer
Chief Financial Officer
    Joe R Micheletto/VP & Controller
Public Relations
    ED Richards/VP & Dir-Pub Rels
General Counsel,Secretary
    James M Neville/VP Gen Counsel & Sec
Corporate Officer (VP)
    Philip J Kennedy/VP & Pres & Chief Oper Officer-Eveready
      Battery Co
Chief Financial Officer
    Ronald D Winney/Treas
Investor Rels Director
    Michael Grabel/Investor Rels Dir
George C Cook/Dir-Video Systems
W W Davis Jr/Dir- Hdqtrs Oper & Corp Services

Board  of  Directors: William P Stiritz;   David R Banks;
John H  Biggs; Theodore  A  Burtis;..... Warren M Shapleigh
```

Example 7.1 (continued)

```
Corporate Family Hierarchy:

=>Ralston Purina Company 1967157<=
    Protein Technologies International (Group) 1967156
    Purina Grocery Products Group (Group) 1967155
    Beech-Nut Nutrition Corporation (Subsidiary) 1967154
        Beech-Nut Nutrition Corporation (Plant) 1967153
        Beech-Nut Nutrition Corporation (Plant) 1967152
        Beech-Nut Nutrition Corporation (Plant) 1967151
    Benco Pet Foods Inc (Subsidiary) 1967150
    Continental Baking Co Inc (Subsidiary) 1967149
    Eveready Battery Co (Subsidiary) 1967148
```

CORPORATE AFFILIATIONS has several ways to search corporate relationships. If you examine the record for Ralston Purina, you will see a ten-digit number called the NRPC number. The first six digits of this number are the same for related companies. One technique is to use the first six digits of the NRPC number to bring together all related companies in the file. For example, to retrieve all company records associated with Ralston Purina:

S   NO = 008858   ["NO" IS THE PREFIX FOR THE NRPC NUMBER]

S1   14   [THERE ARE FOURTEEN RECORDS IN THE FILE
          RELATED TO RALSTON PURINA]

Companies reporting to the "ultimate parent" (the company at the top of hierarchy) can be retrieved by searching the prefix "UP." To retrieve all companies in the database that have Ralston Purina as their ultimate parent:

S   UP = RALSTON PURINA COMPANY

S1   9   [THERE ARE NINE COMPANIES IN THE FILE
         THAT HAVE RALSTON PURINA AS AN ULTIMATE PARENT]

The prefix "IP" can be used to search for "immediate parents." An "immediate parent" is the company that a subsidiary is owned by. It need not be the ultimate parent company. For example, to retrieve all companies in the database that have Ralston Purina as an immediate parent, type:

S   IP = RALSTON PURINA COMPANY

S1   4   [THERE ARE FOUR COMPANIES IN THE FILE THAT HAVE
         RALSTON PURINA AS AN IMMEDIATE PARENT]

In Example 7.2 a "subsidary record" is retrieved by searching for Ralston Purina either as an ultimate parent or as an immediate parent.

Although CORPORATE AFFILIATIONS is an excellent source of corporate relationship information, we sometimes require information on small companies or greater detail concerning the establishments of major corporations. For extensive listings of small U.S. corporations and for details of establishments and their place within a corporate hierarchy, you must use the large online directory files produced by Dun & Bradstreet and TRINET.

Previously discussed as screening databases in Chapter 6, D&B—DUN'S MARKET IDENTIFIERS and TRINET U.S. BUSINESSES contain millions of company records. Both databases use coding systems that allow us to retrieve all of the company records relating to a parent company. The D-U-N-S number system created by Dun & Bradstreet is particularly useful as a retrieval device to discover corporate relationships. D-U-N-S numbers are unique nine-digit numeric identifiers given by Dun & Bradstreet to every company in their database. D-U-N-S numbers have several uses:

- The numbers allow us to distinguish among companies with similar or identical names. For example, there are several companies in the United States that use variations of the name "Allied Medical Laboratories" (e.g., Allied Medical

Example 7.2
Retrieval of a Subsidiary Record

```
            Protein Technologies International
            Checkerboard Square
            St Louis,  MO  63164

            Telephone: 314-982-1000

            NRPC Number: 008858003

            Ultimate Parent:  Ralston Purina Company - 1967157
            Immediate Parent: Ralston Purina Company - 1967157
            Number of US Affiliates: 0

            Business: Isolated Soy Proteins, Plastic Binders & Paper
                      Coatings

            SIC Codes:
               7011   Hotels & motels
               8741   Management services
               3479   Coating, engraving & allied services, NEC
               2821   Plastics materials, synthetic resins &
                      nonvulcanizable elastomers
               2075   Soybean oil mills
            This is a(n) Affiliate, US Company

            Executives:
            Top Officer Of Non-Parent
              P H Hatfield/Pres


            Corporate Family Hierarchy:

              Ralston Purina Company 1967157
              =>Protein Technologies International (Group) 1967156<=

D-U-N-S NUMBER
```

Laboratory, Allied Medical Lab). However, each of the companies can be easily distinguished by its unique D-U-N-S numbers.

• D-U-N-S numbers allow us to identify companies that have changed their names. The numbers remain the same even if the company changes its name.

• D-U-N-S numbers allow us to retrieve all related corporations regardless of name. It is this function we will examine in some detail.

• In addition to their use by Dun & Bradstreet, D-U-N-S numbers are used by other databases as unique company identifiers. The DISCLOSURE database and ABI/INFORM are two examples.

Each location (place of business) in a Dun & Bradstreet file is given one unique D-U-N-S number. A company with one location will be given one D-U-N-S number. A large company with a complex organization may have four D-U-N-S numbers. These will be:

• establishment D-U-N-S number
• headquarters D-U-N-S number
• corporate parent D-U-N-S number
• corporate family D-U-N-S number

For the ultimate parent of the company, all of these D-U-N-S numbers will be the same. An example of a search using D-U-N-S numbers on DIALOG's D&B—DUN'S MARKET IDENTIFIERS will show that the Ralston Purina Company headquarters in Checkerboard Square has the D-U-N-S number 00-626-6811. If we wanted to retrieve the description of the Ralston Purina headquarters from the databases, we would use the following search statement:

S   DN = 00-626-6811   ["S" stands for "Select" and
                         "DN" stands for "D-U-N-S number".]

We also could use the D-U-N-S number to retrieve the headquarters record of Ralston Purina and all of the records of companies with the same name reporting to it—102 records.

S   DH = 00-626-6811   ["DH" stands for "Dun's
                         headquarters number"]

The D-U-N-S corporate number (DC =) will retrieve the ultimate corporate record of Ralston Purina and all family members headed by Ralston Purina regardless of name—492 records.

S   DC = 00-626-6811   ["DC" stands for "Dun's
                         corporate number"]

A final variation is the D-U-N-S parent number. The search statement "S DP = 00-626-6811" will retrieve subsidiary records that report directly to Ralston Purina (37 records).

Example 7.3 is a record from D&B—DUN'S MARKET IDENTIFIERS that shows the name and address of one establishment of one subsidiary of Ralston Purina.

Another important source of information for subsidiary and establishment listings is DIALOG's TRINET U.S. BUSINESSES (File 531). This file contains the records for more than 7 million establishments in the United States. The records for associated companies are linked together with a unique number ("TU" number). To find the TU number for a company, select the company name and display one record (see Example 7.4).

The number in parenthesis (00407149) is the "TU" number. Select this number with the prefix "TU" to retrieve all establishments associated with Ralston Purina.

S TU = 004607149

S2 637 [THERE ARE 637 ESTABLISHMENTS ASSOCIATED WITH
          RALSTON PURINA]

At this point we could display individual records for the establishments. Another choice is to display the establishment locations as a report. We first sort the 637 by a criterion of our choice. In the example below, we have sorted by the state in which the establishments do business (see Table 7.1):

SORT 2/ALL/ST

S3 637 [SET 3 CONTAINS THE SORTED ESTABLISHMENTS]

REPORT 3/CO,ST,CY,TE/1-20 [WE REQUEST A REPORT LISTING
                            THE FIRST TWENTY ESTABLISHMENTS]

Example 7.3
DMI Record

```
        Continental Baking Company Inc
            110 Tices Lane
            P O Box 10
            East Brunswick, NJ  08816-2014

        TELEPHONE: 201-254-8800

        PRIMARY SIC:
            3556       Food products machinery, nsk
            35569901   Bakery machinery

        DUNS NUMBER:            60-180-8157
        HEADQUARTER DUNS:       00-131-7197 Continental Baking Company
        CORPORATE FAMILY DUNS: 00-626-6811 Ralston Purina Company
```

Example 7.4
TRINET Record

```
S  CO=RALSTON PURINA CO

S1     60    CO="RALSTON PURINA CO"  [THERE ARE 60 RECORDS IN

                                     THE DATABASE WITH THE COMPANY

                                     NAME RALSTON PURINA CO]

   T 1/5/1    [TYPE THE FIRST RECORD IN FORMAT 5]



   RALSTON PURINA CO
   3818 WOODVILLE RD
   TOLEDO, OH  43619-1844

   Telephone: 419-697-0100
   County: WOOD
   MSA: 8400  (TOLEDO, OHIO)

   Primary SIC:
     5149  (GROCERIES & RELATED PDTS NEC)

   Number of employees:          16
   Estimated location sales:     $2,300,000
   Share of market (SIC 5149):   0.00500 %

   THIS IS:
     a(n) BRANCH location of a PUBLIC company
   TRINET location number: 315530923    Ticker symbol: RAL

   Ultimate headquarters: RALSTON PURINA   (004607149)
```

A HISTORICAL APPROACH

In addition to determining "who owns whom," we may want to know a history of corporate events ("what happened when"). M&A activity often results in corporate reorganization. For example, between 1981 and 1987 General Electric Company was involved in 14 major acquisitions. During the same period the company disposed of 10 major and over 200 smaller businesses.[7] A frequent point of interest in examining a corporation is the history of its changes.

An excellent source of capsule corporate histories are the printed Moody's Manuals. Moody's Manuals give detailed descriptions of most U.S. public companies (as well as major non-U.S. companies). The first paragraph of the description is headed "History." The following extract from Moody's description of Ralston Purina will give you an understanding of their treatment:

History: Incorporated in Missouri, Jan 8 1894 as Robinson Danforth Commission Co. present title adopted in 1902. For acquisitions before 1977 see Moody's 1984 Manual. In Sept. 1977 acquired the floricultural assets of Stratford of Texas Inc. for $35,000,000 in cash and noninterest-bearing 10-year note in the principal amount of $12,000,000. Principal amount of note is subject to adjust to reflect any

Table 7.1
TRINET Report Format

Company Name	State	City	Telephone Number
WONDER BREAD	AL	MUSCLE SHOALS	205-381-8624
HOSTESS CAKE	AL	BIRMINGHAM	205-945-4655
WONDER BREAD BAKING CO	AR	SEARCY	501-268-2240
WONDER BREAD BAKERY	AR	LITTLE ROCK	501-372-5116
CONTINENTAL BAKING CO	AR	FORT SMITH	501-646-2546
CONTINENTAL BAKING CO	AR	RUSSELLVILLE	501-968-4287
RALSTON PURINA COMPANY	AR	LOWELL	501-770-6193
HOSTESS CAKE DISTRIBUTOR	AR	FAYETTEVILLE	501-521-1112
WONDER BREAD	AR	HARRISON	501-741-6280
WONDER BREAD&HOSTESS CAKE	AR	BATESVILLE	501-793-2260
WONDER BREAD CO	AR	PARAGOULD	501-236-2274
WONDER BREAD CO	AR	JONESBORO	501-932-2441
WONDERBREAD	AR	WEST HELENA	501-572-2241
WONDER BREAD CO	AR	FORREST CITY	501-633-4758
WONDER BREAD	AR	BLYTHEVILLE	501-763-6814
WONDER BREAD BAKERY	AR	LITTLE ROCK	501-565-4446
WONDER BREAD THRIFT STORE	AR	LITTLE ROCK	501-663-2847
WONDER BREAD BAKING CO	AR	H SPGS NAT PK	501-623-8241
WONDER BREAD BAKING CO	AR	PINE BLUFF	501-247-2915
RALSTON PURINA CO	AR	RUSSELLVILLE	501-968-1900

changes in audited books value of assets acquired. . . . In Nov. 1977 acquired WARF Institute. Inc.[8]

Moody's Manuals are the general description of several financial services produced by Moody's Investors Service. They consist of annual bound volume(s) and a loose leaf binder containing current information sheets. Here is a list of the Manuals together with their first date of issue:

Industrials	1900
Transportation	1909
Public Utilities	1917
Banks and Finance	1928
Municipals/Governments	1918
International	1981
O-T-C Industrial	1970
O-T-C Unlisted	1986

Moody's Manuals are an excellent source of subsidiary listings as well as a source for a description of a corporation's plants and properties.

A second source of corporate chronology is the Commerce Clearing House's *Capital Changes Reporter*. This service gives a chronology of changes in corporate capital and debt. *Capital Changes Reporter* is designed to allow security holders to calculate their gain or loss as the result of capital changes. It is kept up to date with weekly supplements. Here are the first few lines of the description of the Ralston Purina Company:

```
Ralson Purina Co       1893   Incorporated in Missouri
1-18-24   Stock split 4-1 $100 to $25 par, and 25% stock dividend
   (equivalent to 5-1 split) Record date 1-8-24.
Nontaxable.................... *20.0000%
1-2-26 20% stock dividend. Record date 12-15-25
Nontaxable..............................................83.3333%
10-19-28 60% stock dividend. record date 10-5-28
Nontaxable..............................................62.5000%
     .      .      .      10-1-70 Merged Foodmaker, Inc. See that
company (continued on next page)
```

```
*Apply percentage to basis per share of original stock to
arrive at new basis per share of original and new stock or shares
resulting from a stock split.[]
```

Source: Reproduced with permission from CCH CAPITAL CHANGES REPORTS published and copyrighted by Commerce Clearing House, Inc., 4025 W. Peterson Ave., Chicago, Illinois, 60646.

Another source of corporate chronologies is the annual *Directory of Obsolete Securities* (Financial Stock Guide Service). Produced by Financial Information Inc., the directory gives brief profiles of U.S. and Canadian companies whose original identities have been lost as a result of name change, merger, acquisition, dissolution, reorganization, bankruptcy, or charter cancellation. Each annual directory covers the period 1927 through the current year. Here is an example of the description of Studebaker Corporation:

```
Studebaker Corp. (DEL)
Merged into Studebaker-Packard Corpt. in 1954
Each share Common $1 par exchanged for (1.5) shares Common $10 par.
```

```
*Studebaker-Packard Corp name changed to Studebaker Corpt (Mich.)
    6/29/62 which merged into Studebaker-Worthington inc. 11/27/67
(see Studebaker-Worthington Inc).[9]
```

Major corporations often have one or more books devoted entirely to their history. You can search for books on corporations in the *Books in Print* directory either in print or online (DIALOG File 470). Lists of books by subject held by major libraries in the United States and Canada are available through electronic bibliographic networks such as RESEARCH LIBRARY NETWORK (RLIN) and OCLC. Records for English language books catalogued by the Library of Congress since 1968 are searchable on LC MARC-BOOK (DIALOG File 426). Another source of corporate history is the five-volume *International Directory of Company Histories.* It contains two-page histories of 1,250 of the world's largest companies.

SCREENING FOR CORPORATE EVENTS

In our discussion of corporate events, we have been emphasizing the individual corporation. Occasionally, we are interested in knowing what events occurred in a larger context. In addition to knowing that an individual company merged, went bankrupt, or was delisted, we may want to know the names of all the companies in an industry, or in a country, or during a particular year that underwent similar change. This type of search is a "screening search" as discussed in Chapter 6. The transaction databases discussed in Chapter 5 are designed to create customized lists of companies involved in M&A activity. In Chapter 6 we give several examples of searches for companies that fit a particular profile in regard to M&A activity. The COMPUSTAT Industrial database (discussed in Chapter 6) can also be used to provide lists of companies that declared bankruptcy, merged, were liquidated, delisted, or went private during the past twenty years. Table 7.2 is an example of a report that can be prepared from the database. It shows the first few alphabetical entries of public companies that went private between 1985 and 1987.

Another type of screening search can be used to determine the names of subsidiaries or parent companies that fit a particular geographic, industry, or financial profile. Here are two examples from the TRINET U.S. BUSINESSES. In the first example, we want to know the names of public companies that have their corporate headquarters in Philadelphia, Pennsylvania. TRINET records have several special indexing tags that allow retrieval on corporate relationships. Called "special fields," they include these terms:

- ULTIMATE (the tag for the corporate headquarters)
- SUBSIDIARY
- BRANCH
- SINGLE (for companies with one location only)
- PUBLIC (for companies that trade on exchanges)
- PRIVATE

Table 7.2
Public Companies That Went Private, 1985-1987

Company	SIC Code	Sales (in millions)	Year
1 POTATO 2 INC	5812	7.185	1986
AARON BROTHERS ART MARTS INC	5990	50.366	1986
ALOHA INC	4512	95.073	1985
AMERICAN AGGREGATES CORP	1400	77.967	1985
AMERICARE HEALTH CORP	6324	143.074	1986
ASSOCIATED GROCERS INC	5141	877.009	1987
AVONDALE MILLS	2200	238.263	1985
BARCO OF CALIFORNIA	2330	20.692	1987
BEDFORD COMPUTER CORP	3575	9.035	1985
BEVIS INDUSTRIES INC	3317	0	1987
BIRDVIEW SATELLITE COMM INC	3663	58.922	1985

To answer our question, we combined the special field tags for corporate headquarters (SF = ULTIMATE) and public company (SF = PUBLIC) with city and state names (see Example 2.5).

Example 7.6 makes use of a DIALOG system feature called "mapping." We want the names of subsidiaries or branches in the state of Delaware whose companies have their headquarters in Pennsylvania. We first retrieve a set of all establishments in Delaware that are either branches or subsidiaries.

Large online directory files such as D&B—DUN'S MARKET IDENTI-FIERS and TRINET U.S. BUSINESSES include about 60 percent of the 17 million companies that file tax returns in the United States. An excellent source for small private U.S. corporations and partnerships as well as for records of companies no longer in existence are the INCORP Files on the LEXIS Service.

INCORP includes records of corporations, limited partnerships, municipal authorities, and nonprofit associations registered to do business

Example 7.5
A TRINET Screening Search

```
SS SF=ULTIMATE AND SF=PUBLIC AND CY=PHILADELPHIA AND ST=PA

   S1    22565   SF=ULTIMATE

   S2    36452   CY=PHILADELPHIA

   S3   309261   ST=PA

   S4   201406   SF=PUBLIC

   S5       22   1 AND 2 AND 3 AND 4   [THERE ARE 22 COMPANIES

                                        THAT HAVE ALL THE

                                        CRITERIA]

T 5/5/1 [TO TYPE THE FIRST RECORD IN THE SET]

5/5/1
0402906
HUNT MFG CO INC
230 S BROAD ST
PHILADELPHIA, PA   19102-4121

Telephone: 215-732-7700
County: PHILADELPHIA
MSA: 6160  (PHILADELPHIA, PENNSYLVANIA-NEW JERSEY)

Primary SIC:
  2521  (WOOD OFFICE FURNITURE)

Number of employees:          117
Estimated location sales:     $21,400,000
Share of market (SIC 2521):   0.54770 %

THIS IS:
  a(n) ULTIMATE location of a PUBLIC company

TRINET location number: 009146176    Ticker symbol: HUN

Executive:                    RONALD J NAPLES / PRESIDENT
```

Example 7.6
DIALOG Mapping

```
SS ST=DE AND SF=(BRANCH OR SUBSIDIARY)

 S1   15833   ST=DE

 S2  378670   SF=BRANCH

 S3    5165   SF=SUBSIDIARY

 S4     968   ST=DE AND SF=(BRANCH OR SUBSIDIARY)
```

[THERE ARE 968 ESTABLISHMENTS IN DELAWARE THAT ARE EITHER BRANCHES
OR SUBSIDIARIES]

```
  MAP TU TEMP S4/TL=      [THE MAP COMMAND ASSIGNS A TRINET LOCATION
                          NUMBER (TL=) FOR EACH CORPORATE NUMBER
                          (TU=) AND SAVES THE RESULTS]

34 SELECT STATEMENT(S)
SERIAL#TB038

EX TB038    [EXECUTES SAVED SEARCH]

             ·1   TL=000073916
              1   TL=000120733
              1   TL=000209700
                  .
                  .

  S5     488   SERIAL: TB038   [THERE ARE 488 HEADQUARTER
                               COMPANIES IN THE U.S. WITH BRANCHES
                               OR SUBSIDIARIES IN DELAWARE]

   S S5 AND ST=PA    [COMBINES SET 5 WITH THE STATE]

          488   S5
       309261   ST=PA
   S5    52   S5 AND ST=PA   [THERE ARE 52 COMPANIES WITH ULTIMATE
                             HEADQUARTERS IN PENNSYLVANIA WITH
                             BRANCHES OR SUBSIDIARIES IN DELAWARE]


      T 12/5/1  [TYPING THE FIRST RECORD IN THE SET]
```

```
84 LUMBER CO
PO BOX 8484
EIGHTY FOUR, PA  15330-8484

Telephone: 412-228-8820
County: WASHINGTON
MSA: 6280  (PITTSBURGH, PENNSYLVANIA)

Primary SIC:
  5211  (LUMBER & OTHER BLDG MATL DLRS)

Number of employees:        500
Estimated location sales:   $80,000,000
Share of market (SIC 5211): 0.13060 %

THIS IS:
  a(n) ULTIMATE location of a PRIVATE company

TRINET location number: 230001026
```

in fourteen states. The LEXIS Service has plans to include all the states' incorporation files as they become available. The files vary greatly in years of coverage, elements covered, and updating frequency. Some state files have records beginning in the eighteenth century! Typically, a company record in INCORP contains the current company name, any prior company name, names of officers, the owners of the business, the type of business, the status of the company, filing date, and a brief history. The complete text of company records can be ordered from the state while online.

For example, PASOS, the Pennsylvania Department of State Corporation and Limited Partnership file, has over 1 million records plus an additional 55,000 records for foreign corporations. The file is updated daily; its earliest record has the date 1785. Example 7.7 shows a search on PASOS for companies located in Philadelphia County that were involved in mergers after January 1, 1989.

In this chapter we have discussed sources of information for answering questions concerning the history and status of corporations. As with most business questions, there is no single comprehensive source of information on this topic. For U.S. public corporations, comprehensive lists of subsidiaries can be found in 10K and related reports filed with the Securities and Exchange Commission.

Names and brief descriptions (name, address, percent ownership by parent company) for 4,000 U.S. public and private corporations can be found in the *Directory of Corporate Affiliations*, which is available both in print and online. Descriptions of individual establishments can be found in D&B—DUN'S MARKET IDENTIFIERS and TRINET U.S. BUSINESSES. Dun & Bradstreet's D-U-N-S number system is particularly effective in grouping establishments by affiliation. Corporate histories can be found in several sources, including Moody's Manuals, the *Capital Changes Reporter*, and the *Directory of Obsolete Securities.* The INCORP files on the LEXIS Service are useful for determining the existence and legal status of corporations within a state.

Despite the variety and apparent comprehensiveness of the sources we have discussed, you will occasionally be given the name of a company for which you can find no information. There are several possibilities to consider in such a case.

The company name that you are trying to find may be garbled or misspelled. For example, you are searching for the E. I. Konics Corporation but the company's actual name is Eikonics. You may be searching for "Crossfield Electronics" instead of "Crosfield Electronics." Searching online dictionary displays of company names (using the "EXPAND" command on DIALOG, for example) can often help clear up ambiguities

Example 7.7
A PASOS Search

```
      COUNTY(PHILADELPHIA) AND MERGER AND FILING-DATE > 1/1/1989

          Twenty-five records were retrieved. We display the first
      record in full format.

PENNSYLVANIA DEPARTMENT OF STATE, CORPORATE/LTD PARTNERSHIP RECORD

NAME:    ADOBE GAS GATHERING AND PROCESSING CO.

TYPE:    FOREIGN PROFIT (BUSINESS)

STATUS:    IN GOOD STANDING

FILING-DATE:    07/ 27/1989

STATE:    DELAWARE

REGISTERED OFFICE:    % C T CORPORATION SYSTEM
                      123 SOUTH BROAD STREET
                      PHILADELPHIA, PA 19109

COUNTY:    PHILADELPHIA

PRIOR-NAMES:    ADOBE GAS GATHERING AND PROCESSING CO.

OFFICERS:

Name                                Title        Effective Date

J K FREEMAN                         CEO          07/13/1989
S E VEAZEY                          SECRETARY    07/13/1989

NUMBER:    1516462

HISTORY:

Date:              07/27/1989
Transaction:       CERTIFICATE OF AUTHORITY - FOREIGN CORP FOR PROFIT
Microfilm Roll:    08954
Start/End:         1697/1699
Date:              07/13/1989
Transaction:       STATEMENT OF  MERGER  OR CONSOL. - CORP FOR PROFIT
Comment:           SURV
Microfilm Roll:    08955
Start/End:         0536/0538
-----------------------------------------------------------------------
```

Source: Reprinted with the permission of Mead Data Central, Inc., provider of the LEXIS® /
NEXIS® services.

in names. Keep in mind, however, that online (and printed) directories
have their own share of misspelled company names.

   The company name that you are trying to find may actually be a trade
or brand name. You are trying to find information about the Medicane
Corporation, but "Medicane" is actually a defunct trade name. Use
Thomas Register (in print or online) to search for U.S. brand names, or
use the printed directory *Brands and Their Companies* (formerly called
the *Trade Name Dictionary*). For non-U.S. brands use the printed
International Trade Names Dictionary.

The company name that you are trying to find may be described as a U.S. company but does not do business in the United States. We will discuss non-U.S. sources of data in Chapter 8.

The company may be very new or no longer in existence. Searching for newly formed companies in online financial newspapers, particularly local financial newspapers, is often helpful. For companies that are defunct, directories such as old Moody's Manuals and the *Directory of Obsolete Securities* are useful as is *F&S Index* (online back to 1972 and in print back to 1960).

Of course, these problems are not mutually exclusive. Consider a request for information concerning a company that is a misspelled, garbled, non-U.S. defunct brand name.

Finally, keep in mind that corporate change is continuous. There are about 600,000 new incorporations and 60,000 business failures each year in the United States. To be made as complete as possible, a search for company information should always include the sources discussed in Chapters 2 and 3 for monitoring corporate events.

NOTES

1. Richard K. Ferris, *The Executive Speaker* 7(9):6 (September 1986).

2. E. C. Lashbrooke, *The Legal Handbook of Business Transactions* (New York: Quorum, 1987), p. 31.

3. Clive Chajet, "Identifying Symptoms of Identity Malaise," *Management Review* 77(9):49-50 (1988).

4. *Coal*, "Restructurings and Dismemberments," March 1988, p. 122.

5. *Directory of Corporate Affiliations* (Wilmette, Ill.: National Register, 1990).

6. *International Directory of Corporate Affiliations* (Wilmette, Ill.: National Register, 1990).

7. "The Welch Years: GE Gambles on Growth," *Industry Week* 233:30-32 (1987).

8. *Moody's Industrial Manual* (New York: Moody's Investors Service, 1989), 2:626.

9. *Directory of Obsolete Securities* (Jersey City, N.J.: Financial Information Incorporated, 1991), p. 1253.

International M&A:
A Cross-Border Perspective

M&A transactions among U.S. companies are declining from the boom period of the 1980s. W. T. Grimm reported that domestic deal activity in the 1990s began with a bust. Potential M&A announced in the first quarter of 1990 fell 13 percent from the previous first quarter. In addition, the total value of deals dropped 38 percent from the same period a year before. Another indication that M&A activity is waning is the decline of the total value of the top ten deals announced in the first quarter of 1990—their value was lower than the value of the single top deal of 1989.[1]

However, one area of M&A activity is increasing—international M&A. In the first quarter of 1990, this was the pattern of U.S. companies attempting to buy foreign companies:

U.S. Companies Seeking Foreign Companies

Number of companies involved	201
Percent change from previous year	0%
Percent change in value of deals	−68%

In contrast, foreign companies seeking U.S. companies increased their activity sharply:

Foreign Companies Seeking U.S. Companies

Number of foreign acquirers	+31%
Value of deals	+65%

The increasing globalization of business, with its lack of regard to national boundaries, has given birth to what *Business Week* describes as the "stateless corporation." One harbinger of the stateless corporation is the surge of international M&A activity past domestic deal activity.[2]

The focus of activity has shifted from the United States to Europe. According to a study of cross-border transactions by KPMG Peat Marwick, the number of transactions in Europe shot up from 847 in 1988 to 1,314 in 1989. The value of the deals increased from $31.6 billion to $50 billion in one year. While acquirers of European firms represented 31 countries, the United Kingdom accounted for 53 percent of the purchases. The Japanese are more active in the United States than in Europe. Of their $12.5 billion in cross-border deals, only 9 percent was spent in Europe.[3] Canada, Germany, France, Italy, and Spain are also players in the international M&A market. In 1989, Germany led all European countries other than the United Kingdom with 129 cross-border deals.[4]

In this chapter we will examine sources of information on international M&A. Our discussion cuts across formats, to include all types of print and electronic sources. There are few publications dedicated to international transactions, but the number may increase as cross-border deals continue to outpace domestic activity. With few publications focusing solely on international deals, researchers will continue to use sources that cover both domestic and international transactions. We will emphasize those techniques that can help you focus your research on deals between two different countries, whether or not the United States is one of the parties.

DEFINITION AND ROOTS OF INTERNATIONAL M&A

M&A can be classified as either domestic or cross-border. A cross-border deal involves a target whose nationality is different from the acquirer or acquirer's ultimate parent.[5] From a U.S. perspective, we define a domestic deal as one that involves two American-owned companies. Cross-border deals include:

- acquisitions by domestic firms of foreign enterprises (e.g., a U.S. firm purchasing a non-U.S. target)
- acquisitions by foreign firms of domestic enterprises (e.g., a non-U.S. firm purchasing a U.S. target)
- transactions between non-U.S. firms (e.g., a British acquirer seeking a Spanish target)

Cross-border M&A has a long history. By 1900, seventy-five U.S. subsidiaries had been established in the United Kingdom.[6] In 1901, for example, J. P. Morgan began buying up U.K. shipping lines. Cross-border deals, particularly by non-U.S. firms, are usually strategic acquisitions. A strategic acquisition is designed to add strength to the organization—a new product, a brand name, or expansion into a new territory. Cross-border M&A deals are booming because industries are globalizing and the players must compete internationally. The companies sought in international deals are often lesser-known firms whose acquisition can round out a global market position, add a foreign-based plant, or provide access to a new technology or a strong brand name.

If a target is considered a key to strategic position, the foreign acquirer is less likely to be deterred by price. For example, in 1988 Bridgestone of Japan acquired Firestone. The Japanese tire company made its bid after Pirelli of Italy had made an initial hostile offer for Firestone. While Pirelli offered $58 a share, Bridgestone countered with $80 a share, a price far too high according to some analysts. Analysts also agreed that the high price was of less concern to Bridgestone than its place in the global tire market and its desire to gain entry to the U.S. marketplace.[7]

There is another reason why non-U.S. firms are able to make costly acquisitions at a fast pace. Foreign companies often can afford to pay more than their U.S. counterparts because they operate under different accounting rules. Unlike a U.S. firm, a British company can write off goodwill against shareholders' equity where it does no damage to earnings per share. If an American company had acquired Pillsbury at the price Grand Metropolitan paid for it in 1989 ($5.1 billion), overall earnings would be sharply reduced because tax regulations require that the expense of goodwill be charged to earnings. This would hurt the company's position with shareholders. Likewise, Japanese and West German accounting rules provide a better climate for costly acquisitions. In short, the large problem of debt repayment for American companies is often no problem for foreign acquirers.[8] Japanese and European companies have other potential advantages over their U.S. counterparts including favorable exchange rates and lower interest rates. These factors add to the global growth of cross-border M&A.

RESEARCHING INTERNATIONAL M&A

Merger & Acquisition Sourcebook

The growth in information sources that exclusively report cross-border transactions has not kept pace with deal activity. Several print sources have tracked both domestic and cross-border deals for several years. The drawback to these sources is their lack of coverage of cross-border deals where a U.S. company is not a target or acquirer. One notable example is the *Merger & Acquisition Sourcebook*, published by Quality Services Company of Santa Barbara, California. Quality Services Company also publishes *Corporate Growth Magazine* and *The Acquisition/Divestiture Weekly Report*. The *Sourcebook* contains a "foreign transactions" section that records transactions occurring in the calendar year previous to the current edition. The only clear criterion for inclusion of information about a deal appears to be that it involve one domestic and one foreign company.

The *Sourcebook* organizes deals by industry code (see Figure 8.1). It provides a description of the target and acquirer, company sales, income, net worth, and deal price in a brief paragraph. Both announced and completed deals are included. In addition to reporting individual transactions, the *Sourcebook* also includes statistical tables on cross-border deals, such as deal activity in Europe. Unfortunately, the *Sourcebook* lacks multiple indexes. There is only a company name index. This makes it impossible, for example, to find all deals in which the target was a Pacific Rim country.

International Merger Yearbook

The *International Merger Yearbook* made its first appearance in 1990. What was previously the *Merger Yearbook* became two separate M&A annual publications, the *Domestic Merger Yearbook* and the *International Merger Yearbook* (the books are subtitled "Corporate Acquisitions, Leveraged Buyouts, Joint Ventures and Corporate Policy"). The domestic version reports only deals involving U.S. corporations. The international version includes only cross-border deals, but it is superior to the *Merger & Acquisition Sourcebook* in that it reports a deal regardless of whether a U.S. company is a party. It also reports many more cross-border deals in a single volume than were previously available in a printed source.

Organized by industry, product, and basic deal information, the *Yearbook* is similar to the *Sourcebook* (see Figure 8.2). One additional feature in each *Yearbook* entry is a code for type of deal. These "types" include deals such as private negotiations, divestitures, and spinoffs. The deals are indexed only by company name or investor, making it impossible to identify cross-border deals by the company's country. Despite this limitation, the *Yearbook* provides much more of a "one-stop" source for cross-border deal information than comparable print sources.

Mergerstat Review

Another useful source for cross-border deal information is the *Mergerstat Review*. Published by the Merrill Lynch Business Brokerage & Valuation firm of Schaumburg, Illinois, the *Review* is a well known source of statistical information on M&A. Unlike the previous two sources that report information on individual transactions, the *Review* provides only a statistical report on deal activity (see Figure 8.3). The *Review's* statistical tables include deal rankings, industry highlights, purchase price analyses, and for international deals, a section for both foreign buyers and foreign sellers. A major limitation of the *Review* for international merger activity is its requirement that a U.S. company must be involved in the deal for inclusion. The foreign buyers section gives data on both the foreign purchase of domestic companies and purchase of foreign-based subsidiaries of U.S. corporations. The foreign sellers section lists U.S. corporations' purchases of foreign companies and units of foreign companies.

M&A JOURNALS

Mergers & Acquisitions

M&A yearbooks lack currency. Published annually, yearbooks are less useful than journals for keeping up-to-date with cross-border deals. There are several business journals providing international M&A information on a more timely basis. A standard journal source is *Mergers & Acquisitions*, published six times a year by MLR Publishing in Philadelphia. Each quarter *Mergers & Acquisitions* includes an "M&A Roster" giving capsule descriptions of deals taking place during the period. Two sections focusing on cross-border deals are included in the roster. One section covers U.S. deals for foreign firms and the other covers deals for U.S. companies by foreign firms. Again, there is no coverage of deals between two non-U.S. firms. In the roster, standard information, such as terms of the deal, is provided for each transaction (see Figure 8.4). There is also an annual index to all deals covered in the roster, but it is an index by company name only. The index always appears in the May/June issue of *Mergers & Acquisitions*, an issue that also includes the "Almanac," a statistical summary of the year's M&A activity. The almanac includes tables such as "countries most active in U.S. acquisitions" and "countries attracting U.S. buyers."

Corporate Growth Report

A comparable M&A journal, *Corporate Growth Report*, is published monthly by Quality Services Company. It is less useful than *Mergers & Acquisitions* for tracking international M&A. Each issue contains only a selected list of major transactions for the past month. This list includes cross-border deals between two non-U.S. firms and those with a U.S.

Figure 8.1
Sample Page from *Merger & Acquisition Sourcebook*

FOREIGN TRANSACTIONS, 1989

DESCRIPTION OF SELLER							DESCRIPTION OF BUYER				PURCHASE PRICE			
SIC-COMPANY NAME type of business		Sales ($ Millions)	Net Income		Net Worth ($mm)	Blk Value ($) Earnings($)	SIC-COMPANY NAME type of business	Sales ($ Millions)	Net Income		Total Amount ($ mm)	Multiple of Seller's Earnings	% of Sire Annl Sales	Multiple of Net Worth
			$ Mis	%					$ Mis	%				
0912-ARCTIC ALASKA FISHERIES CORP., an operator of a fishing fleet amex $10.875	'88 '87 '86	12.1 71.0 48.7	13.9 8.9 2.3	11.8 12.5 4.7	44.3	3.06 1.00	NIPPON SUISAN KAISHA LTD., the largest fishing company in Japan				195.2 for 100% at $13.50/sh	14.0	161	4.41

Arctic Alaska Fisheries Corp. said Nippon Suisan Kaisha Ltd. will buy two million newly issued shares for $13.50 a share, a hefty premium over the market price, in a move that will give the Japanese concern a 12% stake in the fishing company. Under a separate agreement, Nippon Suisan also acquired the right to sell all the surimi -- a protein base made from bottomfish -- produced by two vessels Arctic Alaska will place in service later this year. The Japanese concern has agreed not to exceed a 12% stake for five years, Arctic said. Arctic's total assets: $162.0 mm; current assets: $26.3 mm; current liabilities: $25.1 mm; long-term debt: $83.6 mm. Institutions own 18% of Arctic's shares, while insiders own 43%. Stock price one month prior to announcement: $10.125/sh.

DESCRIPTION OF SELLER							DESCRIPTION OF BUYER				PURCHASE PRICE			
1031-GULF RESOURCES & CHEMICAL CORP., an oil producer nyse $11.375	'87 '86 '85	116.8 121.6 155.8	0.2 65.9 2.0	0.2 nmf 1.3	186.4	19.07 00.03	A unit of INOCO PLC, a British-based real-estate concern				121.1 for 100% at $13/sh	nmf	104	0.65

Gulf Resources & Chemical Corp. said two directors have agreed to sell their 34% stake in the company for $13 a share to a unit of Inoco PLC. The directors, David and Frederick Barclay, will resign from Gulf's board along with Aidan Barclay and Charles Klotz, Gulf said. The $13-a-share price is slightly below the stock's recent trading level of about $13.63 to $14 a share. A Gulf spokesman said it was not known why the men sold their stock below current market price. Gulf said the Inoco transaction, conditioned on clearance under U.S. antitrust law and on other factors, is expected to be completed in about 30 days. Gulf's current assets: $207.3 mm; current liabilities: $41.2 mm; long-term debt: $96.1 mm. Institutions own 29% of Gulf's shares and FMR Corp. owns 14.1%. Stock price one month prior to announcement: $12.875/sh.

1061-FALCONBRIDGE LTD., a nickel mining concern — tse $36.37 (C)

'88	2,123.8	341.1	16.1	1,176.7	15.80	461.8	11.7	2,420.5	5.2	61		1.42
'87	1,339.8	29.7	2.2		4.57	146.0	4.3	for 100%				
'86	1,145.5	d15.5	nmf			d14.6	nmf	at $36.125(C)/sh				

1061-AMAX INC., a natural resource company — nyse $28.375

'88	3,944.0		
'87	3,383.2		
'86	1,307.5		

Amax Inc. has allowed its $2.85 billion (C) offer for Falconbridge Ltd. to expire, leaving the way clear for a competing bid by Noranda Inc. and Sweden's Trelleborg AB. With no other bidder except Noranda in sight, Amax's withdrawal left some speculators facing possible losses. Noranda's vice president and treasurer said the Amax decision was a surprise to the Toronto company and seems to be the end as far as Amax is concerned. Falconbridge's current assets: $749.0 mm; current liabilities: $261.2mm; long-term debt: $761.3 mm. Institutions own 7% of Falconbridge's shares, while Noranda Inc. owns 19.9%; McIntyre Mines Ltd. owns 12.3% and Forstmann-Leff Assoc. Inc. owns 9.6%. Stock price one month prior to announcement $22.75/sh.

1061-FALCONBRIDGE LTD., a nickel mining concern — tse $36.37 (C)

'88	2,123.8	341.1	16.1	1,176.7	15.80	461.8	11.7	2,420.5	5.2	61		1.42
'87	1,339.8	29.7	2.2		4.57	146.0	4.3	for 100%				
'86	1,145.5	d15.5	nmf			d14.6	nmf	at $36.125(C)/sh				

1061-AMAX INC., a natural resource company — nyse $28.375

'88	3,944.0		
'87	3,383.2		
'86	1,307.5		

Amax Inc. has agreed to acquire Falconbridge Ltd. under a proposed tender offer valued at C$36.125 a share. The acquisition would make Amax one of the world's six largest base-metal producers. The agreement came as a surprise to industry analysts who thought it was designed to thwart a year-long creeping takeover of Falconbridge by Noranda Inc., a resource giant indirectly controlled by Toronto financiers Edward and Peter Bronfman. Falconbridge's current assets: $749.0 mm; current liabilities: $261.2mm; long-term debt: $761.3 mm. Institutions own 7% of Falconbridge's shares, while Noranda Inc. owns 19.9%; McIntyre Mines Ltd. owns 12.3% and Forstmann-Leff Assoc. Inc. owns 9.6%. Stock price one month prior to announcement $22.75/sh.

1061-FALCONBRIDGE LTD., a nickel mining concern

'88	2,123.8	341.1	16.1	1,176.7	15.80	2,479.5	7.3
'87	1,339.8	29.7	2.2		4.57	for 100%	117
'86	1,145.5	d15.5	nmf			at $31.49/sh	2.11

NORANDA INC., a natural resource concern, and **TRELLEBORG AB,** a Swedish industrial group

Noranda Inc. and Sweden's Trelleborg AB hastily put together a sweetened offer for Falconbridge after Amax Inc. presented the mining concern with a rival bid. The group's new bid is for $31.49 a share for all of Falconbridge Ltd. shares it doesn't already own. The Amax bid was valued at a total of $2.43 billon. Falconbridge's current assets: $749.0 mm; current liabilities: $261.2mm; long-term debt: $761.3 mm. Institutions own 37% of Falconbridge's shares, while Noranda Inc. owns 19.9%; McIntyre Mines Ltd. owns 12.3% and Forstmann-Leff Assoc. Inc. owns 9.6%. Stock price one month prior to announcement $22.75/sh.

Figure 8.2
Sample Page from *International Merger Yearbook*

Manufacturing

Aerospace and Aircraft

TARGET	SIC	BUYER	VALUE	CURR.
Air Precision SA	3728	FR Group PLC	$2.0	US
Mafr,whl slip rings		Mafr machinery, aircraft parts		Acq. of Assets
France		United Kingdom		Efct: 04/26/89
				Ancd: 04/26/89

FR Group acquired Air Precision of France for 1.2 mil British pounds ($2.0 mil US).

CROSS

TARGET	SIC	BUYER	VALUE	CURR.
Arianespace-Rocket Engine Tech	3764	Brazil	Undisclosed	
Mnfr rocket propulsion units		National government		Acq. of Assets
France		Brazil		Efct: Pending
				Ancd: 07/17/89

Arianespace, the French rocket company, announced negotiations to sell to Brazil the technology to produce large rocket engines, promoting quarries that the sale would give France an unfair advantage in competition for launch business and would violate the spirit of arms-control agreements.

CROSS DIVEST

TARGET	SIC	BUYER	VALUE	CURR.
Avions Marcel Dassault-Breguet	3721	Aerospatiale SA	Undisclosed	
Manufacture jet fighters		Engineering svcs,mnfr aircraft		Merger
France		France		With: 06/28/89
				Ancd: 06/28/89

Aerospatiale withdrew its intention to merge with Avions Marcel Dassault-Breguet Aviation, or the Dassault Group. Although the French government-controlled Aerospatiale had pressured Dassault to merge given Dassault's shrinking market, and the government had held a majority voting state, Dassault used political allies and a reorganization to resist. Dassault had annual profit of 380.1 mil French francs (US$71.4 mil), while Aerospatiale had annual profit of 93 mil francs (US$ 17.5 mil).

TARGET	SIC	BUYER	VALUE	CURR.
Bell Components Ltd	3728	GKN PLC	0.9	STG
Mafr,whl propeller shafts		Mafr auto parts, army vehicles	$1.5	Acq. of Assets
United Kingdom		United Kingdom		Efct: 04/18/89
				Ancd: 04/18/89

TARGET	SIC	BUYER	VALUE	CURR.
Daimler-Benz,Messerschmitt-Nar	3761	Investor Group	Undisclosed	
Missiles, naval strategic sys		Investor group		Acq. of Assets
West Germany				With: 02/05/90
				Ancd: 11/08/89

Daimler-Benz and Messerschmitt-Boelkow-Blohm withdrew from talks to sell their navy and missile technology lines to an investor group including Friedrich Krupp, Salzgitter, Bremer Vulkan, and two smaller shipbuilding companies. State officials in West Germany had insisted that the technology lines be sold prior to Daimler-Benz's acquisition of Messerschmitt Boelkow-Blohm. Thyssen had expressed in the technology lines, but this deal apparently superseded it. It was not stated how Daimler-Benz planned to proceed with the disposal of the lines.

DIVEST

TARGET	SIC	BUYER	VALUE	CURR.
FAC Inc.,Langely Corp	3728	Fleet Aerospace Corp	Undisclosed	
Manufacture aircraft parts		Aircraft parts,radar equipment		Merger
Canada		Canada		Efct: 06/05/89
Drexel Burnham Lambert		Drexel Burnham Lambert		Ancd: 06/05/89

Fleet Aerospace acquired FAC, a unit of Fleet Aerospace Corp, and Langley. Drexel Burnham Lambert acted as financial advisor to Fleet Aerospace Corp.

SFBOR SFLC

TARGET	SIC	BUYER	VALUE	CURR.
Fabrique Nat Herstal-FN Moteur	3724	SNECMA	Undisclosed	
Mnfr aircraft engines, parts		Manufacture aircraft engines		Acq. Maj. Int.
Belgium		France		Efct: 01/16/90
Dillon, Read				Ancd: 06/14/89

Societe Nationale d'Etude et de Construction de Moteurs d'Aviation (SNECMA) acquired a controlling 51% stake in FN Moteurs, a division of Fabrique Nationale Herstal, for an undisclosed amount. Dillon Read initiated the transaction and acted as financial advisor to FN Moteurs.

CROSS DIVEST

TARGET	SIC	BUYER	VALUE	CURR.
Industria de Turbopulsion	3724	Sener,Construcciones,Bazan	Undisclosed	
Manufacture jet engines		Engineering,architectural svcs		Acq. Maj. Int.
Spain		Spain		Ancd: 04/07/89
				Pending

Sener, Construcciones Aeronauticas and Bazaan, all owned by the Spanish Government, were to acquire a 51% stake in Industria de Turbopropulsion (ITP). ITP was capitalized at 6 bil Spanish pesetas ($52 mil US).

GKN acquired Ball Components for 900,000 British pounds ($1.55 mil). GKN made an initial payment of 550,000 pounds ($.94 mil), and was to make further payments of 250,000 pounds ($.43 mil) and 100,000 pounds ($.17 mil) at the ends of 1989 and 1990.

British Aerospace-Missile Div	3761 Thomson-CSF-Guided Missile Div	Undisclosed	Merger
Manufacture guided missiles	Manufacture guided missiles		
United Kingdom	France	Anncd: 10/13/89	Pending

Thomson CSF agreed to combine its guided missile division with that of British Aerospace thus expanding collaboration between the two defense contractors. The new venture, to be called Eurodynamics, was expected to have annual sales of at least $2.2 bil. A final agreement on the combination was reached in January 1990, and gained the approval of both the British and the French governments.

CROSS

Bronzavia Air Equipment	3721 Undisclosed Acquiror	Undisclosed	Acq. of Assets
Mnfr aircraft, aircraft parts	Undisclosed Acquiror		
France	Unknown	Anncd: 06/30/89	Efct: 06/30/89

An undisclosed acquiror acquired the Bronzavia Air Equipement unit of Thomson's Thomson-CSF.

DIVEST

Casa(Instituto Nacional de	3721 Instituto Nacional Industria	Undisclosed	Acq. Part. Int.
Manufacture aircraft	Mnfr industrial equip; hold co		
Spain	Spain	Anncd: 05/05/89	Pending

INI disclosed that it planned to raise its holding in Casa from 73% to 88% through a capital increase.

PRIVNEG

Daimler-Benz,Messerschmitt-Nev	3761 Blohm & Voss AG(Thyssen AG)	Undisclosed	Acq. of Assets
Missiles, naval strategic sys	Shipbuilding firm		
West Germany	West Germany	Anncd: 09/25/89	With: 11/08/89

The Blohm & Voss unit of Thyssen expressed interest in acquiring the navy technology activities of Daimler-Benz and Messerschmitt-Bolkow-Blohm that the German government required the companies to sell as part of the Daimler/Messerschmitt merger. Subsequently, however, an investor group including Fried. Krupp, Salzgitter, and Bremer Vulkan agreed to acquire the technologies.

DIVEST

Industria de Turbopropulsion	3724 Rolls-Royce PLC	Undisclosed	Acq. Part. Int.
Manufacture jet engines	Mnfr turbines and jet engines		
Spain	United Kingdom	Anncd: 04/07/89	Pending

Rolls Royce was to acquire a 45% interest in Industria de Turbopropulsion (ITP). Three state-owned companies were also to take a 51% stake in ITP. ITP was capitalized at 6 bil Spanish pesetas ($52 mil US).

CROSS PRIVNEG

Lucas Inds PLC-Aerostructures	3728 Societe de Construction Avion	Undisclosed	Acq. of Assets
Mnfr thrust reversers,housings	Manufacture aircraft		
United Kingdom	France	Anncd: 06/13/89	Pending

Societe de Construction des Avion Hurel-Dubois agreed to acquire the aerostructures business of Lucas Industries. The transaction was expected to close by the end of July 1989.

CROSS DIVEST

Marston Palmer-Fuel Tank Bus	3728 Westland Group PLC	1.3 STG	Acq. of Assets
Manufacture fuel tanks	Mnfr and service helicopters	$2.3	
United Kingdom	United Kingdom	Anncd: 02/08/89	Efct: 02/08/89

Westland Group acquired the jig built fuel tank business of Marston Palmer from IMI for 1.3 mil British pounds ($2.26 mil).

DIVEST

Matra SA-Space Systems Bus	3761 Shareholders	Undisclosed	Acquisition
Manufacture aerospace products	Shareholders		
France	United States	Anncd: 10/10/89	Pending

Matra planned to spin off its space systems business into a separate subsidiary as a prelude to the creation of a joint venture between GEC's Marconi Space Systems and Matra.

CROSS DIVEST SPINOFF

Salver Co	3728 CIBA-GEIGY AG	Undisclosed	Acq. Maj. Int.
Mnfr aerospace materials,parts	Mnfr, whl pharmaceutical prod		
Italy	Switzerland	Anncd: 09/08/89	Efct: 09/08/89

CIBA-GEIGY acquired a majority stake in Salver, which had been family owned before the acquisition. Terms were not disclosed.

CROSS

151

Figure 8.3
Sample Page from *Mergerstat Review*

INDUSTRIES ATTRACTING FOREIGN BUYERS
1985 - 1989

Seller Industry Category	1985	1986	Number of transactions 1987	1988	1989	Five-Year Cumulative
Miscellaneous Services	11	18	10	31	21	91
Printing & Publishing	13	16	6	14	19	68
Electronics	4	11	7	9	16	47
Chemicals, Paints & Coatings	20	18	12	12	15	77
Banking & Finance	9	7	10	8	13	47
Drugs, Medical Supplies & Equipment	12	14	8	14	12	60
Wholesale & Distribution	10	8	8	10	12	48
Food Processing	8	11	7	17	11	54
Leisure & Entertainment	3	7	6	6	11	33
Oil & Gas	8	4	5	5	10	32
Brokerage, Invst & Mngt Consulting Svcs.	4	2	6	9	9	30
Retail	9	11	15	9	9	53
Office Equipment & Computer Hardware	5	8	6	5	8	32
Plastics & Rubber	3	5	7	4	8	27
Toiletries & Cosmetics	2	2	2	6	7	19
Automotive Products & Accessories	2	3	2	3	7	17
Primary Metal Processing	3	4	7	5	7	26
Beverages	2	2	6	5	6	21
Health Services	1	2	2	0	6	11
Industrial & Farm Equipment & Machinery	7	8	12	24	6	57
Insurance	6	11	3	7	6	33
Computer Software Supplies & Services	5	9	5	12	5	36
Electrical Equipment	6	9	4	12	5	36

Industry						Total
Real Estate	3	1		4	5	11
Cnstr Contractors & Engineering Svcs.		2	2	2	4	13
Communications		2	6	3	4	9
Fabricated Metal Products	2	5	6	9	4	26
Instruments & Photographic Equipment	6	13	9	13	4	45
Mining & Minerals	2	5	1	2	4	14
Aerospace, Aircraft & Defense	2	4	2	4	3	16
Apparel		4	4	3	3	12
Household Goods	1	6	2	3	3	17
Packaging & Containers	4	4	6	1	3	14
Stone, Clay & Glass	5	12	6	9	3	35
Textiles			3	8	3	14
Toys & Recreational Products	1		1	3	3	8
Agricultural Production	2	1	1		2	6
Cnstr, Mining & Oil Field Machinery & Equip.	1	2	4		2	9
Transportation	1	3	3	4	2	13
Building Products & Materials	2	3	3	3	1	9
Electric, Gas, Water & Sanitary Services	1		1	1	1	4
Timber & Forest Products	1				1	2
Valves, Pumps & Hydraulics		3	3	2	1	9
Autos & Trucks	2			1		3
Broadcasting	1	1	1	1		4
Conglomerate	1	3	2	1		7
Energy Services	1					1
Furniture		1		2		3
Miscellaneous Manufacturing	2		6			8
Paper	3	2		1		6
Totals	197	264	220	307	285	1273

SOURCE: MERGERSTAT REVIEW

Figure 8.4
Sample Page from *Mergers & Acquisitions*

Foreign Investment in the U.S.

01-09 AGRICULTURE, FORESTRY, FISHING

Ranks Hovis McDougal PLC	acq.	Sunstar Foods Inc.
Windsor, Berkshire, England		Minneapolis, MN
Revenues: $2,841,626,000		Revenues: $26,572,000
Net Inc.: $138,284,000		Net Loss: $5,075,000
Year End: 9-3-88		Year End: 8-26-89

Terms: Sunstar Foods sold substantially all of its assets to Ranks Hovis McDougal for an undisclosed consideration. Sunstar shareholders also approved a plan of liquidation under which Sunstar will distribute its assets to shareholders over a period of time.

Principals: Ranks Hovis McDougal, through subsidiaries, is primarily engaged in the manufacturing, processing, and marketing of a wide range of food products in the U.S., U.K., Europe, the Far East, and Australia. Its RHM Holdings (USA) Inc. unit is the holding company for Ranks Hovis McDougal's U.S. subsidiaries. The operations of Sunstar Foods consist of its consumer food division, based in Streator, Ill. Its products include honey, peanut butter, syrup, vanilla, and nonalcoholic drink mixes sold through supermarkets in 30 states and food ingredient products sold to major food

Principals: LAC Minerals is engaged in gold mining, and oil and gas exploration and development activities in Canada and the U.S. It is one of the largest gold producing companies in Canada. It expects to produce about 400,000 ounces in 1989. In 1988, it spent an average of $260 to produce an ounce of gold. Bond International is a gold mining company 65-percent owned by companies controlled by Alan Bond, an Australian financier. It currently produces 16,800 kilograms of gold, 32,000 metric tons of copper, and 42,000 kilograms of silver per year. In fiscal 1988, which ended March 31, gold production totaled 342,833 ounces. In 1988, it spent an average of $204 to produce an ounce of gold at mines in North and South America and in Australia. It owns an 83-percent stake in the El Indio mine in Chile, which had 1988 production costs of below $100 an ounce. Dallhold Investments Pty. owns a 58-percent holding and Bell Resources Ltd. holds a 7-percent stake.

Effective Date: 11-15-89

Placer Dome Inc.	acq.	U.S. Gold Corp.
Vancouver, British Columbia, Canada	add.	Denver, CO
Revenues: $660,585,000	int.	Revenues: $9,138,000
Net Inc.: $219,943,000		Net Inc.: $1,628,000
		Year End: 12-31-88

154

companies and bakeries. Upon completion of the sale, Sunstar was to change its name to SUNF Inc.

Effective Date: 12-18-89

10 METAL MINING

Brascan Ltd.	acq.	M. A. Hanna Co.
Toronto, Ontario, Canada	int.	Cleveland, OH
Revenues: $502,585,000		Revenues: $1,019,020,000
Net Inc.: $220,279,000		Net Inc.: $83,223,000
Year End: 12-31-88		Year End: 12-31-88

Terms: Norcen Energy Resources Ltd. sold its 28-percent stake in the outstanding common stock of M. A. Hanna to Brascan for $213 million (Canadian), the equivalent of $182.6 million (U.S.). The holding of 7.7 million M. A. Hanna common shares formed part of the consideration paid by Norcen Energy Resources for the purchase of Westmin Resources Ltd.'s oil and gas assets.

Principals: Brascan is an investment holding company engaged in mining natural resources, manufacturing consumer products, and financial services. It is controlled by the Bronfman family of Toronto, which indirectly controls Norcen Energy Resources and Westmin Resources Ltd. M. A. Hanna is engaged in custom compounding of rubber and plastic polymers and mixes polymers, resins, fillers, and additives. It is the largest distributor of basic plastic shapes, such as sheets, rods, and tubes and is a leading producer of custom formulated colorants and additives for plastic and rubber products. It produces oil, gas, and iron ore pellets and provides insurance services.

Effective Date: 12-1-89

LAC Minerals Ltd.	acq.	Bond International Gold
Toronto, Ontario, Canada	maj.	Inc.
Revenues: $174,221,000	int.	Denver, CO
Net Inc.: $38,409,000		Revenues: $58,547,000
Year End: 12-31-88		Net Loss: $18,656,000
		Year End: 6-30-88

Terms: LAC Minerals acquired the 65-percent stake in Bond International Gold held by Alan Bond for $10 per share, or 373.8 million. The transaction had been subject to regulatory approval and other customary approvals.

Year End: 12-31-88

Terms: Placer Dome increased its holding in U.S. Gold to 22 percent from 16 percent through the exercise of an option to convert a $4.5 million debenture into three million U.S. Gold common shares at $1.50 each.

Principals: Placer Dome engages in the mining of gold, silver, copper, and molybdenum. It also explores for and develops oil and natural gas properties mainly in western Canada and the southern U.S. It operates 10 gold mines in Canada, the U.S., New Guinea, and Australia. At December 31, 1988, it produced 811,606 ounces of gold and 206,238 ounces of copper and silver. It also produced 2.7 million barrels of oil and 16,700 trillion cubic feet of natural gas. U.S. Gold is engaged in the exploration for and mining of gold and silver. At December 31, 1988, it had interests in four mining properties, the Tonkin Springs Gold Project in Eureka County, Nev., the White Pine Project in White Pine County, Nev., the Dee Gold Mine in Elko County, Nev., and the Hayden Hill prospect in Lassen County, Calif. It produced 23,440 ounces of gold and 274 ounces of silver in 1988.

Effective Date: 11-6-89

13 OIL AND GAS EXTRACTION

Mercury Asset	acq.	Energy Ventures Inc.
Management PLC	add.	Houston, TX
London, England	int.	Revenues: $54,191,000
Revenues: $169,487,000		Net Inc.: $882,000
Net Inc.: $49,404,000		Year End: 12-31-88
Year End: 3-31-39		

Terms: Mercury Asset Management increased its holding in the outstanding common stock of Energy Ventures to 15.9 percent from 10.1 percent. The additional 5.8-percent stake, valued at about $5.1 million, includes net purchases of 32,300 shares purchased at prices ranging from $38 to $50 per share between September 19 and October 23, 1989. As a result of the transaction, Mercury Asset holds 369,300 Energy Ventures common shares.

Principals: Mercury Asset Management manages portfolio investments for investment clients and provides advisory services. Energy Ventures is engaged in oil and gas exploration and production. It provides workover and completion services on offshore rigs. It also manufactures downhole sucker rod pumps and downhole packers.

Effective Date: 10-23-89

firm as a party. A companion publication of the *Report* is the *Acquisition/ Divestiture Weekly* newsletter. Also published by Quality Service, the *Weekly* provides timely, thorough, and detailed reporting of international transactions. Several of the M&A newsletters discussed in Chapter 2 for monitoring should be useful for following cross-border deals.

Mergers & Acquisitions International

While *Mergers & Acquisitions* has a distinct U.S. perspective, *Mergers & Acquisitions International*, which is published by Financial Times Business Information in London, has a United Kingdom/European emphasis. This monthly journal provides information on U.K. private and public companies, whether pending, completed, or terminated. There are also detailed sections for areas outside the United Kingdom, and here transactions involving U.S. and European firms are recorded. Deals are indexed by company name and country, both for acquirers and targets.

Other Journal Sources

M&A Europe is a companion publication of *Mergers & Acquisitions*. Both are published by MLR Publishing in Philadelphia. *M&A Europe* focuses on deal activity among European firms. Although articles make up the bulk of the journal, lists of deals and statistical analyses of deal activity are included. *M&A Europe* is also available as a full-text database on the LEXIS Service, in the EUROPE Library.

A non-U.S. perspective on deal activity may be found in the center section of each issue of *Multinational Business*. Published by The Economist in London, the "Acquisitions and Mergers" report provides a summary of major deals in Europe, the United Kingdom, the United States, and other major countries (Japan, Canada, the Mideast).

A more specialized annual report on European merger and acquisition activity is found in the February issue of *Euromoney*. Published by Euromoney Publications PLC, the reports in this magazine emphasize advisor activity. A representative table ranks advisors by all completed deals for European countries buying into the United Kingdom. There are also summary statistical tables on cross-border deals by nation, industry, and deal value. *Euromoney* does not provide specific information for each transaction.

ONLINE DATABASES FOR INTERNATIONAL M&A

Chapter 5 introduced databases for monitoring M&A activity, screening for deal candidates, researching specific transactions, and identifying deals by specific criteria. Most of the databases we described apply to the research of international M&A.

In addition to the general business and newswire databases that are useful for monitoring domestic and global deal activity, there are others that cover developments in non-U.S. countries. These files may be more useful when tracking cross-border M&A activity that does not involve a U.S. firm. DIALOG offers several databases covering business developments in regions and countries outside the United States.

ASIA-PACIFIC (DIALOG File 30) specializes in business events in the Pacific Rim regions. This file is updated biweekly and covers the period from 1985 to the present. It provides abstracts or citations for news items. There are some search codes that may be useful. For example, use the "CN" prefix to search by specific countries. There is also a descriptor for M&A activity; the term "acquisitions" is used. In this database, M&A activity can also be identified by use of foreign investment codes. For example, to locate articles about deal activity in Thailand, the code "FITHAI" would be used to identify information related to foreign investment in Thailand. This could locate articles on other corporate change as well, such as joint ventures. Example 8.1 shows a search using the foreign investment codes.

CANADIAN BUSINESS AND CURRENT AFFAIRS (DIALOG File 262) provides indexing to over 200 Canadian business periodicals and ten newspapers. The file is updated monthly and covers 1982 to the present. This is an index only; there are no abstracts. There is a descriptor for M&A ("Corporate Acquisitions and Mergers") that can be used to increase search precision. When using the database for monitoring, use the DIALOG update (UD =) search technique discussed in Chapter 3 to limit your search to more recent material. Example 8.2 shows a search free text searching. Note that the first citation indicates a descriptor for searching M&A.

EXTEL INTERNATIONAL NEWS CARDS (DIALOG File 501) provides news and basic company information on quoted, major unquoted, and other large international companies. Stories are written by Extel based on information received from firms in the United Kingdom, other European countries, the Pacific Rim, and the Middle East. It is updated weekly, and covers 1989 to the present. There are no special codes related to M&A, but there are country codes. Example 8.3 is a sample record from the database.

FINANCIAL TIMES FULLTEXT (DIALOG File 622) provides the complete text of all articles published in the London and International editions of the *Financial Times* newspaper. This file is updated weekly, and goes back to 1986. There are no descriptors, but there is a "lead paragraph" field tag, so terms like "merger" or "acquisition" can be searched as they appear in lead paragraphs. Example 8.4 shows a search.

JAPAN ECONOMIC NEWSWIRE PLUS (DIALOG File 612) provides the complete text of English language news releases provided by Kyodo

Example 8.1
A Search Using ASIA-PACIFIC

```
ss fithai/de [search the code for foreign investment in Thailand]

    S1      398   FITHAI/DE [there are 398 articles with this
                            code]

?ss s1 and cn=japan and cn=thailand [combine the first set with
                            the country codes for Japan and Thailand to
                            identify articles involving companies in
                            these two countries]

            398   S1
    S2    57819   CN=JAPAN
    S3     5543   CN=THAILAND
    S4      121   S1 AND CN=JAPAN AND CN=THAILAND
?ss s4 and (merger or acquisitions) [there were 121 articles
                            meeting the search criteria, so it is further
                            limited to those articles mentioning a merger
                            or acquisitions]

            121   S4
    S5      282   MERGER
    S6     3688   ACQUISITIONS
    S7        4   S7 AND (MERGER OR ACQUISITIONS)

?t7/3/1-2 [display the first two article citations from the set]


    10/3/1

    09217263   DIALOG File 30: ASIA-PACIFIC
    "Airborne  Express  Venture  [in  venture  with Mitsui & Co Ltd.
    to acquire Griffin Associates Co., an air freight company based
    in Thailand]", in Wall Street Journal, June 29, 1990. p. A4.
    [TXT] LANGUAGE: English

    10/3/2

    09214577   DIALOG File 30: ASIA-PACIFIC
    "Thai  Joint  Venture  Plant  For  Guardian  Industries Cleared
    [with Siam Cement Co., B3 billion, $16.6 million glass plant
    approved; plant ends near monopoly  of Thai-Asahi Glass Co.]", in
    Wall Street Journal, June 29, 1990. p. B3A. White, Helen E.
    LANGUAGE: English
```

News Service of Tokyo. It includes general as well as business news. The file is updated daily, and covers the period 1984 to the present. This is a source for corporate change developments in Pacific Rim nations (as they relate to Japan), but also gives access to important global business events. The file has no special descriptors or codes for M&A searching. Example 8.5 is a sample search.

INFOMAT INTERNATIONAL BUSINESS (DIALOG File 583) is produced by Infomat Ltd., a Predicasts company. This file has concise abstracts of articles on products, markets, companies, and business events from over 400 business newspapers and journals translated into English. Its principal focus is Europe and Third World countries. The file is updated weekly and covers 1984 to the present. As with most Predicasts files, INFOMAT has event codes, but there is not a specific code for

Example 8.2
A CANADIAN BUSINESS AND CURRENT AFFAIRS Search

```
?ss merger? or acquisition? [free text search of two terms,
                            truncated with the question mark]

        S1    10656   MERGER?
        S2    10103   ACQUISITION?
        S3    12356   MERGER? OR ACQUISITION? [there are 12,356
                      documents with either term]

?e co=abit [in this example we want to find deals involving
            the Abitibi Price company of Canada.  Here we use
            the DIALOG "expand" command to locate the most
            correct spelling of the company name.]


Ref   Items   Index-term
E1       1    CO=ABICOM LTD.
E2       1    CO=ABIGNANO INDUSTRIES LTD
E3       0   *CO=ABIT
E4       7    CO=ABITIBI ASBESTOS MINING CO LTD
E5       5    CO=ABITIBI METAL MINES LTD
E6       3    CO=ABITIBI METAL MINES LTD.
E7       1    CO=ABITIBI PRICE LUMBER LTD
E8       1    CO=ABITIBI RESOURCES INC
E9      20    CO=ABITIBI RESOURCES LTD
E10      1    CO=ABITIBI RESOURCES LTD.
E11    300    CO=ABITIBI-PRICE INC
E12    142    CO=ABITIBI-PRICE INC.

        Enter P or E for more
?s e11 [select variation E11 from the expand list]

        S4      300   CO="ABITIBI-PRICE INC"

?ss s3 and s4 [combine the merger/acquisition set with
               documents about Abitibi Price]

        12356   S3
          300   S4
        S5    8   S3 AND S4 [there are eight documents]

?t5/5/1-2 [display documents one and two]

   5/5/1
   01881620
   COMPANY: Abitibi-Price Inc; Datarex Systems Inc
   Abitibi-Price Inc - Datarex Systems Inc // Acquisition/Merger
   Globe and Mail (Toronto) - Metro Edition  April 26, 1988 pg B12
   DESCRIPTORS: Corporate acquisitions and mergers - By company

   5/5/2
   1741515
   COMPANY: Abitibi-Price Inc
   Abitibi-Price Inc. seeks acquisition in United States
   Halifax Chronicle Herald  July 2, 1987 pg 52
   SPECIAL FEATURES: Canadian Press NewsFile
```

M&A. Predicasts country codes are available. Example 8.6 is a sample search using country codes.

DIALOG has other general business databases that, although of U.S. origin, have international coverage of the business literature that may prove useful in cross-border M&A research. Predicasts PROMT (File 16) is a good example. It provides abstracts and full-text records for about 1,500 of the world's important trade and business journals, newspapers,

Example 8.3
An EXTEL INTERNATIONAL NEWS CARDS Record

```
BLENHEIM EXHIBITIONS GROUP PLC
Country: England  (EN)

EXTEL Services: UK Listed Companies
EXTEL Company Number: EXT003078
SEDOL Number: 0104559
Topic Code: BEH

                        GROUP ORGANIZATION
Acquisition
On 2-5-90, and in accordance with acquisition agreement, a
further consideration of L206,910 in cash was paid to vendors of
business and assets of Southern and Sussex Craft Exhibitions Ltd
and Maw Promotions Ltd. Total consideration was therefore
L540,243 in cash.

                            DIVIDEND
Dividend
Interim dividend of 6p (4p) per share for year to 31-8-90 payable
27-7-90 to holders registered 13-7-90 (xd 25-6-90).

                   PROFIT AND LOSS ACCOUNTS
Interim Results
Interim results to 28-2-90, figs in Lm: Turnover 51.0 (15.0).
Interest payable 0.6 (nil). Profit before tax 14.5 (3.5). Tax 5.5
(1.2). Net profit 9.0 (2.3). EPS 40.7p (15.2p).
Analysis of turnover in Lm: UK 10.5 (7.1), France 31.5 (4.5),
Germany 6.6 (3.4), Switzerland 0.3 (nil), USA 1.6 (nil), Belgium
0.5 (nil), total 51.0 (15.0). Chairman states that organic growth
continues at a good level across the spectrum of group. Growth
was supplemented in first half year by significant first time
contribution from 5 major exhibitions, of which 2 are biennial.
Timing and scale of these events will cause profits in
current year to be heavily biased towards first half, but
Directors anticipate another successful outcome. Overall,
bookings for exhibitions to be held in the next 12 months are
buoyant.
   Section Heading(s): Acquisition;  Dividend;  Interim Results
```

Source: Extel Financial News Cards (Dialog File 501). Reproduced with kind permission of Extel Financial Ltd. © Extel Financial Ltd 1991. A UK Company registered in London No. 949387.

analysts' reports, press releases, and annual reports. Nearly 50 percent of the information in PROMT is international in scope. The file is updated daily, goes back to 1972, and features Predicasts' comprehensive product searching code scheme. There is also a code for M&A acquisitions. Example 8.7 shows a sample search.

Although it is not a news and event-oriented database like PROMT, international M&A researchers should also investigate the ABI/INFORM file (available on BRS and the NEXIS Service as well as DIALOG). Its abstracts of articles from over 500 business journals and magazines provide overviews, analyses, and case studies of global business developments. There is a descriptor for M&A and geographic descriptors to help country searching. For scholarly research articles, ABI/INFORM is an excellent source as it covers many academic journals.

DOW JONES NEWS/RETRIEVAL (DJNR) offers several databases applicable to the research and monitoring of cross-border M&A activity. The "menus" files in DJNR provide limited access to business informa-

Example 8.4
A FINANCIAL TIMES FULLTEXT Search

```
ss acquisition? or merger? [free text search of terms]

        S1    21111   ACQUISITION?
        S2    11667   MERGER?
        S3    29126   ACQUISITION? OR MERGER?

?ss s3 and france and germany [refine search to identify
    documents that relate to merger and acquisition
    activity between French and West German firms]

              29126   S3
        S4    18469   FRANCE
        S5    20504   GERMANY
        S6     1154   S3 AND FRANCE AND GERMANY [there are too many
                          documents that meet the search criteria,
                          so we further refine the search]

?ss s3 and france(15n)germany [locate documents where france
                          and germany occur together within 15 words]

              29126   S3
        S7    18469   FRANCE
        S8    20504   GERMANY
        S9     4814   FRANCE(15N)GERMANY
        S10     676   S3 AND FRANCE(15N)GERMANY [there are still many
                          many documents; here is a sample]
?t10/5/1
```

Sweden 5: Aggressive buying spree: Profile: Nobel Industries
Financial Times 90.07.03 London Page 5 (V): S45 Survey
Special Feature: Company; Photograph; In Survey
Word Count: 781

Author: JOHN BURTON

TEXT:
  THE principal shareholder of Nobel Industries and its new
chairman, Mr Erik Penser, vowed several years ago that the
chemicals and armaments conglomerate would be one of Sweden's
five biggest companies by the end of 1991. The company already
has achieved the distinction of being one of the country's
fastest growing industrial concerns during the second half of the
1980s after its creation out of a 1984 merger between the defence
concern Bofors and the chemicals group Kema Nobel. A string of
acquisitions totalling SKr16bn had tripled Nobel's size by the
end of last year, making it Sweden's 18th largest company with
sales of SKr22bn.
.
.
.

  The Dollars 107m purchase of the European skin and hair care
operations of Gillette has broadened Nobel's marketing of
chemical-based consumer products into southern Europe from its
operations in Sweden, **France** and West **Germany**. More acquisitions
in this business area are expected. Nobel has deviated from its
emphasis on chemicals in one respect by building up its
high-technology subsidiary, Pharos. The separately-listed
concern, in which Nobel has an 80 per cent shareholding, has seen
its turnover triple in the last few months to SKr4bn.

Example 8.5
A JAPAN ECONOMIC NEWSWIRE PLUS Search

```
?ss sony(7n)cbs and acqui? [search for documents that discuss
                           the Sony acquisition of CBS]

        S1     3502   SONY
        S2      175   CBS
        S3       29   SONY(7N)CBS
        S4     1795   ACQUI?
        S5       10   SONY(7N)CBS AND ACQUI?

?t5/3/1-2


  15/3/1
  0605250
SONY AND WARNER END ROW OVER HOLLYWOOD PRODUCERS
Dateline: New York     Date: November 16, 1989   Word Count: 183

  15/3/2
  0601265
U.S. CONGRESSWOMAN URGES BAN ON SONY-COLUMBIA DEAL
Dateline: Washington     Date: October 1, 1989   Word Count: 210
```

Example 8.6
An INFOMAT INTERNATIONAL BUSINESS Search

```
?ss takeover? or acquisition? or merger?

        S1     7190   TAKEOVER?
        S2    14932   ACQUISITION?
        S3     6525   MERGER?
        S4    26577   TAKEOVER? OR ACQUISITION? OR MERGER?

?ss s4 and germany and france

       26577   S5
        S6    57379   GERMANY
        S7    44346   FRANCE
        S8      529   S5 AND GERMANY AND FRANCE

?t8/3/1-2

  8/3/1
  0867853
     SPAIN - URBIS TO INCREASE CAPITAL AFTER MERGER
     Cinco Dias (CDS)   June 13, 1990   (Page 10)

  8/3/2
  0867831
     FRANCE - CONCERN VOICED OVER MERGERS IN AVIATION FIELD
     Financial Times (FT)   June 26, 1990   (Page X)


  8/5/2
  0867831
     FRANCE - CONCERN VOICED OVER MERGERS IN AVIATION FIELD
     Financial Times (FT)   June 26, 1990   (Page X)
```

The French airline field has courted controversy over the past 12 months, with concern from smaller airlines and competition authorities in the European Commission. Air France took control in January 1990 of UTA, the only leading privately owned airline in France. The transaction established the third largest airline in the West and the largest in Europe and puts Air France in a prominent position, with its linkup with Lufthansa (W Germany), national airline, in mind. Article assesses the state of the French airline field, amid concern over the trend towards alliances and mergers.

```
   PRODUCT: General Aviation (AVGA)
   EVENT:   General Business & Commercial (BUS)
   COUNTRY: France (FRA); European Economic Community (EEC)
```

Example 8.7
A PROMT Search

```
ss ec=15 and cc=4fra and cc=4wge [combine the event code for M&A
                                   with the country codes for France and
                                   West Germany]

        S1   212015   EC=15   (ACQUISITIONS & MERGERS)
        S2    71481   CC=4FRA  (FRANCE)
        S3    80239   CC=4WGE  (WEST GERMANY)
        S4      241   EC=15 AND CC=4FRA AND CC=4WGE

?t4/4/1

   4/4/1
02581272
France: France's Aerospatiale and West Germany's Deutsche Aerospace

EuroBusiness    April 00, 1990    p. 52
ISSN: 0953-0711

        Aerospatiale and Deutsche Aerospace have agreed to merge
   their helicopter activities, but need to settle several problems
   before the marriage. Aerospatiale is 2X as big as Deutsche
   Aerospace, its suitor, and had sales of F6.65 bil in 1989 vs F3
   bil for Deutsche. Also, Aerospatiale at first wanted 80% of the
   new company, with Deutsche owning the remaining 20%. Aerospatiale
   has now agreed to a 60-40 deal but wants Deutsche to pay a
   'dowry.' Lastly, the French govt wants the German govt to make a
   commitment on the M-90 military transport helicopter, mainly
   because its development will be crucial to the joint venture. The
   Germans originally agreed to contribute 25% to the project but
   unofficially have said they will not pay more than 21%. Any less
   of a contribution could endanger the program and the
   Aerospatiale-Deutsche Aerospace merger.
```

tion. Searches must be done with company names, ticker symbols, or news codes. There are three foreign origin files in the menu portion of DJNR. JAPAN ECONOMIC DAILY (//KYODO) is comparable in content to the JAPAN ECONOMIC NEWSWIRE on DIALOG, although it has a more limited search system on DJNR. DJNR provides access to the current day's information plus four earlier editions. The top economic, political, and business stories from Japan are retrievable through menus. Summaries are provided, but the full text may be found in the TEXT segment of DJNR. DJNR news codes do not work in JAPAN ECONOMIC NEWSWIRE.

CORPORATE CANADA ONLINE (//CANADA) is useful for searching over 2,200 public and private Canadian firms. Most of the information available is financial and unrelated to M&A. One menu selection in the database will provide recent news articles from *The Globe and Mail*, Canada's national newspaper. For global company news try INTERNATIONAL DOW JONES NEWS (//DJINS). This file is updated continuously, and stories coded with a ticker symbol are retained for six months. Locate your company's ticker in the SYMBOL database on DJNR, and then use it to retrieve a list of all stories in the database. Limited code searching is available. For example, the DJNR news code for mergers will not work, but the country codes (e.g., R/GE for Germany) are operable. DJNR users should consider the various files available in the

TEXT portion of DJNR. With access to the full text of the *Wall Street Journal*, including European and Asian editions and hundreds of other business publications, stories on cross-border M&A activity are likely to be located in TEXT. The primary advantage of TEXT searching is that more sophisticated keyword search techniques are available.

A lesser known databank in the United States is DATA-STAR. It provides access to familiar business databases, including Predicasts and the ABI/INFORM file. However, DATA-STAR is a Swiss-based system and offers databases unique to Europe. For example, there are several company directory files, not available on other databanks, that could be applicable for identifyng acquisition targets. A weakness of DATA-STAR is a lack of business news files providing unique coverage of European developments. Despite this weakness, DATA-STAR is worth considering for international M&A research.

INTERNATIONAL ASPECTS OF SPECIALIZED M&A DATABASES

Earlier we discussed the features of several specialized M&A databases. These included ADP's M&A DATA BASE, SDC's MERGERS AND CORPORATE TRANSACTIONS, and IDD's M&A DATABASE (on DIALOG). The majority of the transactions found in these three databases involve a U.S. company, and many of these are strictly domestic deals. Each file does track cross-border deals to varying degrees, and offers search techniques to identify deals involving firms of particular countries or regions.

While each of the databases can be used to identify cross-border deals, there are some subtle differences in their coverage. All track cross-border activity involving either a U.S. target or acquirer. However, only SDC and IDD may be used to identify deals in which both target and acquirer are non-U.S. companies. ADP, by nature of its coverage, includes only transactions where a U.S. company is one of the parties. Therefore, identifying deals between England and Japan would be possible only in the M&A databases of SDC and IDD. All three databases have different dates of coverage.

An important criterion in selecting a database is ease of use. These files offer completely different search languages and approaches to information retrieval. SDC is a menu-driven system that is easy to master, although navigating the menus is sometimes time-consuming when a search involves multiple variables. SDC's response time is noticeably fast, however, so total search time is comparable to that of a command-driven system. ADP is a command-driven system that requires some time to learn, even for experienced searchers. ADP offers a software front-end ("INQUERY") that provides menu access to all of its data-bases. The version of IDD available on DIALOG is also command-driven. IDD is more accessible to those familiar with DIALOG and will be easier to search. Yet although it can perform many types of searches it is not as sophisticated as ADP, nor do the individual records provide as much deal data as ADP and SDC. For example, a typical record in ADP may provide as many as 400 data items while a record in the IDD file yields no more than 200. All three offer the user a choice of preformatted reports, such as a deal overview report, or the option to create custom-ized reports. Some sample searches follow.

Example 8.8 shows an SDC search.

Since we plan to base our search on the countries of the acquirer and target, we need to identify the appropriate usage for each country name (they can be obtained from the user manuals for both SDC and ADP). For example, a search for "United Kingdom" will not work because the correct name to use is "Great Britain." In DIALOG we can do this by ex-panding on the country name with the appropriate code for acquiring or target country. The codes are "CN" for target and "AN" for acquirer. The EXPAND command will provide a list of country names and show us the correct usage. Example 8.9 is a sample expand list for the com-mand E CN = A, just to illustrate the beginning of the list for target countries.

IDD's coverage of cross-border deals begins later than SDC's. While deals involving a U.S. target are covered back to 1984, deals involving a non-U.S. target begin in any of three years, depending on the target's country. Deals with U.K. targets are covered from 1984, deals with targets from continental Europe are covered from 1989, and deals with targets from the Pacific Rim are covered from 1989. SDC's coverage of deals involving a non-U.S. target extends back to 1985, regardless of the parent country.

With little accumulation of transactions for continental Europe and the Pacific Rim, the bulk of the non-U.S. cross-border data from IDD's data-base on DIALOG is for deals involving a U.K. target. In our example above, we found 34 deals with a Japanese acquirer and a U.K. target. If we reversed the search and requested a U.K. acquirer and a Japanese target, we would retrieve fewer than 10 deals. Moreover, the informa-tion on deals between two non-U.S. firms is more limited. Most of the deals are between two European firms, with far fewer involving two firms from different continents. The majority of the cross-border deals appear to involve the United States and United Kingdom. For example, there were over 800 deals with a U.K. acquirer and a U.S. target, but only 7 involving a West German acquirer and a French target. Granted, there are more deals between U.S. and U.K. firms. The United States and

Example 8.8
An SDC Search

```
Choose one of the following

1.  Domestic Merger and Corporate Transactions      (US Targets)
2.  International Merger and Corporate Transactions (Non-US Targets)
3.  Combined Domestic and International              (All Targets)
```

[**SDC allows you to limit your retrieval at the start of your search
to either deals for domestic targets or non-U.S. targets. For the
most complete cross-border searching you need to select the
combined file. Why? A deal from menu option two includes U.S.
acquirers (only targets are non-US), so deals with two non-U.S.
parties won't be found there.**]

> 3 [**choose menu option three**]

```
Specify start date, end date for announcement date range
   (e.g. 1/1/88, 6/30/88)
```

> 1/1/90,7/13/90 [**we only want deals between January and July 1990**]

```
Company Information               Transaction Information
  1.  Industry/SIC Codes            12.  Transaction Type
  2.  Specific Deal/Company/Investor 13.  Transaction Value
  3.  Location                      14.  Acquisition Techniques
  4.  Financial Information         15.  Defensive Tactics
  5.  Public Status                 16.  Consideration Offered/Sought
                                    17.  Percent Acquired
Advisor Information                18.  Attitude
  6.  Financial Advisors           19.  Source of Funds
  7.  Financial Advisor Assignments 20.  Effective Date
  8.  Legal Advisors               21.  Announcement Date
  9.  Fee Information               22.  Unconditional Date
 10.  Depositaries/Registrars      23.  Regulatory Agencies
 11.  Information Agents            24.  Status

  A.  All deals in date range    R.  Report/Rank    U.  Utilities
  O.  Screen any other data item Q.  Quick Display  X.  Exit
```

```
Enter a search item, LIST to display selections, MORE for more
   selections, R to print reports, or X to exit
```

> 3 [**We choose option 3 from SDC's menu for selecting your search criteria.
   Since we want to screen primarily by nation of target and acquirer,
   a location search is appropriate**]

```
Select a screening criterion

  1.  Target Company
  2.  Acquiring Company
  3.  Either Target or Acquiring Company
  4.  Target Company's Parent Nation
  5.  Acquiring Company's Parent Nation
  6.  Either Target or Acquiring Company's Parent Nation
  7.  Cross Border Transactions
```

> 4 [**we begin by selecting the target parent country**]

```
Specify nation(s). (see user manual for codes; e.g. US;UK;AU)
```

> UK [**we provide the user code for the United Kingdom**]
Query begins.

```
1070 deals selected from International Mergers deal table.
59 deals selected from Merger/Corporate Transactions deal table.
0 deals selected from Original SDC Mergers, 1979-84 deal table.
Total deals selected:  1129. [there are 1129 deals where the UK
                             is the target's nation]
The current query number is 1.
```

```
Enter a search item, LIST to display selections, R to print reports,
   or X to exit
```

166

Example 8.8 (continued)

```
> list [we type list to redisplay the menu for search options]
```

Company Information	Transaction Information
1. Industry/SIC Codes	12. Transaction Type
2. Specific Deal/Company/Investor	13. Transaction Value
3. Location	14. Acquisition Techniques
4. Financial Information	15. Defensive Tactics
5. Public Status	16. Consideration Offered/Sought
	17. Percent Acquired
Advisor Information	18. Attitude
6. Financial Advisors	19. Source of Funds
7. Financial Advisor Assignments	20. Effective Date
8. Legal Advisors	21. Announcement Date
9. Fee Information	22. Unconditional Date
10. Depositaries/Registrars	23. Regulatory Agencies
11. Information Agents	24. Status

```
A.  All deals in date range    R.  Report/Rank    U.  Utilities
O.  Screen any other data item Q.  Quick Display   X.  Exit

Enter a search item, LIST to display selections, MORE for more
   selections, R to print reports, or X to exit

> 3 [once again we search by location, this type for acquirer]

Select a screening criterion

   1.  Target Company
   2.  Acquiring Company
   3.  Either Target or Acquiring Company
   4.  Target Company's Parent Nation
   5.  Acquiring Company's Parent Nation
   6.  Either Target or Acquiring Company's Parent Nation
   7.  Cross Border Transactions

> 5 [now we will further limit our prior search by screening by
      acquiring company's country]

Specify nation(s). (see user manual for codes; e.g. US;UK;AU)

> JP [we enter the code for Japan]
Query begins.

17 deals selected from International Mergers deal table.
2 deals selected from Merger/Corporate Transactions deal table.
Total deals selected:   19. [there are 19 deals with UK as the target's
                            country and Japan as acquirer's country]
The current query number is 2.

[At this point we would return to the main menu to select options for
 printing a report.  SDC offers preformatted reports, but allows you
 to create reports by selecting specific data items.  The sample report we
 created shows information on the target, acquirer, and their nations]
```

Target Name	Acquiror Name	Acq. Nation	Target Nation
Technitron PLC	Oki Electric Industry Co	JP	UK
LSI Systems Ltd	Japan Digital Laboratories	JP	UK
Triefus PLC	Asahi Corp	JP	UK
JV-Greycoat, Park Tower Realty	Mitsubishi Estate Co	JP	UK

Source: From Securities Data Company's "Mergers and Corporate Transactions Database."
   Copyright 1991. Reprinted with permission of Securities Data Company.

Example 8.9
A DIALOG Expand List and IDD Search

```
Ref    Items   Index-term
E1        2    B4=  1100000000.00
E2        1    B4=  1200000000.00
E3        0    *CN=A
E4      351    CN=AUSTRALIA
E5       26    CN=AUSTRIA
E6        5    CN=BAHRAIN
E7        2    CN=BARBADOS
E8       97    CN=BELGIUM
E9       33    CN=BERMUDA
E10      37    CN=BRAZIL
E11    1637    CN=CANADA
E12       3    CN=CAYMAN ISLANDS
```

[Having expanded to identify the correct form of the countries we want to search, England (target) and Japan (acquirer), we can now begin our search]

?SS CN=GREAT BRITAIN [search for records where the target company's country is England]

```
     S1   10135  CN=GREAT BRITAIN [there are 10,135 deals
                        where a UK company is the target]
```

?SS AR=JAPAN

```
     S2    421  AR=JAPAN [there are 421 deals where a
                        Japanese firm is the acquirer]
```

?SS S1 AND S2

```
          10135  S4
            421  S5
     S6      34  S4 AND S5 [there are 34 deals with a
                        UK target and Japanese acquirer]
```

?T6/3/1-2 [we display the first two deals in the set in an abbreviated format. Note that this format does not show the country names; that name will show in a full format display]

```
  6/3/1
00050063                    This record changed on 06/21/90
Target Company:
---------------
Voyager Travel Holdings

Acquirer Company:
-----------------
Seibu Saison

Deal Specifics:
---------------
Announcement Date:    05/14/90    Deal Value ($MIL):    60.53
Effective Date:       05/14/90
First Offer Date:     05/14/90

Transaction Type:     Acquisition of Partial Interest
Status:               Completed
Attitude:             Friendly

Source of Data:  Financial Times
Supplier ID:  2819901349289A5000
This is an UK record.

  6/3/2
00049324                    This record changed on 05/24/90
Target Company:
---------------
Apricot Computers PLC
Computer Hardware Division

Acquirer Company:
-----------------
Mitsubishi Electric Corp
```

Example 8.9 (continued)

```
Deal Specifics:
---------------
Announcement Date:      04/11/90     Deal Value ($MIL):    63.76
First Offer Date:       04/11/90

Transaction Type:       Acquisition
Status:                 Pending
Attitude:               Friendly

Source of Data:  LSE Company News Service
Supplier ID:   2619901010368A1000
This is an UK record.
```

?T6/5/3 **[display document three in full format]**

```
 6/5/3
00049324                            This record changed on 05/24/90
Target Company:
---------------
Apricot Computers PLC
Computer Hardware Division
FF
Great Britain

CUSIP Number: 0368A1
Parent CUSIP: 01990C

Company is Subsidiary

Target Business Description
---------------------------
Primary SIC Code:       3572
Secondary SIC Codes:    3577

Description of Business:
  Engaged in the manufacture of computer file-servers  and
high-end workstations.

Acquirer Company:
-----------------
Mitsubishi Electric Corp
FF
Japan

DUNS Number: 69-054-3699
CUSIP Number: 606776

Company is Public

Acquirer Business Description
-----------------------------
Primary SIC Code:       3511
Secondary SIC Codes:    3531; 3532; 3549; 3632

Description of Business:
  Turbines and generators for the production of electricity


Deal Specifics:
---------------
Announcement Date:      04/11/90     Deal Value ($MIL):    63.76
First Offer Date:       04/11/90

Transaction Type:       Acquisition
Status:                 Pending
Attitude:               Friendly


Advisor Information:
-------------------
Target Advisors:
  Financial -           Barclays de Zoete Wedd
                        Daiwa Securities
  Legal -               Martineau Johnson
  Accountants -         Peat Marwick McLintock
```

Example 8.9 (continued)

```
Acquirer Advisors:
  Financial -           Kleinwort, Benson
  Legal -               Baker McKenzie
  Accountants -         Ernst & Young

Deal Terms:
-----------
  Apricot Computers PLC has agreed to dispose of its computer
hardware division to the Mitsubishi Electric Corporation, for a
cash consideration of Stg39mil. The division is a major UK based
manufacturer of computer file servers and high-end workstations.
In the year to 31 March 1989, the division made a profit before
group charges and interest of Stg2.49mil on a turnover of
Stg70.76mil.  The hardware division will trade as Apricot
Computers Ltd, a UK subsidiary of Mitsubishi Electric (UK) Ltd.


Techniques:    Divestiture; Cross Border


                        Consideration ($MIL)
---------------------------------------------------------------
Cash:                                                    63.76
---------------------------------------------------------------
Total Dollar Value of Transaction:                       63.76

Target Financials
-----------------
Date of Financials                03/31/89
Total Revenue ($MIL)                118.59
EBIT ($MIL)                           4.17

Source of Financial Data: LSE Company News Service

Deal Value to Target Financials
--------------------------------------------------------
Deal Value/Total Revenue                          0.54

Currencies and Exchange Rates
--------------------------------------------------------
Deal Currency                               Sterling
Deal Exchange Rate($)                        1.63500
Target Currency                             Sterling
Target Exchange Rate($)                      1.67600

Source of Data:  LSE Company News Service
Supplier ID:  2619901010368A1000
This is an UK record.
```

United Kingdom are two of the most active countries. Despite this, cross-border deal activity outside of the United Kingdom and United States is under-represented in IDD, and is less complete than found in SDC.

Example 8.10 shows an ADP search. The use of ADP's M&A DATA BASE should be limited to researching cross-border deals that involve a U.S. firm. Although ADP's command language and search syntax are more complicated than those of the two other systems, searches can be performed quickly when the correct strategy is used. New users can obtain search assistance from the ADP hotline.

Price is an important criterion for comparing databases offering similar information. ADP, SDC, and IDD on DIALOG all have different pricing structures. Search costs are based on any of the following: a per hour connect rate; computer processing time; standard report costs (e.g.,

Example 8.10
An ADP Search

```
* FIN ACNTRY CT 'JAPAN'[ACNTRY is the deal item mneumonic
                       for acquiring company's country.  This search
                       statement translates to "find deals where the
                       ACNTRY field contains the word string 'JAPAN']

366 TRANSACTIONS found in subset # 1 [there are 366 deals in the
                       database where the acquiring company is Japanese
                       In order for these deals to be included, the target
                       of these deals must be a U.S. firm.]

* FIN TCNTRY CT 'ENGLAND' [this is the command to find all deals
                       in the prior set of 366 deals where the target
                       company's nation is England]

0 TRANSACTIONS found in subset # 4 [the result is zero because
                       ADP does not include a deal in the database unless
                       the target is a U.S. company]
```

Source: © Copyright ADP BISG Data Services/MLR Publishing. The ADP/MLR M&A Data Base is jointly researched and updated by ADP BISG Data Services and MLR Publishing. The M&A Data Base is easily accessed through a window-driven PC interface InQuery℠, which also provides push-button access to historical stock price and foreign exchange data, as well as corporate and banking fundamentals. For more information, call 1-800-ADP-DATA.

$10.00 for a summary report per deal); or number of data items reported. Searches can cost several hundred dollars to perform. Online searchers may find some advantage in the database offering predictable costs.

IDD, because it is on DIALOG, offers the "COST" command that provides the cost of the search session as you proceed, much like a taxi's meter. The database is expensive, but the ability to track the cost as the search session occurs can help in meeting cost constraints. ADP does inform the user how much printed data will cost (before a report is displayed) but otherwise it is difficult to determine how much was spent on a total search session immediately after a search was run. Pricing based on connect hours and CPU time makes it difficult to estimate cost. SDC is straightforward in its database pricing. It costs $50 to log on and execute an initial search strategy. There are no costs for connect or CPU time or for additional searches. There are varying fees for standard reports, and data items are charged at $.30 each.

IDD offers a more powerful and complete (more data items, more deals) version of its M&A TRANSACTIONS than is available on DIALOG. This file can be subscribed to directly or the IDD firm will perform custom searches by request. IDD's own version of M&A TRANSACTIONS is available in three subsets that are particularly useful for international research. There is a separate file for deals involving U.K. firms, one specifically for European M&A activity, and a third general database for all cross-border activity. The U.K. transactions database became available in the DIALOG version of IDD in 1990.

IDD also mounts a version of its database on the DATA-STAR system. It is similar in content and record structure to the DIALOG IDD M&A TRANSACTIONS file. One important difference for cross-border M&A research is that the DATA-STAR file is divided into three separate versions, much like the version available directly from IDD. A concatenated version contains over 62,000 deals dating back to 1984, and includes targets and acquirers of many countries. To limit your research to deals involving target companies from specific countries, there are other files that include only U.S. targets (1984 to present), only U.K. targets (1987 to present), or only targets in continental Europe (1989 to present).

DATA-STAR's option of selecting targets within a certain country or continent is useful, and might be faster than IDD's DIALOG file. On close inspection, the DIALOG version does offer some additional data items and searchable fields. Again, in either IDD file, users should pay close attention to the dates of availability of deal information.

A system less familiar to online searchers in the United States is FT INFORMATION ONLINE, a service of the Financial Times. In the United States, FT databases are searched in a system called PROFILE, which is marketed by Knight-Ridder's VU/TEXT system. Here is yet another M&A database covering the details of deals in the United Kingdom, Europe, the United States, and elsewhere. FT MERGERS & ACQUISITIONS INTERNATIONAL is more than a transaction database. It also includes news stories on ongoing deals and rumored deals. Individual records in the databases do not include as much detailed data as the other files discussed. One strong area is financial data. Bid prices, bid premiums, price/earnings multiples, profits forecast, and asset information are included. The FT file does include deals between continental European companies and companies from the Asia/Pacific region.

SCREENING INTERNATIONAL DATABASES FOR
DEAL CANDIDATES

In chapter 6 we discussed the DIALOG databases appropriate for screening domestic acquisition candidates. DIALOG also provides access to international directory databases that may be useful in identifying targets in non-U.S. countries. The majority of these files are country- or region-specific. These files are considerably smaller than the D&B—DUN'S MARKET IDENTIFIERS or TRINET databases that contain more than 6 million firms each. Most of the international directory databases contain hundreds of thousands of companies. Also, the familiar Standard Industrial Classification code may not be available for an industry screening. The text of a business description field can provide clues to the company's industry.

The directory database with the most complete global coverage is D&B—INTERNATIONAL DUN'S MARKET IDENTIFIERS (File 518). It includes businesses in Asia, Africa, the Middle East, South America, Australia, the Pacific Rim, and other countries outside Europe and North America (covered in other D&B files). Despite the world coverage, the file contains only about 200,000 records. As a Dun's file, D-U-N-S number searching is possible. Searching by primary Standard Industrial Classification (SIC) codes or by brief textual business descriptors is available for industry screening. Of course, there is a search prefix (CN) for limiting searches to specific countries. Full country names are used; therefore, expand the name before using it in a search to make sure of the correct spelling or usage. Sales data is given in local and U.S. currency.

D&B—INTERNATIONAL DUN'S MARKET IDENTIFIERS has several special fields that allow the searcher to partition the database by company ownership. For example, you may wish to limit your retrieval to publicly held companies or those that are privately owned. Alternatively, you may wish to drop from your search those companies that are government-controlled. To search by special name use the search prefix "SF" in tandem with the special field (found in the DIALOG documentation). For example, to limit your retrieval to subsidiaries, the command is SF = Subsidiary.

Although more a financial file than a directory, EXTEL INTERNATIONAL FINANCIAL CARDS (File 500) includes information on 7,000 companies in Europe, Australia, Hong Kong, Japan, the Middle East, Thailand, Singapore, and Malaysia. Each company record provides full financial statements plus key financial ratios. You can screen by industry with either primary or secondary SIC codes. The codes, it is important to note, are U.K., not U.S. codes. Countries may be searched by either name or code. Although it is far smaller than a directory file such as INTERNATIONAL DUN'S MARKET IDENTIFIERS, EXTEL offers advantages to those who want to identify acquisition targets according to financial criteria. At best, other directory files may have sales data. EXTEL is far more detailed. It also offers considerably more text, such as the company's Director's Report (from the annual report), which can be searched to identify unusual circumstances.

To search for Canadian or European companies, try Dun's other directory databases. CANADIAN DUN'S MARKET IDENTIFIERS (File 520) covers both public and private firms. Over 350,000 firms are included in the database. Record content and structure are similar to other Dun's databases, with SIC searching, sales in U.S. and Canadian dollars, and D-U-N-S number searching. EUROPEAN DUN'S MARKET IDENTIFIERS (File 521) includes 1.5 million companies selected from 29 European countries. Most Eastern European countries are excluded. Public, private, and government-controlled companies are covered. Because the European DMI was previously included in the INTERNATIONAL MARKET IDENTIFIER'S database, the record content and search features are virtually the same in both files. The European DMI offers the SF category "EEC" for limiting searches to countries in the European Economic Community.

KOMPASS is a recognized name as a provider of directory information for European countries. There are two KOMPASS databases on DIALOG. KOMPASS EUROPE (File 590) covers primarily manufacturing firms in West Germany, Denmark, Norway, Sweden, France, Italy, and the United Kingdom. With a few exceptions, the record content is standard for directory databases. The product codes, which extend to five digits, are not the same as those used in the U.S. SIC manual. However, detailed product code listings, which may be searched textually, are provided. Product names are also searchable in Italian, French, Spanish, and German.

KOMPASS UK (File 591), also primarily a file containing manufacturing firms, is a compilation of several print directories of U.K. firms including *Kelly's Directories*, *British Exports*, *U.K. Trade Names*, and *Directory of Directors*. With over 110,000 companies, the individual company records in this file are much more detailed than in KOMPASS EUROPE. In addition to the detailed product listing, there is trade name information, selected financial information, a more complete textual business description, and listing of management personnel.

There are several country-specific directory databases in the DIALOG system. The ICC BRITISH COMPANY DIRECTORY (File 561) provides 2 million records on companies in England, Wales, Scotland, and Northern Ireland. A major weakness of this database is its lack of industry classification. You can search by SIC code in the companion file to the Directory, the ICC BRITISH COMPANY FINANCIAL DATASHEETS (File 562). It covers only 150,000 companies, but includes detailed financial information. In addition to SIC (U.K.) codes, there are also ICC industry codes.

The HOPPENSTEDT DIRECTORY OF GERMAN COMPANIES (File 529) covers approximately 35,000 public and private West German companies. The firms in this database account for 70 percent of all sales volume in Germany., There is moderate detail in each company record with SIC codes, list of officers, product listing, and subsidiaries. Financial data is limited to sales. Records are available in both English and German. There are Hoppenstedt databases for other European countries. Currently, DIALOG includes only Germany, but DATA-STAR has several others.

More detailed information for Canadian firms may be found in CAN-CORP CANADIAN CORPORATIONS (File 491), although as with most of the financially detailed databases, there are many fewer firms than directory files. CANCORP covers approximately 6,000 companies. Industry screening can be accomplished with either primary or secondary SIC code or textual business description. Unique to this file is the company's rank in several Canadian business rankings. The "mergers and acquisitions" section of each record may also be of interest as it summarizes the company's annual activity in divestitures and acquisitions.

Availability of information on cross-border transactions is likely to be dependent on the nation of the target and acquirer. If either the United States or United Kingdom is involved in the deal, finding deal data should not be difficult. Information on transactions involving two firms from other countries is more difficult to locate. At this point, world region may be important as more deal information may be available for European firms than for Asian firms. Statistics in this chapter indicate that global cross-border deal activity is increasing. We hope that providers of business information tools will acknowledge this trend and produce more resources for research.

NOTES

1. Merrill Lynch, First Quarter Press Release, "Merger/Acquisition Transactions Announced in 1990 First Quarter Fell 13%" (Schaumburg, Ill.: Merrill Lynch Business Brokerage & Valuation, 1990).
2. "The Stateless Corporation," *Business Week* 3159:98-106 (1990).
3. "Cross-border Mergers Rose by 8% in 1989 Study Says," *Wall Street Journal Database on Dow Jones News Retrieval*, Document Number 900126-0089, January 26, 1990.
4. Barrick Holmes, "Europe's Shopping Spree," *Mergers & Acquisitions* 24(6):12-15 (1990).
5. Evan Simonoff, ed., *The International Merger Yearbook: Corporate Acquisitions, Leveraged Buyouts, Joint Ventures & Corporate Policy* (New York: Securities Data Corporation, 1990), p. 16.
6. Brian Sturgess, "Booming International Mergers and Acquisitions," *International Mergers & Acquisitions* London: IFR, 1989), p. 19.
7. John J. Curran, "What Foreigners Will Buy Next," *Fortune* 119(4):94-98 (1989).
8. Ibid.

9

Information Checklist

The potential targets of a merger or an acquisition are scrutinized carefully by their acquirers. Handbooks on M&A often include checklists of facts to be established about a company's business before a takeover bid or merger offer. A particularly complete checklist (over thirty-five pages long) is included in *Mergers, Acquisitions and LBOs*.[1] Although checklists provide useful lists of facts to be discovered about a target company, they never include the sources of information where these facts can be found.

In this chapter we will use a checklist of facts for finding information about both acquirers and their targets as a framework for reviewing sources of information. The checklist will serve as a review of the sources discussed in previous chapters. It will also be used to illustrate several general business information sources not mentioned previously. We have divided the list into these categories:

- Company Background Information
- Company Financial Information
- Industry Information
- Marketing Information
- Legal Information
- Strategic Information

We have excluded the specialized M&A transaction databases described in detail in Chapters 5 and 8.

For each category we will give a list of typical questions and a selected list of databases. We will then discuss how the databases may be used. It is not our intention to list sources exhaustively, but only to give representative databases. We will describe some international databases, but our emphasis is on U.S. sources. With a few exceptions, the databases we list are available either through time sharing or in CD-ROM. Keep in mind that the sources we list for a particular category often have multiple uses. For example, an information resource that is useful for industry analysis frequently is helpful for market research. We give bibliographic details for each of the sources in Appendix 1.

As we mentioned earlier, the amount of published information available varies greatly by subject. Information about large, publicly traded companies will be available in scores of printed and online sources. Published information about small, private companies may be scarce or nonexistent. The information we seek may be single facts (What are the current annual sales of a company?) or complex combinations of facts, opinions, and judgments (What effect do LBOs have on the U.S. economy?). In our search for information, we will frequently discover that what we want does not exist in published form.

COMPANY BACKGROUND

Typical Facts needed are:

Company name, address, locations
State of incorporation
Officers' names
Annual sales
Number of employees

Name of Source	Coverage
CORPORATE TECHNOLOGY DIRECTORY	U.S.
DUN & BRADSTREET INTERNATIONAL	International
DUN'S MARKET IDENTIFIERS	U.S.
DUN'S MILLION DOLLAR DIRECTORY	U.S.
INCORP	U.S.
KOMPASS EUROPE	Europe
S&P REGISTER	U.S.
THOMAS REGISTER	U.S.
TRINET U.S. BUSINESSES	U.S.

Finding even "simple" facts, such as annual sales, for smaller companies often can be difficult. When screening for companies with particular characteristics e.g., sale size, geographic location, or industry) keep these potential problems in mind:

- The certainty that some of the records in the database will be inaccurate because of miscodings, reporting inaccuracies, or because the information is out of date
- The difficulty, when searching for information on non-U.S. companies, of comparing sales figures in U.S. dollars with those in foreign currencies
- The lack of agreement among databases in assigning industry codes to companies

We recommend searching more than one database for company information whenever possible. Agreement among databases gives some guarantee of factual accuracy.

The multimillion-record electronic files, such as D&B—DUN'S MARKET IDENTIFIERS and TRINET U.S. BUSINESSES, allow us to search for many, but not all, U.S. companies. The INCORP files (on the LEXIS Service) are useful for locating state records for existing and defunct companies. There are hundreds of more specialized industry and geographic directories online and in print. For a comprehensive list of printed directories, consult *Directories in Print.* For a list and description of online directories, we recommend Cuadra Associates' *Directory of Online Databases*, available both in print and online.

COMPANY FINANCIAL DATA

Typical Facts needed are:

Earning estimates
Financial statements
Financial time series
Ratio analyses
Security prices
Type of securities issued

Name of Source	Coverage
BEST'S REVIEWS	U.S.
CAPITAL CHANGE REPORTER	U.S.
COMPUSTAT	U.S.
D&B—DUN'S FINANCIAL RECORDS PLUS	U.S.
DISCLOSURE/SEC	U.S.
EXTEL	International
ICC INT BUSINESS RESEARCH	International
ICC INTERNATIONAL ANNUAL REPORTS	International
INVESTEXT	International
LASER DISCLOSURE	International

MOODY'S MANUALS	International
S&P CORPORATE DESCRIPTIONS	U.S.
SEC ONLINE	U.S.
TRADELINE	International
WORLDSCOPE	International

Company reports (in the United States, annual reports and SEC filings) are the main sources of information for many of the databases listed above. The examination of company reports is an essential part of company research. For all companies filing with the U.S. SEC, complete reports are available on CD-ROM from DISCLOSURE. DISCLOSURE publishes the complete annual reports of several thousand non-U.S. companies on CD-ROM as well. Time-sharing access to the full text of many of the reports of New York and American Stock Exchange companies is available through SEC ONLINE. Full-text annual reports for all U.K. companies as well as the largest 500 European companies are available through ICC INTERNATIONAL ANNUAL REPORTS.

The complete texts of company reports are often awkward to search when doing a preliminary screening for company characteristics or seeking a few individual facts. For example, finding the sales figures for IBM for the past twenty years directly from annual reports would be a chore. This information is directly available on COMPUSTAT.

Dun and Bradstreet is the only online source for detailed financial information on small private companies. On the DIALOG system,. the DUN'S FINANCIAL RECORDS PLUS file provides up to three years of financial statements for over 650,000 U.S. public and private companies. In addition, corporate histories and operations background are provided for an additional 1.2 million companies.

Expert analysis and interpretation of company and industry finances are available through INVESTEXT and ICC INTERNATIONAL BUSINESS RESEARCH. Both online files have the complete text of thousands of investment bank reports. INVESTEXT's focus is on U.S. companies and ICC's emphasis is on U.K. companies, although both services include analyses of major European and Asian corporations.

CORPORATE AFFILIATIONS

Typical Facts needed are:

Separate Hierarchy
Who owns whom

Name of Source	**Coverage**
DIRECTORY OF CORPORATE AFFILIATIONS	International
DUN'S INTERNATIONAL	International

| DUN'S MARKET IDENTIFIERS | U.S. |
| TRINET U.S. BUSINESSES | U.S. |

For large international companies, the question of "who owns whom" can be easily answered with DIALOG'S CORPORATE AFFILIATIONS. For smaller companies the Dun & Bradstreet files can be searched using D-U-N-S numbers. The TRINET U.S. BUSINESSES file can also be used to group corporate families in the United States. There are several country-specific online files for corporate affiliations. One example is WER GEHOERT ZU WEM, a German language "who owns whom" online with DATA-STAR. The databases listed above are discussed in detail in Chapter 7.

RECENT DEVELOPMENTS

Typical facts needed are:

Bankruptcy
Dividend announcements
Joint ventures
M&A announcements
Name changes
New product announcements
Reorganization plans

Name of Source	Coverage
AP NEWS	International
BANKRUPTCY DATASOURCE	U.S.
BUSINESS DATELINE	U.S.
BUSINESSWIRE	International
DOW JONES NEWS	International
DOW JONES' NEWS RETRIEVAL	International
NEWSWIRE ASAP	International
PR NEWSWIRE	International
PROMPT	International
RELEASE	International
UPI NEWS	International

The speed, comprehensiveness, and flexibility of time-sharing systems are especially important in monitoring corporate developments. All the machine-readable databases listed above are examined at length in Chapter 3. A source we have not described is *The Bankruptcy DataSource*, a monthly print service that follows all publicly traded companies that are in bankruptcy proceedings.

INDUSTRY ANALYSIS

Typical facts needed are:

Business growth rates
Competition
Degree of industry concentration
Factors affecting growth
Industry structure
Number of companies by size category

Name of Source	Coverage
COUNTY BUSINESS PATTERNS	U.S.
INVESTEXT	International
ICC INTERNATIONAL BUSINESS RESEARCH	International
MEDIA GENERAL	U.S.
PREDICASTS FORECASTS/WORLDCASTS	International
PREDICASTS BASEBOOK	U.S.
STANDARD & POOR'S INDUSTRY SURVEYS	U.S.
U.S. INDUSTRIAL OUTLOOK	U.S.
U.S. ECONOMIC CENSUSES	U.S.

The crucial consideration in finding information about an industry is defining the industry. Many of the databases above use the U.S. Standard Industrial Classification Code (SIC code) to describe companies and industries.

County Business Patterns, the *U.S. Industrial Outlook*, and the various U.S. economic censuses are U.S. government publications. All three publications arrange their data by SIC codes. The annual *U.S. Industrial Outlook* is an excellent starting place for industry analysis. Divided into 35 major industry groups, this work describes over 300 industries both narratively and statistically. *County Business Patterns* is useful for determining the number of business establishments in an industry by employment size. U.S. economic censuses (such as the *Census of Manufacturers*) are published every 5 years. They supply information on industry value of shipments, employment size, and payroll. In addition, the censuses include several volumes of special studies such as measures of industry concentration. Industry concentration ratios (the number of companies that account for a given percentage of an industry's value of shipments) are important for determining whether an M&A transaction has antitrust implications. In addition to their print formats, *County Business Patterns*, the economic censuses, and many statistical tables from the *U.S. Industrial Outlook* are available in CD-ROM.

Predicasts' Basebook describes thousands of U.S. economic time series and arranges the information by SIC number. The *Basebook* is a convenient source for examining growth trends for an industry or product. *Predicast's Forecasts* and *Worldcasts* are abstracts of published industry and product projections. *Predicast's Forecasts* reports U.S. projections; *Worldcasts* reports projections for the rest of the world.

The Predicasts and U.S. publications we have been describing report aggregate economic statistics. They may tell us, for example, that the ice cream industry has 400 manufacturing establishments, but they will not tell us the names of the establishments. Media General and Standard & Poor's *Industry Surveys*, in their analysis of large public companies, report both industry totals and individual company finances.

MARKETING DATA

Typical facts needed are:

Patents
Product lines
Share of market
Trademarks
Market structure
Nature of customer

Name of Source	Coverage
COMPUSTAT SEGMENT DATA	U.S.
ICC INTERNATIONAL BUSINESS RESEARCH	International
INVESTEXT	International
LEXPAT	U.S.
M.A.I.D.	International
PATDATA	U.S.
S&P STOCK REPORTS	U.S.
TRADEMARKSCAN—FEDERAL	U.S.
TRADEMARKSCAN—STATE	U.S.
TRINET U.S. BUSINESS ESTABLISHMENTS	U.S.
WORLD PATENTS INDEX	International
WORLDSCOPE	International
PROMT	International
FIND/SVP	International

For M&A research, estimating a company's share of market is important for purposes of financial evaluation and as a way of determining if the merger has antitrust implications. The U.S. Federal Trade Commission determines whether an acquisition is in violation of antitrust law in large part by estimating the control of the market a merged company will exert. There are many problems involved with collecting data on market share. Sometimes the market is so narrowly defined that no published data exist. For example, in determining whether Nestle's acquisition of Stouffer Foods violated antitrust law, the Federal Trade Commission tried to define the market for "frozen high priced non-ethnic entrees."[2] Often we are asked to find market share information for an industry that is too vaguely defined. Consider the problems of defining market share for the "U.S. Computer Industry."

Detailed product line information, particularly for private companies, is also difficult to obtain. Companies divulge only the product line information required by law. The U.S. SEC requires disclosure of lines of business that account for 5 percent or more of revenue or profit. This rule allows many companies to be vague about their product lines. In 1989, IBM for example, reported four lines of business: processors/peripherals, workstations, programs, and federal systems. Segment data is included on a company's 10K report. The information is also available from Standard & Poor's Stock Reports or from their COMPUSTAT database. The product line information for companies available from the TRINET U.S. BUSINESSES database includes both private and public companies. TRINET derives product line information by aggregating the production of individual establishments. Unfortunately, the estimates are only for company sales within the United States.

The "industry reports" from INVESTEXT and ICC INTERNATIONAL BUSINESS RESEARCH often have information that is useful for marketing. ICC includes a "Keynote Series" of "market research overviews" in its database.

Published market research reports can often supply direct answers to questions such as a company's market share. There are thousands of market research reports. They often have a very narrow focus (e.g., "The Market for Super Premium Ice Cream") and a very high price ($1,000 per report and up!). Findex is a directory of published market reports that gives description and price. Findex is available both in print and online (DIALOG File 196). Market reports are available in full text online from the M.A.I.D. (Market Analysis and Information Delivery) database. M.A.I.D. has thousands of reports and is international in scope.[3]

The Encyclopedia of Associations can be a useful source of marketing information. The Encyclopedia includes descriptions of U.S. national and regional associations as well as international groups. Industry associations can sometimes provide expert opinion or internal publications. The Encyclopedia of Associations is available online as well as in print.

If there are no published sources for the information you want, you can have market research performed for you. The *International Directory of Marketing Research* will provide you with the names and descriptions of firms that do customized research.

LEGAL ANALYSIS

Typical facts needed are:

Federal and state merger laws

Antitrust rulings

Tax rulings

Accounting literature

Name of Source	Coverage
LEXIS AICPA	U.S.
LEXIS LITIGATION SUPPORT	U.S.
LEXIS M&A	U.S.
LEXIS TRADE	U.S.
WESTLAW M&A FILINGS	U.S.
WESTLAW ANTITRUST	U.S.

Legal research on mergers is a complex subject that we only touch upon here. Two comprehensive sources of online legal material are the LEXIS Service (Mead Data Service) and WESTLAW. Both systems are detailed sources of U.S. legislative, judicial, and administrative law. In addition to their primary sources (court cases, administrative rulings, and statutes), both systems have extensive supplementary material, including the complete text of many legal services, law reviews, and practitioner materials. The LEXIS Service, in addition, has a large selection of European national laws.

The LEXIS Service has several "libraries" of legal material that relates to M&A. The most important of these, called M&A, contains federal and state cases, federal regulations, and SEC filings and abstracts. Because M&A activity may involve antitrust law, the TRADE library is often useful. It includes Federal Trade Commission regulation cases and FTC decisions, opinions, and orders. In addition, the TRADE library contains several journals and newsletters relating to antitrust. Examples are the BNA *Antitrust and Trade Daily* and the *FTC Watch*. The *FTC Watch* has a column ("Merger Watch") that gives brief statements of antitrust rulings by the FTC.

M&A transactions often involve detailed accounting questions. U.S. accounting standards are determined in large part by the Financial Accounting Standards Board (FASB). In their decisions regarding accounting matters, courts give much weight to the rulings of the FASB. The complete text of FASB pronouncements is available through the LEXIS Service.

The LEXIS Service can also be used to search for expert assistance regarding M&A. The Litigation Support Service library contains the names of individuals and companies that are "experts" in some aspect of merger litigation. For example, one service listed promises up-to-the-minute delivery of Williams Act filings.

WESTLAW's M&A FILINGS database contains the same information available on DIALOG's M&A FILINGS—abstracts of SEC forms relating to M&A.

CONCEPTUAL QUESTIONS

The types of M&A factual questions we have discussed are often the building blocks of answers to more complex conceptual questions. Answers to such questions involve interpretation, judgment, or opinion. The following questions are examples of conceptual questions:

- What are the strategic objectives of the acquiring company?
- What motivates the acquisition?
- Has the quality of the product produced by the target changed after the acquisition?
- Has the acquiring company gained any competitive advantage?
- What are the possible synergies between the acquirer and target?
- Does the acquisition have any antitrust implications?
- What are the tax implications of the acquisition?

Name of Source	Coverage
ABI/INFORM	International
DOW JONES TEXT	International
ECONOMIC LITERATURE INDEX	International
LEXIS—LAW REVIEWS	U.S.
NEXIS—NEW YORK TIMES	International
DIALOG—FINANCIAL TIMES	International

The financial, marketing, and industry data sources we have discussed earlier in this chapter usually will not provide a direct answer to conceptual questions although they often provide the facts you need to draw a conclusion.

We can sometimes find explicit answers to complex conceptual questions in business, economic, or legal literature. For example, an article by William C. Hunter and Larry D. Wall discusses the motivation for merger in the bank industry.[4] The larger the acquisition the more likely we are to find interpretations of the event in journals, newspapers, and books. The RJR Nabisco LBO inspired two books within two years of the event.[5]

TRENDS IN M&A RESEARCH

The availability of online databases has increased the efficiency of researchers enormously. However, online databases have several limitations for M&A research:

1. The search systems lack standardization. To be comprehensive in our research, we have to be familiar with the search systems of a half-dozen databanks and the individual idiosyncracies of scores of databases.
2. Important M&A research material is either not available online or is available only in abstract form. Examples of important material missing from commercial online sources include U.S. state documents and most non-U.S. M&A documents. The text of U.S. tender offers is available online only in abstract form.
3. The M&A material that is available online is limited chronologically. For example, although the full text of Proxy Reports is available for New York and American Stock Exchange companies online, coverage does not begin until 1987.
4. M&A material that is online is often poorly integrated. Transactions databases, filings databases, and monitoring databases exist as separate blocks of information that the researcher must integrate.

There is nothing in this list of shortcomings that current technology could not fix. More M&A materials will become available online as storage costs continue to fall and as the ability to scan materials into computer-readable form continues to improve. When the SEC's EDGAR system becomes fully operational, we will have all SEC filings in text-searchable form shortly after their release.

We have the beginnings of a natural language search system in Dow Jones News Retrieval's DOWQUEST. DIALOG's ONESEARCH give us the ability to search and retrieve from many databases simultaneously. We have the foundations of a "super" databanks in the Easylink System. Faster retrieval speed and display together with the integration of text and image seem assured as the natural result of technological evolution.

In ten years, we expect to be able to say to a computer, "Get me information on the IBM Fujitsu deal" and instantly have a comprehensive list of full text and images available for display, downloading, or printing. The material will be translated into any language we choose. We hope that ten years is too conservative an estimate.

NOTES

1. Robert Lawrence Kuhn, ed., *Mergers, Acquisitions, and Leveraged Buyouts.* (Homewood, Ill.: Dow Jones-Irwin, 1990).

2. Franklin M. Fisher, John J. McGowan, and Joen E. Greenwood, *Folded, Spindled, and Mutilated: Economic Analysis and U.S. v. IBM* (Cambridge, Mass.: MIT, 1983), p. 45.

3. Michael Halperin, "M.A.I.D. for Marketing," *Online* 12(1):51-52 (January 1988).

4. William C. Hunter and Larry D. Wall, "Bank Merger Motivations: A Review of the Evidence and an Examination of Key Target Bank Characteristics," *Economics Review* (Federal Reserve Bank of Atlanta) 75(5):2-19 (September/October 1989).

5. Bryan Burrough and John Helyar, *Barbarians at the Gate: The Fall of RJR Nabisco* (New York: Harper & Row, 1990); Hope Lampert, *True Greed: what Really Happened in the Battle for RJR Nabisco* (New York: Nal Books, 1990).

Appendix 1

Online Database Chart

DATABASE	DATABANK	TYPE	COST
ABI/Inform	DIALOG BRS DATASTAR NEXIS	J	1.90
ACQUIS	LEXIS	Fi	*
AP News	DIALOG NEXIS	N	1.40
Asia-Pacific	DIALOG	N,J	1.50
Bectel SEC	Newsnet	Fi	
Business Dateline	DIALOG BRS Dow Jones NEXIS	N	2.10
BusinessWire	DIALOG Dow Jones	N,PR	1.60
Canadian Business & Current Affairs	DIALOG	N,J	1.20
Cancorp Canadian Corporations	DIALOG	D,F,S	1.40
Corporate Canada Online	DIALOG	D,N,S	

DATABASE	DATABANK	TYPE	COST
Corporate Affiliations	DIALOG	D	1.40
Disclosure	DIALOG BRS Dow Jones	D,F	.75
Dow Jones News	Dow Jones	N	1.93
Dun's Canadian Market Identifiers	DIALOG	D,S	1.75
Dun's Electronic Business Directory	DIALOG	D,S	1.75
Dun's European Market Identifiers	DIALOG	D,S	1.75
Dun's Financial Records Plus	DIALOG	D,F,S	1.75
Dun's International Market Identifiers	DIALOG	D,S	1.75
Dun's Market Identifiers	DIALOG	D.S	1.75
Economic Literature Index	DIALOG		
Extel International News Cards	DIALOG	N	1.60
Fedfiles	Dow Jones	Fi	1.93
Find/SVP	DIALOG		
Financial Times (full text)	DIALOG	N	1.40
Hoppenstedt Directory of German Companies	DIALOG	D	1.75
ICC British Company Directory	DIALOG	D,S	1.40
ICC British Company Financial Datasheets	DIALOG	D,F,S	1.60
IDD M & A Transactions	DIALOG	T,S	1.40

DATABASE	DATABANK	TYPE	COST
Incorp	LEXIS	F	*
Infomat Int'l Business	DIALOG	N,J	1.60
Insider Trading Monitor	DIALOG	F	
International Dow Jones News	Dow Jones	N,PR	1.93
Investext	DIALOG Dow Jones LEXIS	I,F	1.60
Japan Economic Daily	Dow Jones	N	1.93
Japan Economic Newswire Plus	DIALOG	N	1.60
Knight-Ridder Financial News	DIALOG	N,F	1.60
KOMPASS Europe	DIALOG	D,S	1.60
LEXPAT	LEXIS	Ip	*
M & A Corporate Transactions	SDC	T,S	#
M & A Data Base	ADP	T,S	#
M & A Filings	DIALOG	Fi	1.40
M.A.I.D.	Pergamon	M	
Media General	DIALOG Dow Jones		
New York Times (full text)	NEXIS	N	*
Newswire ASAP	DIALOG	N,PR	1.60
PATS	BRS	Ip	
PR Newswire	DIALOG Dow Jones	PR	1.60

DATABASE	DATABANK	TYPE	COST
PTS Basebook	DIALOG	E,M	
PTS Forecasts	DIALOG	E,M	
PTS PROMT	DIALOG BRS DATASTAR	J,N	2.10
PTS Worldcasts	DIALOG	E,M	
Release	Dow Jones	PR	1.93
SEC Online	DIALOG NEXIS	Fi	1.40
SECNEW	LEXIS	Fi,N	*
Thomas Register	DIALOG		1.67
Tradeline	Dow Jones		*
TrademarkScan (Federal)	DIALOG	P	2.17
TrademarkScan (State)	DIALOG	P	2.17
Trinet U.S. Businesses	DIALOG NEXIS	D,S	1.40
UPI News	DIALOG NEXIS	N	1.42
U.S. Copyrights	DIALOG	Ip	2.00
Wall Street Journal (full text)	Dow Jones	N	1.93

Note 1: All costs listed are based on prime time connect rates, per minute charges.

Note 2: Where multiple databanks are listed, cost and frequency information is for the first databank listed.

Note 3: DIALOG also requires a per record display charge, which averages from less than $1.00 to $5.00. An exception is Dun's Financial Records Database which charges $96.00 per full record. Display charges may be less if a format other than "full" is used in any database.

Note 4: Dow Jones prices are based on use of a 1200 baud modem. At
        2400 baud, an additional $.36 a minute is charaged. There
        may be additional charges for displaying documents in some
        Dow Jones databases.

*Note 5: LEXIS/NEXIS database charges are based on a standard connect
        rate for any database searched. The current rate is $36.00
        per hour. Additionally, a per search charge is assessed. A
        search is one search statement. Search charges may range from
        $7.00 to $30.00, depending on the file or combination of files
        searched. There are no document display charges.

#Note 6: These databanks calculate costs based on a combination of
        factors which generally include computing costs (CPU time), an
        hourly connect rate, and either pre-formatted reports charges
        or per data item charges, depending on the type of output
        the user requests.

Type Codes

D - Directory
E - Economics
F - Financial
Fi - Filings
I - Investment Reports
Ip - Intelectual Property
J - Journals
M - Marketing
N - News
PR - Press Releases
S- Screening
T - Transactions

Appendix 2

Directory of Time-Sharing Database Systems

ADP Data Services
175 Jackson Plaza
Ann Arbor, MI 48106
800-ADP-DATA
313-769-6800

BRS Information Technologies
8000 Westpark Drive
McLean, VA 22102
800-289-4277
703-442-0900

Data-Star Marketing, Inc.
Suite 110, 485 Devon Park Drive
Wayne, PA 19087
800-221-7754
215-687-6777

Dialog Information Services, Inc.
3460 Hillview Avenue
Palo Alto, CA 94304
800-3-DIALOG
415-858-3777

Dow Jones News/Retrieval
P.O. Box 300
Princeton, NJ 08543-0300
609-520-4000

LEXIS/NEXIS
Mead Data Central
P.O. Box 933
Dayton, OH 45401
800-227-4908
513-865-6800

M.A.I.D.
Market Analysis and Information Database
South Park Tower
124 West 60th Street
New York, NY 10023
212-245-3513

Newsnet, Inc.
945 Haverford Road
Bryn Mawr, PA 19010
215-527-8030

Securities Data Company (SDC)
1180 Raymond Boulevard
Newark, NJ 07102
201-622-3100

Glossary

Acquisition—the acquiring of control of one corporation by another.

Arbitrager—a speculative investor who purchases a stock with the intent of selling it quickly for a profit, especially if the company is the rumored or real target of a takeover.

Asset Play—a firm whose underlying assets are worth substantially more (after paying off the firm's liabilities) than the market value of its stock.

Bankruptcy—the conditions under which the financial position of an individual, corporation, or other legal entity are such as to cause actual or legal insolvency.

Bidder—the person, group, or company making an offer for control of another company.

Black Knight—a potential acquirer that management opposes and would prefer to find an alternative to (i.e., a white knight).

Block Purchase—the acquisition of a large number of a company's shares. The purchaser can exert pressure on the company even without making a formal takeover bid.

Blue Sky Laws—state securities laws that generally require registration of broker-dealers and securities. Although a Uniform Securities Act exists, the field is far from uniform and only analysis of particular state statutes is definitive.

Breakup Value—the sum of the values of a firm's assets if sold off separately.

Conglomerate Merger—a merger of companies from different fields.

Consolidation—a combination of two or more organizations into one, to form a new corporate entity.

Creeping Takeover—the gradual accumulation of a company's stock through purchases in the open market. Since public disclosure is not required until 5 percent of a company's shares are owned, a bidder can control a substantial portion of stock before the outset of an actual takeover.

Crown Jewels—a firm's most valuable assets. The "crown jewels" may be sold or optioned to a third party, in order to make the company less attractive to a hostile bidder.

Databank—an organization that makes multiple databases available for public access, via time-sharing networks.

Database—a file of organized information covering a specific subject or discipline. The data contained may be either textual or numeric, and is retrievable through multiple access points.

Defensive Tactics—actions taken by a target company to resist a takeover.

Delist—removal of a company's security from an organized exchange because of changes in the company's status that prevent it from meeting listing requirements.

Divestiture—the process of disposing of all or part of a business.

Dutch Auction—a type of auction or bidding process in which bidding begins at the highest price sought and is reduced until prospective buyers are enticed to buy.

Edgar—(Electronic Data Gathering, Analysis and Retrieval)-a project of the Securities and Exchange Commission to implement computerized filing of reports with the SEC.

Friendly Takeover—a merger supported by the management and board of directors of a target company.

Going Private—method by which corporate management fends off a potential hostile takeover. By buying the company from its shareholders, the entrenched management can secure control of the firm, often completed through a leveraged buyout.

Golden Handshake—method by which a raider gains acquiescence of the corporate management of a takeover target. The raider influences management with promises of generous retirement packages.

Golden Parachutes—employment contract provisions that guarantee very substantial severance payments to top management if they lose their jobs as the result of a takeover.

Greenmail—a payment received from a company by a "raider" who has purchased a block of stock and threatens to make a hostile takeover bid. The company agrees to buy the stock back from the raider at a premium, usually lowering the value of all the company's stock.

Horizontal Merger—a merger between firms selling a similar product within the same geographic area.

Hostile Takeover—a merger resisted by the target firm.

In Play—term referring to a company whose status is that of a recognized takeover target.

Junk Bond Financing—method to raise capital for investment that uses low-rated bonds that are speculative in nature. The bonds are usually rated below BBB. If successful, these bonds return outstanding profits.

Leveraged Buyout—a transaction in which a group of investors acquires and "takes private" a publicly owned company (or a division or subsidiary of a firm). The transaction also depends on borrowing most of the purchase price, using the firm's assets as collateral.

Liquidation—the winding up of the affairs of a business by converting all assets into cash, paying off all outside creditors in the order of their preference, and distributing the remainder, if any, to the owners.

Lockup—an agreement between a target company and a proposed acquirer giving that acquirer an advantage over other potential bidders. Lockups usually involve an option to acquire certain company assets not available to other parties.

Mezzanine Financing—a method of obtaining financing often used by those doing a leveraged buyout. The mezzanine financier, often an insurance company, takes a subordinated debt position between a senior secured lender and the equity interest.

Merger—the combining of two or more entities through the direct acquisition by one of the net assets of the other. A new corporate entity is not created.

Minimum Offering Period—the shortest time a tender offer may remain open (twenty business days under current federal law).

Pacman Defense—a tender offer made by the target of a hostile takeover bid for the stock of the original bidder. The defense is summed up by the phrase "Eat your opponent before he eats you."

Poison Pill—an issue of securities, usually preferred stock, designed to discourage a hostile takeover. Upon completion of a hostile takeover, the typical "pill" stock becomes convertible into cash or the common stock of the acquiring company. The effect is to raise considerably the cost of the acquisition.

Raider—a person, group, or company attempting to execute a hostile takeover. The term is frequently applied to those who specialize in hostile takeovers.

Recapitalization—altering the capital structure of a firm by increasing or decreasing its capital stock.

Reorganization—the altering of a firm's capital structure, often resulting from a merger, that affects the rights and responsibilities of the owners.

Retructuring—a collection of activities, which may include divestitures, spinoffs, stock repurchases, or acquisitions, designed to maximize shareholder wealth by maximizing the value of corporate assets.

Screening—a search technique to retrieve only those companies that meet specified characteristics.

Scorched Earth Policy—an antitakeover measure in which the target company takes on large amounts of debt, cripples its subsidiaries, or otherwise makes itself less desirable as a takeover target.

Self-tender—a company's purchase of its own shares. This is frequently done to remove the shares from the reach of a hostile bidder, thereby lessening the prospect of the bidder's obtaining a majority of shares.

Shark Repellent—provisions in corporate bylaws designed to prevent hostile takeover bids.

Spin-off—a subsidiary that becomes an independent company.

Standstill Agreement—an agreement whereby the bidder agrees to buy no more of the target's stock for a specified period.

Statutory Merger—acquisition of a corporation through a merger in conformity with state corporation law.

Synergy—the creation of additional value through a combination beyond the sum of the separate values of the acquirer and acquired companies.

Target—the company that is the subject of an acquisition.

Tender Offer—a public offer to buy some or all of the stock of a corporation within a specified time period. Notice of the offer is reported to the Securities and Exchange Commission on Schedule 14-D1. The price offered is generally well above current market price to induce stockholders to tender their shares to the bidder.

Time-sharing Network—a telecommunications network that provides access to databanks through local telephone nodes.

Tombstone Ad—an advertisement that is run to satisfy a legal requirement to make certain disclosures or give certain notice, the contents and format of which are specified by statute or regulation. These ads are used in making public information about a tender offer.

Two-tiered, Front-end Loaded Tender Offer—in this complex form of tender offer, the first step or "front-end" is to make a tender offer to buy enough shares to establish a controlling position in the target company. Next, the remaining shares of the target are merged into a new entity or bought in the "back end" of the deal, which is usually an offer on less favorable terms and at a lower price than the front-end loaded offer.

Vertical Merger—a merger of firms which the acquired firm is a supplier or customer of the acquiring firm.

White Knight—the party in a takeover defense that is an alternative and presumably more friendly acquirer than the present acquirer.

Select Bibliography

Andrews, Edmund L. "LBO Firms Meet Their Maker." *Venture* 11(2):47-49 (1989).

Andrews, Suzanna. "Just How Hostile Is Carter Bacot?" *Institutional Investor* 23(2):56-62 (1989).

Anonymous. "Retailers of the Year: Post-LBO 7-Eleven Gets Tough." *Chain Store Age Executive* 64(2):36-42 (1988).

Anonymous. "Small Business Has Merger Mania Too." *Business Week* 3107:61 (1989).

Anonymous. "Target and Hills Get Gold Circle." *Discount Merchandiser* 28(10):14, 16 (1988).

Anonymous. "Texaco: Catch a Fallen Star." *Economist* 310(7585):66-67 (1989).

Anonymous. "The Welch Years: GE Gambles on Growth." *Industry Week* 233:30-32 (1987).

Anonymous. "1988: The Market Struggles Through." *Going Public: The IPO Reporter* 13(1):1427-28 (1989).

Bartlett, Charles M. "When the Broker Calls with a Hot New Issue." *Forbes* 141(14):290-92 (1988).

Bell, Steven J. "Corporate Change: Impact on the Corporate Document Collection." *Special Libraries* 79(4):265-70 (1988).

BenDaniel, David J. *The Handbook of International Mergers and Acquisitions.* Englewood Cliffs, N.J.: Prentice-Hall, 1990.

Bibler, Richard S., ed. *The Arthur Young Management Guide to Mergers and Acquisitions.* New York: Wiley, 1989.

Browne & Co. *Regulations 14D, 14E and Rule 14F1: Tender Offers under the Securities and Exchange Act of 1934.* New York: Browne, 1987.

Byrnes, Jane Cameron, and Melanie W. Smith. "Adventures in M & A Searching." *Database* 11(5):64-71 (1988).

Capital Changes Reporter. Chicago: Commerce Clearing House, 1990.

Chajet, Clive. "Identifying Symptoms of Identity Malaise." *Management Review* 77(9):49-50 (1988).

Cooke, Terence E. *International Mergers and Acquisitions.* New York: Blackwell, 1988.

Curran, John J. "What Foreigners Will Buy Next." *Fortune* 119(4):94-98 (1989).

Directory of Corporate Affiliations. Wilmette, Ill.: National Register, 1990.

Directory of Obsolete Securities. Jersey City, N.J.: Financial Information Incorporated, 1991.

Dorn, Philip. "Change and Change Again at IBM." *Computerworld* 22(44):19 (1988).

Ferdinandson, Connie, ed. *Merger & Acquisition Sourcebook.* Santa Barbara, Calif.: Quality Services, 1989.

Ferris, Richard K. *The Executive Speaker* 7(9):6 (1988).

Financial Stock Guide Service. *Directory of Obsolete Securities.* New York: Financial Information, 1990.

Finch, Peter. "Joe Rive's Fight to Fend Off the Bank of New York." *Business Week* 3044 (Industrial/Technology ed.):44 (1988).

Galante, Steven P., and John A. Chiappinelli, eds. *Buyouts: Director of Intermediaries.* Needham, Mass.: Venture Economics, 1989.

Geahigan, Priscilla Cheng. "Leveraged Buyouts, Junk Bonds, Spinoffs, Poison Pills." *RQ* 29:182-87 (Fall 1989).

Greer, Jana W. "Broad Inc. Announces Move of Its $7 Billion Financial Services Operation to Los Angeles." *PR Newswire* pg. 0427035 (April 27, 1989).

Greve, J. T. *How to Do a Leveraged Buyout for Yourself, Your Corporation, or Your Client.* 3d ed. San Diego: Business Publications, 1987.

Haggerty, Alfred C. "Broad Inc. to Quicken Financial Services Pace." *National Underwriter(Life/Health/Financial Services)* 93(2):19-20 (1989).

Halperin, Michael, and Steven J. Bell. "Business Students Find Leverage Online: Searching the M & A Files." *Online* 12(4):58-62 (1988).

Hedden, Judy. "Online Information for Merger and Acquisition Analysis." *Proceedings of the National Online Meeting.* Medford, N.J.: Learned Information, 1987.

Holmes, Barrick. "Europe's Shopping Spree." *Mergers & Acquisitions* 24(6):12-15 (1990).

Hopkins, Thomas Hollis. *Mergers,* Acquisitions and Divestitures: A Guide to Their Impact for Investors and Directors. Homewood, Ill.: Dow Jones-Irwin, 1983.

International Directory of Corporate Affiliations. Wilmette, Ill.: National Register, 1990.

Ivey, Mark. "Manville Starts to See a Glimmer of Daylight." *Business Week* 3074 (Industrial/Technology ed.):58, 60 (1988).

Jenkins, James W. *Mergers and Acquisitions: A Financial Approach.* New York: American Management Association Extension Institute, 1986.

Kight, Leila K., ed. *How to Find Information about Divisions, Subsidiaries, and Products.* Washington, D.C.: Washington Researchers, 1990.

Laderman, Jeffrey. "When One Plus One Equals No. 1." *Business Week* 3108:92, 94 (1989).

Lashbrooke, E. C. *The Legal Handbook of Business Transactions.* New York: Quorum, 1987.

Levine, Sumner N. *Business and Investment Almanac.* Homewood, Ill.: Dow Jones-Irwin, 1987.

McCarroll, Thomas, and William McWhirter. "The Proxy Punchout." *Time* 135(16):40-41 (1990).

Madrick, Jeff. *Taking America: How We Got from the First Hostile Takeover to Megamergers, Corporate Raiding and Scandal.* New York: Bantam Books, 1987.

Mergerstat Review. Schaumburg, Ill.: Merrill Lynch Business Brokerage & Valuation, 1989.

Merrill Lynch. First Quarter Press Release: "Merger/Acquisition Transactions Announced in 1990 First Quarter Fell 13%." Schaumburg, Ill.: Merrill Lynch Business Brokerage & Valuation, 1990.

Mickey, Melissa B. "Dun & Bradstreet." *Business Information Alert* 2(1):3 (January 1990).

Moody's Industrial Manual. Vol. 2 New York: Moody's Investors Service, 1989.

Nagler, George E., and Kenneth B. Schwartz. "Choosing the Best Alternative in a Chapter 11 Case." *Journal of Commercial Bank Lending* 70(2):48-53 (1987).

Newport, John Paul. "A New Era of Rapid Rise and Ruin." *Fortune* 119(9):77-88 (1988).

Ojala, Marydee. "A Patently Obvious Source for Competitor Intelligence: The Patent Literature." *Database* 12(4):46 (August 1989).

Ojala, Marydee. "Dealing with a Full Deck: Mergers and Acquisitions Databases." *Database* 12(3):85-95 (1989).

O'Neal, Michael. "Sears Faces a Tall Task." *Business Week* 3079 (Industrial/Technology ed.):54-55 (1988).

Pagell, Ruth, and Michael Halperin. "SIC Codes: The SIC Confusion in Comparing Codes." *Online* 7(6):49-55 (November 1983).

Parker, Marcia. "Goodyear Ready to Roll Again." *Pensions & Investment Age* 16(17):30-31 (1988).

Reed, Stanley F., and P. C. Edson. *The Art of M & A: A Merger, Acquisition, Buyout Guide.* Homewood, Ill.: Dow Jones-Iwin, 1989.

"Restructurings and Dismemberments." *Coal* March 1988, p. 122.

Rock, Milton L. *The Mergers and Acquisitions Handbook.* New York: McGraw-Hill, 1987.

Rosenberg, Gerald I. *How to Find Information about Acquisitions Candidates.* Washington, D.C.: Washington Researchers, 1987.

Rosenberg, Jerry M. *Dictionary of Banking and Finance.* New York: Wiley, 1982.

Rufa, Karen M., ed. *The Directory of M & A Professionals.* New York: Dealers' Digest, 1989.

Sikora, Martin. "M & A Activity Hit a Record $226.3 Billion in 1988." *PR Newswire* pg. 0126032 (January 26, 1989).

Simonoff, Evan, ed. *The Domestic Merger Yearbook: Corporate Acquisitions, Leveraged Buyouts, Joint Ventures & Corporate Policy.* New York: Securities Data Corporation, 1990.

Simonoff, Evan, ed. *The International Merger Yearbook: Corporate Acquisitions, Leveraged Buyouts, Joint Ventures & Corporate Policy.* New York: Securities Data Corporation, 1990.

Smith, Nathaniel B. "Defining 'Tender Offer' under the Williams Act." *Brooklyn Law Review* 53:189-203 (Winter 1987).

Standard Industrial Classification Manual. Executive Office of the President, Office of Management and Budget, Washington, D.C., 1987.

"The Stateless Corporation," *Business Week* 3159:98-106 (1990).

Steinberg, Marc I., ed. *Tender Offers: Developments and Commentaries.* Westport, Conn.: Quorum, 1985.

Sturgess, Brian. "Booming International Mergers and Acquisitions." *International Mergers & Acquisitions.* London: IFR, 1989.

U.S. Senate Committee on Banking, Housing and Urban Affairs. *Securities and Exchange Commission Report on Tender Offer Laws.* Washington, D.C.: U.S. Government Printing Office, 1980.

Index

ABI/INFORM, database, 42-43
Accounting literature, 185-86
ACQUIS, database, 63-66
Acquisition, definition, 2-3
ADP, 81, 84-87
ALERT service, 44-45
Annual reports, 180
Antitrust, 185
AP NEWSWIRE, database, 39-40, 48
ASIA-PACIFIC, database, 157

Bankruptcy, definition, 3
Bankruptcy DataSource, 181
Blue Sky Law Reporter, 60
Brands and Their Companies, 141
BUSINESS DATELINE, database, 42-43, 48
Business directories, comparison, 99
Business information, availability, 10-14
Business magazines, 23-24
Business newspapers, 21-23
Business organization, 123
Business research, 10-14; company background, 178-79; company financial data, 179; industry analysis, 182-83; marketing, 183-85
Business Week, 23-24

BUSINESS WIRE, database, 41, 46, 48
Buyout, definition, 4-5
Buyouts, Directory of Intermediaries, 97-98

CANADIAN BUSINESS AND CURRENT AFFAIRS, database, 157
CANADIAN DUN'S MARKET IDENTIFIERS, database, 173
CANCORP CANADIAN CORPORATIONS, database, 175
Capital Changes Reporter, 125-36
Chapter 11, 3
COMPNY LIBRARY, database, 126-27
COMPUSTAT, database, 110-11, 137, 184
Consolidation, definition, 3-4
CORPORATE AFFILIATIONS, database, 128-31, 181
CORPORATE CANADA ONLINE, database, 163
Corporate change, 1-2, 9-10, 142; monitoring, 17-18, 27, 32, 181
Corporate Finance Sourcebook, 97-98
Corporate Growth Report, 147, 156
Corporate hierarchy, 125-26, 180-81
Corporate identity, definition, 124

CORPTECH, database, 120
County Business Patterns, 182
Cross-border transactions. *See* International M&A
Current awareness, 27, 38-39, 44-45, 48-49, 181

D&B—DUN'S ELECTRONIC BUSINESS DIRECTORY, database, 105-8
D&B—DUN'S FINANCIAL RECORDS PLUS, database, 111-13, 180
D&B—DUN'S MARKET IDENTIFIERS, database, 97-104, 138-40
D&B—INTERNATIONAL DUN'S MARKET IDENTIFIERS, database, 173
Databanks, 30-33
Database screening. *See* Screening
Databases. *See* names of specific databases
Databases, types, 14, 28-30
DATA-STAR, 164
DIALOG, 31, 38-45; ALERT service, 44-45; mapping command, 138-39; newswire databases, 38-42; ONE-SEARCH, 45-46; update command, 39
Directory databases, comparisons, 104
Directory of Corporate Affiliations, 128
Directory of Obsolete Securities, 136
Directory of Online Databases, 179
DISCLOSURE, database, 109-10
Divestiture, definition, 4
DJNEWS, database, 33-36
Domestic Merger Yearbook, 146
DOW JONES NEWS/RETRIEVAL, 29, 31
DOWQUEST, 187
D-U-N-S Number, 131-33

EDGAR (Electronic Data Gathering and Retrieval), 76
Encyclopedia of Associations, 184
Euromoney, 156
EUROPEAN DUN'S MARKET IDENTIFIERS, database, 173-74

EXTEL INTERNATIONAL NEWS CARDS, database, 157, 173

FASB (Financial Accounting Standards Board), 185
Federal Trade Commission, 185
FEDFILES, database, 66, 70-73
Financial Times, 22
FINANCIAL TIMES FULLTEXT, database, 157
FINDEX, 184
Fortune 500, 10
14D-1, 57-59
14D-9, 57-59
FT MERGERS & ACQUISITIONS INTERNATIONAL, database, 172

HOPPENSTEDT DIRECTORY OF GERMAN COMPANIES, database, 174

ICC BRITISH COMPANY DATASHEETS, database, 174
ICC BRITISH COMPANY DIRECTORY, database, 174
IDD, 43-44, 164-72
INCORP LIBRARY, database, 138-40
Incorporation records, 138, 140-41
INFOMAT INTERNATIONAL BUSINESS, database, 158-59
Initial Public Offering, definition, 4
International Directory of Marketing Research, 185
INTERNATIONAL DOW JONES NEWS, database, 163
International M&A: databases, 157-64; definition, 144-45; overview, 143-45
International Merger Yearbook, 146
International Trade Names Dictionary, 141
INVESTEXT, database, 120, 180, 184
Investor's Daily, 21

JAPAN ECONOMIC DAILY, database, 163
JAPAN ECONOMIC NEWSWIRE

PLUS, database, 157-58
Journal of Commerce and Commercial, 21

KNIGHT-RIDDER FINANCIAL NEWS, database, 41-42, 46
KOMPASS EUROPE, database, 174
KOMPASS UK, database, 174

LaserD, 62-63
LBO, 4-5
Legal research, 185-86
Leveraged buyout, definition, 4-5
LEXIS Service, 31-32, 45-48, 61, 185-86
LEXPAT, database, 116-18
Line of business report, 119
Liquidation, definition, 5

M&A: growth of literature, 8-9; international (*See* International M&A); trends, 187
M&A data, users, 12
M&A DATA BASE, database, 81, 84-87
M&A Europe, 156
M&A FILINGS, database, 43, 64, 66-70
M&A journals, 24, 147, 156
M&A transaction databases: characteristics, 79-80; comparisons, 91, 94-95, 164-72; searching, 87, 89-94
M&A transactions, brokers, 97: statistics, 1-2, 7-10, 53, 143-44
M&A TRANSACTIONS, database, 43-44, 164-72
MAID (Market Analysis and Information Delivery), 184
Market share, 113, 184. *See also* Business research, marketing
Mead Data Central. *See* Lexis Service; Nexis Service
Merger, definition, 5
Merger & Acquisition Sourcebook, 145-46
Merger & Acquisitions, 8, 147
Mergers & Acquisitions International, 156

MERGERS AND CORPORATE TRANSACTIONS, database, 84, 87-89, 164-72
Mergerstat Review, 53, 146-47
Metropolitan newspapers, 21-23
Moody's Manuals, 134-35
Multinational business, 156

Name change, corporation, 9-10, 124
NEWSFLASH, 49-51
Newsletters, 25-26, 48
NEWSNET, 32, 48-51
NEWSNET, NEWSFLASH, 49-51
Newspapers, 21-23
News releases, 18-19
News stories, discrepancies, 22
NEWSWIRE ASAP, database, 38, 40
New York Times, 21
NEXIS Service, 31-32, 45-48

ONESEARCH, 45-46, 187
Online searching. *See* Timesharing databases

Parent-subsidiary relationship, 125-26
PASOS, database, 140-41
PATDATA, database, 116
Patents, 115-17
Predicasts' Basebook, 183
Predicasts' Worldcasts, 183
Predicasts' Forecasts, 183
Predicasts' Index of Corporate Change, 10
PREDICASTS' NEWSLETTER DATABASE, database, 32-33
Private companies, 54, 80
PR NEWSWIRE, database, 38-40, 48
Product lines, 114
Proxy fight, 54-55
PTS NEW PRODUCT ANNOUNCEMENTS/PLUS, database, 120
PTS PROMT, database, 42-43, 159-60
Public companies, 80

Recapitalization, definition, 5-6
Regional newspapers, 21-23

RELEASE, database, 35-36
Reorganization, definition, 6
Restructuring, definition, 6

S&P Industry Surveys, 183
Screening, 99-100; corporate events,
    136-42; financial variables, 108-13;
    non-U.S. companies, 119; service
    companies, 107; share of market,
    113
SDC, 84, 87-89, 164-72
SECABS, database, 48
SEC documents. *See* Williams Act
    Filings
SEC FILINGS INDEX, database, 71,
    73-75
SEC News Digest, 61
Securities and Exchange Commission,
    53
Securities Exchange Act of 1934,
    53
Self-Tender, stock buyback, 57
Self-Tender acquisition, 56-57
Service companies, 107
Share of market, 113, 184
SIC (Standard Industrial Classifica-
    tion) code, 101-3, 107
Spin-off, definition, 6
Stock buyback, 56-57

Telecommunication networks, 28
Tender offer, 57-59; amendments, 59,
    64; definition, 57-58; filings (*See*

Williams Act Filings)
10-k, 114, 127
TEXT, database, 36-38, 164
13D, 54-55
13E-3, 56-57
13E-4, 57
13-G, 55-56
Thomas Register, 141
THOMAS REGISTER ONLINE,
    database, 119-20
Timesharing databases, advantages,
    47; disadvantages, 49
Trade and industry journals, 24-25
Trademarks, 117-19
TRADEMARKSCAN, database, 117-19
Transaction rosters, 24, 147
TRINET U.S. BUSINESSES, database,
    102-5, 113-14, 131, 133-35

UPI NEWS, database, 39-40, 48
U.S. Economic Censuses, 182
U.S. Industrial Outlook, 182

Valuation, 118-19
VU/TEXT, 172

Wall Street Journal, 21
WER GEHOERT ZU WEM, database,
    181
WESTLAW, 185-86
Williams Act Filings, 61-62, 80;
    CD-ROM, 62-63; monitoring, 62-63;
    overview, 54-60
World M&A Network, 98

About the Authors

MICHAEL HALPERIN is Librarian, Lippincott Library of the Wharton School, University of Pennsylvania, and adjunct professor at Drexel University's College of Information Studies. In addition to information resources for M & A research, his research interests include machine readable resources for business, and the publications of industrial scientists.

STEVEN J. BELL is Head, Circulation Services and Reference Librarian at the Lippincott Library of the Wharton School, University of Pennsylvania. His research interests include information resources for M & A, telecommunications software, end-users of online databanks and the journals *Online, Database, Link-Up, Special Libraries,* and *Education for Information.*